DATA
COMMUNICATIONS

DATA COMMUNICATIONS

A Beginner's Guide to Concepts and Technology

SCOTT A. HELMERS

PRENTICE HALL

Englewood Cliffs, New Jersey 07632

Library of Congress Cataloging-in-Publication Data

Helmers, Scott A.
    Data communications.

    Bibliography: p.
    Includes index.
    1. Data transmission systems.   2. Computer networks.
I. Title.
TK5105.H44   1989   621.398'1   88-32431
ISBN 0-13-198870-0

Editorial/production supervision
    and interior design: GERTRUDE SZYFERBLATT
Cover design: LUNDGREN GRAPHICS, LTD.
Manufacturing buyer: MARY ANN GLORIANDE

PRENTICE-HALL INTERNATIONAL (UK) LIMITED, London
PRENTICE-HALL OF AUSTRALIA PTY. LIMITED, Sydney
PRENTICE-HALL CANADA INC., Toronto
PRENTICE-HALL HISPANOAMERICANA, S.A., Mexico
PRENTICE-HALL OF INDIA PRIVATE LIMITED, New Delhi
PRENTICE-HALL OF JAPAN, INC., Tokyo
SIMON & SCHUSTER ASIA PTE., LTD., Singapore
EDITORA PRENTICE-HALL DO BRASIL, LTDA., Rio de Janeiro

To Sara

*who won the race between
the baby and the book, and*

To Marilyn

who made all of this possible

CONTENTS

PREFACE

If you know a reasonable amount about computers but know little or nothing about data communications, this book is for you. In fact, this book is a direct result of having taught data communications to numerous students who fit that description, including coworkers at the companies where I have been employed, students in continuing education classes in the State-of-the-Art Engineering program at Northeastern University, and seminar attendees of Systems Technology Forum.

The students in these classes have had diverse backgrounds but few have had strong technical credentials; the common trait they shared was an interest in learning more about an increasingly important topic. Consequently, the challenge has always been to teach the basics of a very technical subject in a non-threatening manner yet to impart sufficient knowledge to allow the students to proceed with further technical study if they desired.

As a result, this book is not a rigorous, technical dissertation on data communications; there are other books that fill that need. Rather, this book was written for the thousands of people who need an informative and readable treatment of the subject. I assume only that the reader has a basic familiarity with computers but does not have an engineering or mathematics background.

I intend this book to be used in two seemingly contradictory ways, both as a primer that can easily be read from front to back and as a reference book that can be used to answer questions long after it has been placed on a bookshelf. I believe both are possible in the same volume and have used several techniques to achieve that goal.

First, this book is organized around the **three key building blocks** of data communications: **the computer, the conversion device, and the communication channel** as shown in the section summary below and, in more detail, in the Contents.

PART I   - THE FUNDAMENTALS

PART II - COMPUTERS AND NETWORK ARCHITECTURES

PART III - CONVERSION DEVICES

PART IV - COMMUNICATION CHANNELS

This structure provides readers with a simple framework for the subject matter and allows them to fit each new subject into the overall structure.

Second, each main section header is accompanied by a variation of a simple diagram showing the relationships among the computer, the conversion device, and the channel. The relevant portion of each **section header diagram** is highlighted to reflect the position of the current subject within the overall structure. (See Chapter 1 for a detailed explanation of the section header diagrams.)

Third, every chapter ends with a **recap** of the key points for the reader to remember.

Fourth, data communications **terms are printed in italics** at the point in the text where they are first used or explained.

Fifth, most **glossary entries are cross-referenced** back to the primary use of the term in the main part of the book in order to provide context in addition to the definition. For terms that are depicted in a figure in the book, the glossary entry also contains a reference to that diagram.

Sixth, most figures have **longer than usual captions** so the reader need not necessarily refer back to the text to fully understand the concept being presented. In cases where additional explanation is necessary it is easy to locate the correct point in the text because all references to "Figure x-x" in the text are printed in boldface.

Seventh, the **annotated bibliography** provides the reader with comments on the usefulness, style, and content of many of the sources.

If this book is successful in introducing future students to data communications, it will be a fitting tribute to the hundreds of former students who, both knowingly and unknowingly, have contributed to its present content.

Scott A. Helmers
Andover, Massachusetts

ACKNOWLEDGMENTS

No one has had more to do with the successful completion of this book than my wife, Marilyn. Her typing, editing, and proofreading, while significant, were actually the least of her many contributions. Had it not been for her love and support and her willingness to assume far more than her share of the household and parenting responsibilities, I would never have completed this project.

Of the many friends and associates who responded willingly to my requests for assistance, four stand out. I am grateful to Steve Lane who read almost the entire manuscript and who contributed his insight, humor, and thoughtful criticism. Peter Bates provided excellent reviews and improved both the content and the style of several chapters and the glossary. Marc Hopkins drew upon his vast technical expertise and offered precise and significant suggestions for improvements in the chapters dealing with network architectures and OSI. Sharon Shelton reviewed numerous chapters and all of the illustrations, often with extremely short deadlines, and offered valuable advice in several other areas.

I also appreciate the assistance of Bill Bowe, Richard Geiger, Kathy Maple, Maryanne Devine, Holly Bradbury, and Rob Taylor who donated some of their evening and weekend hours to critique or proofread portions of the manuscript. All of them are responsible for improvements in the quality of the finished text.

Finally, I would like to thank my parents, Art and Jane Helmers, who were gentle, yet resolute, in their insistence that I pay attention to style as well as content as I was growing up. They provided me with numerous examples of written and verbal elegance, and instilled in me an appreciation for the power of language.

Part I

THE FUNDAMENTALS

Part I of this text provides the fundamental information required for assimilating the material in the remainder of the book. In addition, it provides an introduction to more advanced subjects and refers the reader to the subsequent section in which each topic is more fully developed. Part I is divided into four chapters.

Chapter 1 introduces a number of basic concepts and definitions. It also explains the structure and format of the book.

Chapter 2 describes the various categories of computer devices that can be used in a data communications network. It provides a very brief review of the internal operation of digital computers as a prelude to describing the ASCII and EBCDIC coding schemes that are commonly used to represent data in computers and on communication channels.

Chapter 3 introduces the signal-conversion devices that are required to convert the data-carrying, digital signals from a computer into a form that is acceptable to a transmission circuit. It also includes a discussion of modems, carrier frequencies, and terms such as baud rate and bits per second.

Chapter 4 presents the general characteristics of communications channels and defines such terms as circuit, bandwidth, full duplex, analog, digital, asynchronous, and synchronous.

1

INTRODUCTION

Ten years ago, most data communications were used by businesses to move information from one corporate location to another. Either the information was sent from a remote corporate location to a central location for processing, with the results returned to the remote site, or a communications facility was used to allow a remote location to have immediate access to a central corporate database. The average person had very little direct contact with either computers or data communications.

Today, however, most of us are very likely to come in contact with several computers and communications links throughout the day. This contact may result from:

- Using an automated teller machine to withdraw cash from a bank account
- Calling a stock broker to get a quotation on a security
- Making a purchase with a credit card whose use is authorized by a telephone transaction with the issuing company's computer
- Using a word processor to create a document and then mail it electronically
- Paying bills by connecting a personal computer to a bank's computer and transferring funds to appropriate merchants' accounts

Because many of us come into contact with various communicating computers in the course of our daily lives, there is a growing curiosity about the subject of data communications. This book will provide the fundamental knowledge needed to understand how computers communicate.

ORGANIZATION

The subject matter in this book is arranged into one of three categories: computers, conversion devices, or communication channels. The next three chapters in **Part I** bear those titles and present an introduction to the three subjects. These chapters are intended to pique your interest and to lead you into the subsequent sections of the book.

Part II discusses the data communications functions of the computers on both ends of a communications link. It also describes network architectures and communication protocols.

Part III describes the conversion devices that are required in order to transmit computer data across a communications channel to another computer.

Part IV describes the many types of communication channels that are used to communicate data, both over local and wide area networks.

FORMAT

Throughout the text you will see variations on one simple diagram that depicts the total communications connection from one end-point computer to another. The basic diagram is shown in **Figure 1-1**, and is printed at the beginning of each new section with a portion of it highlighted (see **Figure 1-2**) to show where, within the total communications diagram, the current subject matter lies. This visual reminder will help you to maintain a sense of perspective on the current material and on the relationship between that part and the whole.

As the text discussion of a particular subject narrows in focus, the relevant portion of the basic communications diagram will be expanded to show more detail, while still retaining its correct relationship with the other parts of the diagram. For example, in Chapter 15 on packet switching, the simple communications circuit in the basic diagram will be replaced with the "cloud" that

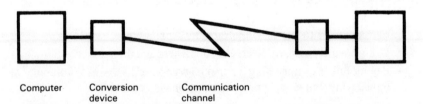

Computer   Conversion   Communication
            device   channel

Figure 1-1   Basic communications diagram. The basic communications diagram is used throughout this book and provides a structure into which all the subjects in the book can be placed. It shows the three primary components of a data communications network: the computer, the conversion device, and the communication channel.

is typically used to depict a packet-switching network, shown here in **Figure 1-3.** In Chapter 16 on the local loop, the diagram will highlight the local portion of the communications line as shown in **Figure 1-4.**

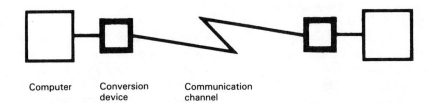

Computer   Conversion   Communication
               device   channel

Figure 1-2 Basic communications diagram with conversion devices highlighted. Whenever conversion devices are discussed in the text, this version of the basic communications diagram is used to show where the current topic fits into the overall communications structure.

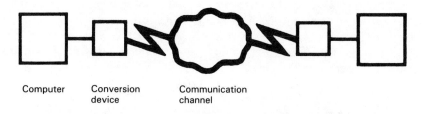

Computer   Conversion   Communication
               device   channel

Figure 1-3 Basic communications diagram with packet-switching "cloud." This format is used during discussions of packet switching to show the differences in the communication channel for packet-switching networks.

Computer   Conversion   Communication
               device   channel

Figure 1-4 Basic communications diagram with details of local loop connection. This format is used during discussions of the local loop which is the connection from the user's premises to the nearest telephone company central office.

DEFINITIONS

New terms are printed in italics where they are defined. In a few cases, the italicized entry is not the first occurence of a word, but is at the place in the text where the definition is located. In addition, the glossary contains page references to the italicized entries and to a relevant figure (if any) so that you may refer to an example of usage for each term.

The focus of this book is on *data communications*, which is the movement of data between computers. *Voice communications* is the movement of voice traffic between telephones. However, the two are closely related and some knowledge of voice communication is essential to understanding data communications, since so many data are transmitted through the telephone network.

The term *telecommunications,* or *telecom,* is used by some people to mean voice communications and by others to mean data communications. An increasingly common meaning is for telecommunications to be more inclusive than either data communications or voice communications, referring to any movement of information in electrical form.

Distinctions between data and voice communications are becoming less important as computer and communications technology merge. To some current and most future networks, the original source of a particular set of bits, whether computer data, a video image, a voice telephone call, or any combination of these, is irrelevant. If a distinction is necessary in this text, you will see data and voice communications used as defined above; however, an increasing percentage of the technology applied to one can be applied to the other.

R E C A P

- The book is organized around three network components: the computer, the conversion device, and the channel.
- The diagrams at the beginning of each section highlight the relationship between the current subject and the "big picture."
- The distinction between data communications and voice communications is diminishing, although the prime focus of this book is on the former.

COMPUTERS

COMMUNICATING COMPUTERS

This book is concerned primarily with the ways that computers communicate and not with the computers themselves; consequently, it will not examine the internal aspects of computer operation in any great detail. Instead, it will look at the ways that computers have been adapted over the years in order to communicate data more efficiently.

The set of rules by which two computers communicate is called a communications *protocol*. Implementing communication protocols involves a considerable amount of processing, as you will learn in Part II. In an attempt to free the central processing unit (CPU) from the complexities of data communications and to let the CPU do what it does best, that is, process data, most computer manufacturers have designed specialized hardware to implement the datacomm functions.

For large mainframe computers, such as an IBM 3090 or a Burroughs A15, the communications processor is usually a separate, special-purpose computer, often called a *front-end processor (FEP)*. For minicomputers, such as a DEC VAX 8700 or a Wang VS, the FEP function may be implemented as a separate box as in the mainframe case, or it may be accomplished by using specialized communications processor boards inside the CPU cabinet. For microcomputers, such as an IBM PC, the communications function may be handled either by the main processor or, increasingly, by a specialized communications board that plugs into one of the option slots inside the PC.

Regardless of the physical implementation for data communications processing, the intent of off-loading communications-related work from the CPU is the same.

Terminals

Many of the communications devices that are discussed will not be full-fledged computers, but will belong to the general category of computer terminals. A *terminal* is a device that is capable of communicating with a computer and has a means of accepting data from the user, typically a keyboard, and either a display screen or a printer, or both, for output of received data. Some terminals are very specialized, such as the automated teller machines used to allow access to banking services; others are very general purpose, such the workstation that allows an employee to access his or her company's computer to run accounting programs or to use word processing.

Terminals are often referred to as "dumb" and "smart" depending on their capabilities. While there are no strict guidelines, the following paragraphs will provide a generally accepted description of the difference between dumb and smart terminals. Smart terminals are occasionally referred to as intelligent terminals, and while some authors further distinguish between these two categories, this book will only differentiate between the dumb and smart categories.

Dumb terminals. A typical *dumb terminal* has little or no data-processing capability of its own. It is able to communicate to a computer using one simple set of rules, probably using an asynchronous protocol or IBM's bisync protocol (see Chapter 6). It either offers no capability to edit the data that are entered by the user, or it provides limited editing capability. A dumb terminal might, for example, be able to verify that a particular field is numeric or alphabetic or that the data entered do not exceed a specified number of characters.

The screen on a dumb terminal probably has several display modes allowing it to show data that are highlighted or underlined or that are displayed in reverse video (for example, black on green instead of green on black). Dumb terminals are relatively inexpensive, ranging upward from only a few hundred dollars apiece. Typical examples of dumb terminals include the Lear-Siegler ADM 3A, DEC VT100, and devices that are described as teletype replacements.

Smart terminals. A *smart terminal* on the other hand, has its own local processing capability and may even have its own local storage device, for example, a disk drive, although this is not required for the terminal to be considered a smart device. Many smart terminals have the ability to communicate using several different protocols, usually employing synchronous transmission (see Chapter 4) and can probably talk to several different types of computers.

Smart terminals have considerable editing capabilities, including those mentioned above, as well as the ability to perform data validation, perhaps by computing check digits or by verifying data against a local database before passing the data on to the computer. Smart terminals also have the capability to display data in a variety of different formats on the screen. Smart terminals may be priced from under $1000 to several thousand dollars apiece depending on their features.

Figure 2-1 provides a quick reference summary to the capabilities of the dumb and smart terminal categories. Bear in mind, however, that there are no firm rules about what is considered to be dumb and what is considered to be smart. Also, do not assume that a dumb terminal is dumb because it does not contain a microprocessor; the capabilities of many dumb terminals are built around software written for a microprocessor because it allows the designers more flexibility than a pure hardware solution.

Feature	Dumb Terminal	Smart Terminal
Communications	Single protocol usually TTY	Sophisticated or multiple protocols
Local processing	Limited	Extensive
Local disk storage	None	Limited to extensive
Data edit/validation	Simple	Complex
Price	$100s	$100s to $1000s

Figure 2-1   Characteristics of dumb and smart terminals.

Throughout the rest of this book, unless the distinction is particularly important, the word terminal will be used in a very general sense to mean a device that is communicating to a computer.

Digital Signaling

Modern computers are referred to as digital computers because their internal operation relies on *digital signaling*. Digital signaling is an electronic technique that uses a small number of discrete values of an electrical signal to represent data. Typically, the electrical signal has two values. It is either on or off; it is either +5 volts or -5 volts; or it has one of two other values at any given instant in time.

While the actual values of the signal may be significant to a computer designer or an electrical engineer, most of us are only concerned with the meaning represented by the signal states. The computer industry has adopted the convention of assigning a value of 0 and 1 to the two signal states, thereby establishing a binary counting system. Each binary digit, or *bit*, has a value of 0 or 1, and the bits are combined to represent larger numbers, just as the *decimal* digits 0 through 9 are combined to form larger decimal numbers.

DATA REPRESENTATION

Over the years, computer designers have created many different ways to combine bits into patterns in order to represent the data that they wished to store inside a computer. While many different coding schemes are still in use, the ASCII and EBCDIC character sets that are described next are the dominant coding schemes used for data communications.

ASCII

The American Standard Code for Information Interchange, or *ASCII*, was proposed by the American National Standards Institute (*ANSI*) in an attempt to provide a uniform way for data to be represented by all the vendors in the fledgling computer industry. ASCII defines a unique combination of 7 bits to represent each possible character. Because each of these 7 bits can have one of two values, there are 2^7 (2*2*2*2*2*2*2), or 128, unique characters that comprise the ASCII chart. **Figure 2-2** is a copy of the 7-bit ASCII chart.

Note that there are positions in the ASCII chart for all the letters of the alphabet (both upper- and lowercase), for the numbers from zero through nine, and for many common symbols, such as the equal sign (=) and dollar sign ($). There are also two columns containing control characters, specifically, columns zero and one. Some of these control characters are special characters that are used for controlling devices attached to computers; for example, the form feed character tells a printer to advance the paper to the top of the next page. Other control characters are used to control the communication of data between computers. **Figure 2-3** contains a list of all the ASCII control characters. Many of the data communication control characters are defined in Chapter 7.

An ASCII character is usually referred to in one of two ways. It may be specified by combining two hexadecimal digits, one to designate its column in the ASCII chart and another to designate its row number. For example, the letter A has an ASCII value of 41, and the letter Z has a value of 5A. (**Figure 2-4** shows the 16 hexadecimal digits and their corresponding decimal values.) The alternative is to specify it by using the decimal equivalent of its hexadecimal value. For example, the letter A has a decimal ASCII value of 65, and the letter Z has a decimal value of 90.

EBCDIC

Often the 128 unique characters allowed by ASCII are not enough. IBM Corporation developed a different encoding scheme called the Extended Binary Coded Decimal Interchange Code, or *EBCDIC*. EBCDIC uses 8 bits per character yielding 2^8, or 256, unique bit patterns.

Bit 4	Bit 3	Bit 2	Bit 1	Row Number	0	1	2	3	4	5	6	7
Bit 7					0	0	0	0	1	1	1	1
Bit 6					0	0	1	1	0	0	1	1
Bit 5					0	1	0	1	0	1	0	1
0	0	0	0	0	NUL	DLE	SP	0	@	P	'	p
0	0	0	1	1	SOH	DC1	!	1	A	Q	a	q
0	0	1	0	2	STX	DC2	"	2	B	R	b	r
0	0	1	1	3	ETX	DC3	#	3	C	S	c	s
0	1	0	0	4	EOT	DC4	$	4	D	T	d	t
0	1	0	1	5	ENQ	NAK	%	5	E	U	e	u
0	1	1	0	6	ACK	SYN	&	6	F	V	f	v
0	1	1	1	7	BEL	ETB	'	7	G	W	g	w
1	0	0	0	8	BS	CAN	(	8	H	X	h	x
1	0	0	1	9	HT	EM	)	9	I	Y	i	y
1	0	1	0	A	LF	SUB	*	:	J	Z	j	z
1	0	1	1	B	VT	ESC	+	;	K	[	k	{
1	1	0	0	C	FF	FS	,	<	L	\	l		
1	1	0	1	D	CR	GS	-	=	M·	]	m	}
1	1	1	0	E	SO	RS	.	>	N	^	n	~
1	1	1	1	F	SI	US	/	?	O	—	o	DEL

First hexadecimal digit

Second hexadecimal digit

Bits are numbered in the order of transmission.

Figure 2-2 The American Standard Code for Information Interchange (ASCII). The ASCII value of any character is determined by locating the character in the chart and noting the hex value for its column number and row number, in that order. The letter A, for example, has an ASCII value of 41 and the letter Z has a value of 5A.

In the EBCDIC chart in **Figure 2-5** you will find not only the letters of the alphabet, the numbers from zero to nine, many symbols, and the special control characters, but because there are now twice as many possible positions in the chart, you will also find some extra symbols, as well as a considerable number of undefined positions. The EBCDIC chart is always read using the first method described above for the ASCII chart, that is by referring to each character with a pair of hexadecimal digits that represent the column and row numbers, in that order. For example, the letter A has an EBCDIC value of C1, and the letter Z has a value of E9.

ASCII Value	Symbol	Name/Meaning
01	SOH	Start of header
02	STX	Start of text
03	ETX	End of text
04	EOT	End of transmission
05	ENQ	Enquiry
06	ACK	Acknowledgment
10	DLE	Data link escape
15	NAK	Negative acknowledgment
16	SYN	Synchronous idle character

Figure 2-3   Selected ASCII control characters. Columns 0 and 1 in the ASCII chart are device and communications control characters. They are included in a message in order to give the receiver special instructions for handling a particular device such as a printer or to control the flow of communications on the line. This figure provides the meaning of selected ASCII control characters; refer to [ANSI]* for descriptions of all ASCII control characters.

ASCII and EBCDIC Variations

Although ASCII and EBCDIC are in widespread use in the form printed in **Figures 2-2** and **2-5** there are many variations of each. For example, a vendor of word-processing equipment needs additional characters to represent special function codes for word processing, such as the characters to cause text in a document to be centered or underlined. Similarly, a computer used in a manufacturing environment needs additional device control codes to cause a conveyor belt to turn on and off or to instruct a robot arm to move to the left or right.

One common adaptation of the ASCII chart adds an extra bit to each character, giving it the same number of characters as the EBCDIC chart. The specific way that these extra characters are defined, however, can vary considerably from one vendor to another. Similarly, the undefined characters in the EBCDIC chart may be used for different purposes by different vendors. In general, the user should exercise caution and not assume that any two variations of ASCII or EBCDIC are identical without examining them closely.

Other Code Sets

ASCII and EBCDIC are the dominant coding schemes used in the communications industry, but they are by no means the only ones. Other computer or communications companies have developed special-purpose code charts to

Decimal	0	1	2	3	4	5	6	7	8	9	10	11	12	13	14	15
Hexadecimal	0	1	2	3	4	5	6	7	8	9	A	B	C	D	E	F

Figure 2-4   Hexadecimal and decimal equivalents.

* Citations in brackets refer to the Bibliography at the end of the text.

Figure 2-5 — EBCDIC code chart

Bits are numbered in the order of transmission.

First hexadecimal digit →

Bit 1	Bit 2	Bit 3	Bit 4													
0	0	0	0													
0	0	0	1													
0	0	1	0													
0	0	1	1													

Bit 5	Bit 6	Bit 7	Bit 8	Column Number → Row Number	0	1	2	3	4	5	6	7	8	9	A	B	C	D	E	F
0	0	0	0	0	NUL	DLE			SP	&	-									0
0	0	0	1	1	SOH	SBA					/		a	j			A	J		1
0	0	1	0	2	STX	EUA		SYN					b	k	s		B	K	S	2
0	0	1	1	3	ETX	IC							c	l	t		C	L	T	3
0	1	0	0	4									d	m	u		D	M	U	4
0	1	0	1	5	PT	NL							e	n	v		E	N	V	5
0	1	1	0	6			ETB						f	o	w		F	O	W	6
0	1	1	1	7			ESC	EOT					g	p	x		G	P	X	7
1	0	0	0	8									h	q	y		H	Q	Y	8
1	0	0	1	9		EM							i	r	z		I	R	Z	9
1	0	1	0	A					¢	!		:								
1	0	1	1	B					.	$	,	#								
1	1	0	0	C		DUP		RA	<	*	%	@								
1	1	0	1	D		SF	ENQ	NAK	(	)	_	'								
1	1	1	0	E		FM			+	;	>	=								
1	1	1	1	F		ITB		SUE			¬	?	"								

Second hexadecimal digit

Figure 2-5 The Extended Binary Coded Decimal Interchange Code (EBCDIC). The EBCDIC value of any character is determined by locating the character in the chart and noting the hex value for its column number and row number, in that order. The letter A, for example, has an EBCDIC value of C1 and the letter Z has a value of E9.

13

satisfy their specific requirements. In this book, all examples will refer to either ASCII or EBCDIC due to their widespread use.

R E C A P

- A communications protocol is a set of rules for communicating between computers.
- Computers often have specialized processors to implement data communications protocols.
- Terminals, both dumb and smart, are devices that communicate over a channel to a computer.
- Computers use digital signaling and binary representation of data.
- ASCII and EBCDIC are the commonly used code sets for representing data on communications lines.

CONVERSION DEVICES

CHARACTERISTICS OF ELECTRICAL SIGNALS

A signal-conversion device is usually required to connect a computer to a communication circuit because the form of electrical signal that is used to move data inside a computer is seldom the same as the type of electrical signal that is used on the communications channel. In particular, internal computer signaling is digital, and a significant percentage of the communication channels available use analog signaling.

Chapter 4 will provide a more complete definition of both digital and analog signaling. For this chapter, it is sufficient to understand that there *is* a difference, and that since computers tend to be digital and communication circuits tend to be analog, some type of signal conversion is required.

MODEMS

The most common type of conversion device is the *modem* that is used to connect a computer to a telephone line. See **Figure 3-1**. The purpose of the modem, the name of which is an acronym for modulator/demodulator, is to combine the digital signal from the computer with a constant-frequency analog signal

Computer A   Modem A   Modem B   Computer B

Figure 3-1 Telephone line modem location. A modem is required to convert the electrical signals from the digital format of a computer to the analog format used on most telephone lines. Modems are always used in pairs since the signal that is modulated on one end of the line must be demodulated at the other so that the data can be extracted and passed to the receiving computer.

called the carrier and then to transmit the combined signal across the line. Modems are always used in pairs since the modulated signal that is received at the far end of the line must be demodulated so that the original data can be extracted and passed on to the other computer.

The *carrier* signal is an electrical signal that oscillates at a constant frequency, that is, a constant number of cycles per second, providing a reference point for the sending and receiving modems and allowing the data to be carried along the circuit. To visualize the need for the carrier signal, imagine that you have a message to deliver to someone across the room. If you try to deliver the message by throwing the piece of paper across the room, you are not likely to succeed. However, if you are walking in the proper direction, you can take the message with you, acting as a carrier for your message in the same way that the carrier signal does for the computer data. **Figure 3-2a** shows an analog carrier signal that is capable of having data added to it for transport across a circuit. **Figure 3-2b** shows the same signal after it has been modulated by the addition of data.

Chapter 11 describes several common modulation techniques that are employed in telephone modems. Chapter 12 describes the operation and use of a number of other kinds of signal-conversion devices. Although there are significant differences in the operation and design of the various conversion devices, they all exist because of the signaling difference between computers and communication channels.

BAUD RATE VERSUS BPS

The two most common measures of the speed of a circuit are the baud rate and the number of bits per second. The two terms are often used interchangeably, but they do not have the same meaning. The *baud rate* is a measure of the signaling speed of a line and defines the number of times per second that the condition of the electrical signal on the line is changing. The data rate, measured

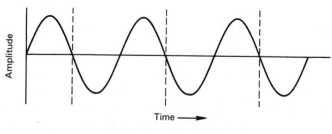

(a) Analog carrier signal

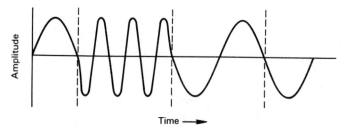

(b) Modulated analog carrier signal

Figure 3-2 Telephone modem signaling. *Part a* shows an unmodulated carrier signal, that is, a constant frequency signal that can be used to carry data on a communication circuit. *Part b* shows the results of modulating the carrier signal from *part a* by the addition of data. In this figure it is the frequency of the carrier signal that has been modulated (see Chapter 11 for descriptions of modulation techniques). By knowing the modulation technique and the characteristics of the original carrier signal, the receiving modem can extract the data.

in *bits per second* (*bps*) is a count of the actual number of data bits that are moving past a given point on the circuit each second.

The baud rate, then, is a measure of an electrical property of a circuit, while the bps rate is a measure of data movement across a line. For example, if a modem can alter the frequency of the carrier signal on a circuit 1200 times per second, then the baud rate of the line is 1200. If each baud interval represents 1 bit of data, then the data rate for this circuit would also be 1200. Thus, whenever the modulation technique conveys 1 bit of data in each baud interval, the bit rate and the baud rate are the same.

The maximum baud rate for a conventional telephone circuit is approximately 2400 baud. However, many telephone circuits that are used for data transmission operate at 4800 bps, 9600 bps, or even faster. If the maximum baud rate on a phone line is 2400, how is it possible to transmit data at any speed faster than that? The secret, which will be explained in Chapter 11, lies in being able to carry multiple bits of data in each change in the electrical signal, that is, packing several bits per baud. For example, if a conversion device uses a technique that can carry 2 bits' worth of data in each signal change on a 1200-baud line, the data rate will be 2400 bps.

For slower transmission speeds that employ less sophisticated modulation techniques, the bps rate and the baud rate are usually equal, so referring to a 1200-bps modem as a 1200-baud modem is probably correct. However, modem manufacturers and even the telephone companies frequently refer to 9600-baud modems for use on telephone circuits; as you should understand from the preceding paragraphs, the device in question is actually a 9600-bps modem using a much lower baud rate, but packing multiple bits of data into each baud interval.

While most people will probably understand if you talk about a 9600-baud modem, the explanation here and in Chapter 11 should allow you to use the correct terminology.

R E C A P

- Conversion devices are required because of signaling differences between computers and communication channels.
- Modems are commonly used conversion devices for connecting computers to telephone lines.
- Baud and bits per second (bps) are measures of signaling speed and data rate, respectively; the terms are not necessarily interchangeable.

$$=============================4$$

COMMUNICATION CHANNELS

CHANNEL BASICS

A communication *channel* or *circuit* is a path for the movement of electrical signals. Also called a *line* or a *link,* the circuit may be several inches or several thousand miles long. The line may consist of copper wire, a satellite connection, or a combination of the many other types of transmission media that will be discussed in Part IV.

Parallel and Serial Circuits

Communication circuits are classified in several ways. *Parallel* circuits are able to move multiple bits of data simultaneously. Many of the paths inside a computer are parallel paths because the connections are short; however, the cost of running multiple wires for long distances becomes prohibitive very quickly. Consequently, most data outside a computer are moved on *serial* data links on which each bit follows the previous one down the wire. All circuits described in this text are serial paths unless specifically mentioned otherwise. **Figure 4-1** illustrates the difference between a parallel and a serial circuit.

Bandwidth

The carrying capacity of a circuit is called the *bandwidth.* For an analog circuit, the bandwidth is the difference between the highest and lowest frequencies

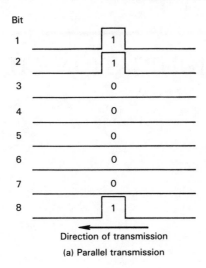

Direction of transmission

(a) Parallel transmission

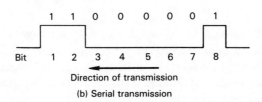

Direction of transmission

(b) Serial transmission

Figure 4-1   Circuit types. A parallel circuit contains a separate path for each bit of the character to be transmitted. In *part a*, there are eight wires for the 8 bits of the letter A encoded in EBCDIC; all bits move simultaneously along the circuit. Parallel circuits are generally used for short distances, typically within a computer system, since running multiple wires over long distances can be very expensive. In a serial circuit, there is only one path for each bit of the character to be transmitted. In *part b*, the 8 bits for an EBCDIC A must travel sequentially down the same wire. Serial transmission is used for almost all long-distance communication circuits.

that a medium can transmit and is expressed in *hertz*. One hertz, abbreviated *Hz*, is equal to one cycle per second. Because there is a direct mathematical relationship between the bandwidth and the maximum data rate that can be carried on a circuit [McNamara]*, and because we are often more concerned with how fast we can move data rather than with the frequency characteristics of a line, the bandwidth is usually expressed in bits per second rather than hertz. On a digital circuit where the frequencies of a signal are largely irrelevant, the bandwidth is always expressed in bits per second. The characteristics of and differences between analog and digital circuits are described later in this chapter.

*Citations in brackets refer to the Bibliography at the end of the text.

Some media types, such as copper twisted-pair wire, have relatively limited bandwidth, capable of moving from several thousand bits per second up to several million bits per second. Other types of media, such as coaxial cable, have a bandwidth measured in millions of bits per second. The bandwidth of fiber-optic cable is measured in megabits and gigabits per second (the prefix mega- means millions; the prefix giga- means billions). Chapters 13 and 16 explore the concept of bandwidth and the characteristics of various transmission media in more detail.

Directional Characteristics

Circuits that are capable of moving data in only one direction are called *simplex* circuits. Circuits that can move signals in both directions but not simultaneously, that is, circuits with alternating traffic flows, are called *half-duplex* circuits. Circuits capable of simultaneous, bidirectional data flow are called *full-duplex* or *duplex* circuits.

As illustrated in **Figure 4-2,** a simplex channel is like a one-way street: the entire bandwidth of the circuit (or the entire width of the street) is always used to carry traffic in the same direction. A half-duplex circuit is like a road that is under repair and has a flagperson to control the movement of cars, first in one direction and then in the other. A full-duplex line is like a road with two or more separate lanes that allows cars to pass in either direction at all times. Just as the multilane road has a yellow line down the center to divide the roadway into two separate directions of travel, a full-duplex circuit uses one of several techniques to subdivide its bandwidth in order to allow signals to move in both directions simultaneously.

In most cases, it is not the circuit but the equipment on either end of the circuit that determines whether a particular link is used in simplex, half-duplex, or full-duplex mode. The same circuit is probably capable of being used in any of the three modes, but the communication requirements will dictate which type of equipment will be used. As a general rule, simplex equipment costs less than half-duplex equipment, which in turn is less expensive than full-duplex gear.

Chapter 11 provides details of the ways that duplex communication is achieved by various signal-conversion devices.

SIGNALING TECHNIQUES

Transmission Impairments

The relative strength of an electrical signal is called the *amplitude*. If there were no resistance to the flow of electricity, the amplitude of a signal

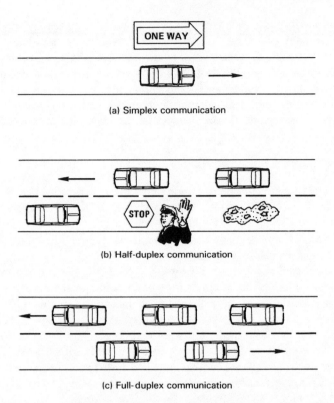

(a) Simplex communication

(b) Half-duplex communication

(c) Full-duplex communication

Figure 4-2   Directional characteristics. Simplex communication occurs in only one direction, just as traffic on the one-way street in *part a* can only travel in one direction. Half-duplex circuits are capable of carrying signals in both directions, but can do so in only one direction at a time, much like the traffic flow on the road-under-construction in *part b*. Traffic flow on the road is regulated by the flag person, who periodically stops the traffic flow in one direction to allow movement in the other direction. Full-duplex circuits allow simultaneous communication in both directions as depicted in *part c* by a conventional two-lane street. Various electronic techniques are used to divide the circuit bandwidth into two separate paths, just as the yellow line in the center of the road divides the roadway into two separate lanes.

would remain constant over distance and time. In the real world, however, any signal traveling through a wire *attenuates,* or weakens, as it overcomes the resistance of the medium to its passage. Therefore, the amplitude of a signal must be boosted periodically to ensure that the signal can travel through a wire and still be usable at the other end.

The notable exception to signal attenuation occurs in a *superconductor,* because a superconductor passes electrical signals without attenuation. While there are no practical superconducting transmission media today, other than for very short distances, there were remarkable breakthroughs during 1987 in achieving superconductivity at temperatures above the supercold of liquid helium. The higher the temperature at which superconductivity can be achieved, the sooner there can be practical, inexpensive superconductors on the market. In the meantime, attenuation is a fact of life in the transmission of electrical signals.

In addition to attenuation, all signals traveling through a transmission medium are subject to corruption by *noise*. Noise is electrical interference that may result from signals passing through mechanical connections such as splices or the junctions between the end of a wire and a piece of electronic equipment. Noise also results from external sources that insert unwanted energy into the circuit, such as an electrical storm or signals leaking from an adjacent wire. The overall effect of noise is to make it more difficult to determine the correct amplitude of the received signal at any given point in time.

Many other transmission impairments affect the passage of electrical signals through transmission media, but most are beyond the scope of this text. Consult [Black] or [Sherman] for more detailed discussions of transmission impairments.

Analog Circuits

Most telephone communication links are designed to carry analog signals because the human voice produces analog waveforms. An *analog signal* is one whose amplitude varies continuously over time, and it is usually drawn as a sine wave, as depicted in **Figure 4-3.**

A device that is designed to receive an analog signal must be able to differentiate among all the possible signal values in order to correctly interpret the received signal at each instant in time. The human ear, for example, interprets the differences in amplitude of an incoming signal as differences in the loudness

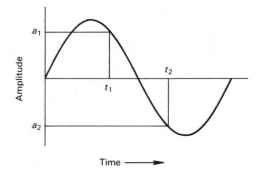

Figure 4-3   Analog sine wave. An analog signal, drawn as a sine wave, has a continuously variable amplitude. At any given time the amplitude can have one of many possible values. In this figure, amplitudes a_1 and a_2 occur at times t_1 and t_2, respectively. Contrast the properties of this analog signal with the digital signal in Figure 4-6, in which the amplitude always has one of two distinct values.

of the sound. An electronic receiving device must be able to perform the same subtle differentiation. To understand how difficult this can be when noise and attenuation affect an analog sine wave, compare **Figure 4-3** with **Figure 4-4**. The latter diagram illustrates the potential for incorrect amplitude measurements that result from a noisy, attenuated signal.

An *amplifier* is a device that boosts the strength of an analog signal to overcome attenuation. An unfortunate property of analog amplifiers is that they have no way to distinguish a good signal from the background noise that is also present. As a result, when an analog signal is amplified, any noise that is present is also amplified. As the signal travels toward the next amplifier, it attenuates again and it also picks up additional noise. At this point, the new noise, the old noise, and the original signal are all amplified. See **Figure 4-5**.

While two people on a noisy telephone line may still be able to converse because the human ear and brain offer a powerful mechanism for rejecting background noise, an electronic device usually has much more stringent requirements and much less ability to perform this discrimination. The combination of attenuation and noise is a major detriment to communicating data over analog circuits. It is even possible that the strength of the accumulated noise will grow to exceed the strength of the useful signal, at which point the information carried by the original signal will be lost.

The ratio of the strength of the desired signal to the background noise is called the *signal-to-noise ratio (S/N)*. Stereo equipment manufacturers use the same ratio to describe the ability of an FM receiver, for example, to discriminate the desired FM radio station out of the background noise that is

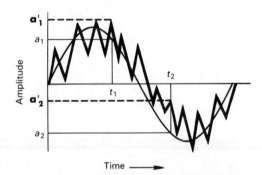

Time ——▶

Figure 4-4 Effects of noise and attenuation on analog signals. Noise on a circuit can cause incorrect amplitude values to be read from an incoming analog signal. Sometimes the difference between the received and original values is very small, as at time t_1, where the received amplitude (a_1') is nearly the same as the original amplitude (a_1). In other cases the difference may be very significant, as shown at time t_2, where the received amplitude (a_2') is markedly different from the original amplitude (a_2). Contrast this with Figure 4-7 for digital signals.

always present to some degree. For data communications, the limiting factor on the length of an analog circuit is its ability to maintain a sufficient S/N ratio to allow the received information to be separated from the accumulated background noise. Chapter 11 describes some of the techniques that modems use to increase their ability to transmit data over inherently noisy analog circuits.

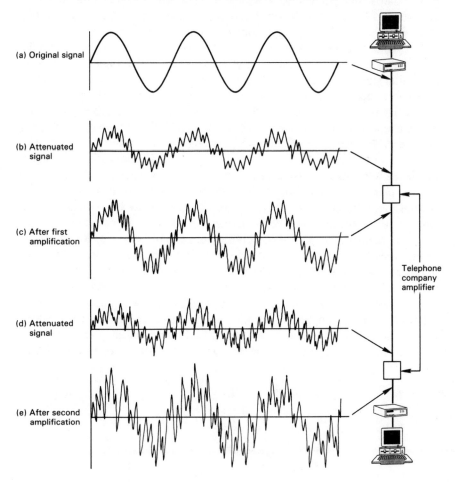

(a) Original signal

(b) Attenuated signal

(c) After first amplification

Telephone company amplifier

(d) Attenuated signal

(e) After second amplification

Effects of amplification on analog signals.

Figure 4-5 Effects of amplification on analog signals. This figure shows the same portion of an analog signal at various locations along a transmission line and illustrates an unfortunate property of analog amplifiers: they cannot distinguish between the original signal and any noise that has been picked up along the way. As a result, each successive amplifier compounds the problem for the receiver by amplifying the signal *and* the noise. If the noise level is too great or if there are too many amplifiers, it is possible for the amplified noise to obscure the signal completely.

Digital Circuits

You have already seen that computers produce *digital signals* and that digital signals always have one of a small number of discrete values. (You should assume that it takes no time for a digital signal to change from one value to the other so that you may ignore the fractional part of a second during which the signal is in transition between values.) Digital signals are usually drawn as square waves like the sample signal in **Figure 4-6**.

Like analog waveforms, digital signals also attenuate and are susceptible to noise; however, the combination of the two has significantly less effect on the digital signal because of its discrete nature. Since the receiver of a digital signal only needs to look for a small number of values and not an infinite number of possible values, its job is much less complex than that of an analog receiver. For example, a digital signal with 2 possible values means that the receiver only needs to determine whether the incoming signal is above or below some reference value, but not by what amount. Consequently, the weak, noisy signal in **Figure 4-7** looks the same to a digital receiver as does the clean, perfect looking signal in **Figure 4-6**. As long as the receiver's location in the circuit is such that it receives the signal before it gets so weak or so noisy that its value actually changes, it is very simple to detect the correct value.

The equivalent of an analog amplifier for a digital signal is called a *repeater* or *regenerator*. A repeater scans the incoming signal at a predetermined rate in order to determine which value the signal has at each instant. It then creates a new output signal that is a nearly perfect replica of the original signal. The noise is essentially thrown away. The real power of a digital circuit for transmitting data, then, lies in its ability to continually recreate a nearly perfect copy of the original signal each time the signal strength needs to be increased. Compare the analog signal traveling through a wire in **Figure 4-5** with the digital

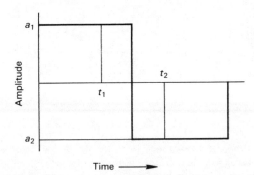

Figure 4-6   Digital square wave. A digital signal, drawn as a square wave, has only a small number of possible amplitude values. In this figure, the amplitude at any time (for example, t_1 and t_2) is always either a_1 or a_2. Contrast this with the analog signal in Figure 4-3, in which the amplitude at a given time has one of many possible values.

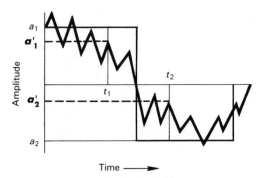

Figure 4-7 Effects of noise and attenuation on digital signals. The effects of noise are minimal on the digital signal in this figure because the receiver is only required to distinguish between the two possible values. Consequently, although the received amplitudes (a_1' and a_2') are different from the original amplitudes (a_1 and a_2), there is no question about which of the two digital values has been received. Contrast this with Figure 4-4 for analog signals.

signal in **Figure 4-8**; the potential for higher-quality output signals at the end of a digital line should be obvious.

Signaling and the Telephone Network

An obvious question at this point is: If digital signaling is so superior to analog signaling, why aren't all data transmitted on digital circuits? The answer lies in the historical development of the telephone network and in its nearly universal availability. Since the telephone network was designed to transmit analog voice signals, the vast majority of the existing telephone network is only able to carry analog signals. The network does, however, offer the considerable advantage of having circuits installed, or installable, in virtually every location. As a result, the cost-effective approach for most data communications is to use the existing analog facilities.

There is a definite trend, however, toward digital signaling within the telephone network, because the phone companies themselves benefit from the nature of digital signals. The various local and long-distance carriers are spending billions of dollars per year to upgrade their facilities to digital operation.

Because of the economies of scale, it is almost always the high-speed trunk lines between telephone company offices that are converted to digital signaling first. The Bell System began installing digital circuits between their offices in the 1960s. However, the connection of individual users to the nearest telephone company office, often referred to as the "last mile," is most often still an analog link.

One of the great ironies of communicating data over analog telephone links in the 1980s is that users spend hundreds or thousands of dollars for equipment to convert signals from digital to analog format for transmission over the telephone network. And yet, once those signals arrive at the nearest telephone

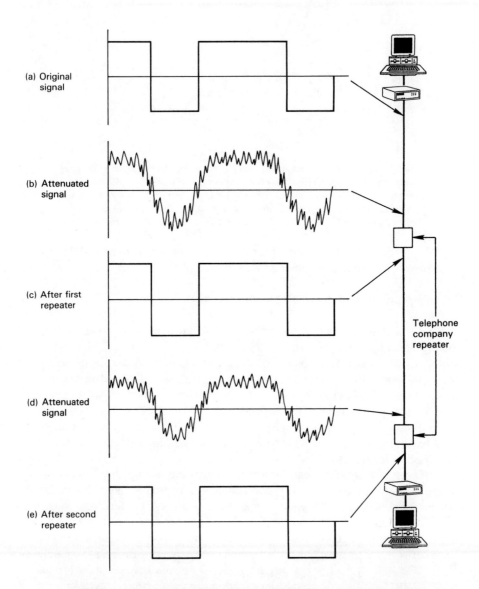

Figure 4-8   Effects of repeaters on digital signals. This figure illustrates the same portion of a digital signal at several different locations along a transmission line. Even though the signal has been corrupted by noise prior to entering the repeater, the repeater can usually build a perfect replica of the original signal because it only needs to determine whether the amplitude is above or below the reference value. Regardless of the number of repeaters through which it must pass, the signal at the receiver in this diagram is an exact copy of the original, despite a less than perfect transmission medium.

company office (or, perhaps, some other more distant office), they are probably converted to digital format for long-haul transmission, only to be converted to analog once again to travel across the last mile to the end user, where the user's equipment converts them back to digital form for use by the computer. See **Figure 4-9** for an illustration of this digital-to-analog paradox.

Despite the significant increase in customer availability of digital circuits in the last five years, the demand far exceeds the supply. Consequently, the pattern of multiple conversions will continue to be true into the foreseeable future for many data communications users.

Part IV describes the nature of telephone company facilities very thoroughly, including both the long-distance and local parts of the network.

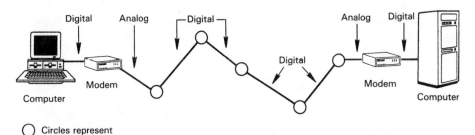

○ Circles represent
telephone company
central offices.

Figure 4-9   Analog transmission paradox. Users of analog telephone lines buy modems to convert their computers' digital signals into analog form. Internal to the telephone network, however, a significant and growing percentage of the long-distance lines employ digital transmission. Consequently, the user's carefully converted analog signal probably gets converted back to digital form for long-distance transmission, before being converted back to analog form so that the receiving modem can convert it back to digital for the computer. This paradox results from the widespread use of digital facilities for long-distance communications and of analog facilities for local communication.

SYNCHRONOUS/ASYNCHRONOUS TRANSMISSION

Depending on the nature of the equipment connected to the ends of a circuit, the line will be used in either synchronous or asynchronous transmission mode. Synchronous transmission maintains a fixed time relationship, as the Greek root of the word, *chronos*, meaning time, suggests. Asynchronous is the opposite of synchronous (just as atypical is the opposite of typical) and implies that there is no rigid time relationship for this type of transmission.

Asynchronous Transmission

In *asynchronous* mode, also called *async* or start-stop mode, each character of data is transmitted as soon as it is available, without regard to the preceding or succeeding characters. Since the receiver of asynchronous data has no fixed time interval to tell it when to expect the next character, this transmission mode employs special "packaging" around each character to indicate where it begins and where it ends. The packaging consists of an extra bit, called the *start bit*, that signals the beginning of a character, and another extra bit, called the *stop bit*, to signal its end.

In between the start and stop bits, there must be a previously agreed on number of bits that represents each character. ASCII code is usually used for async transmission so that there are typically 7 bits of data between the start and stop bit. There may also be another bit called the parity bit that is used for error detection (see Chapter 6 for more details on parity). **Figure 4-10** shows the ASCII character A with a parity bit and start and stop bits.

Between characters on an asynchronous circuit, the line is left in an idle condition consisting of the continuous transmission of one bits. For historical reasons related to early telegraph equipment, one bits are referred to as *mark* bits; hence the idle condition is occasionally still referred to as "marking the line." In the same nomenclature, zero bits are called *space* bits.

Since an idle transmitter sends continuous one bits, the only possible way that a start bit can expect to wake up the receiver for the next data character is for the start bit to have a value of zero. By the same logic, the only way for the stop bit to always return the line to the idle state at the end of each character is for it to have a value of one. **Figure 4-11** shows the bit value and the format of the corresponding digital signal that is generated to transmit the three ASCII characters ABC, in that order.

Some communications equipment requires that each character be followed by more than one stop bit in order to allow the receiver sufficient time to process each new character before the next character arrives. Typically, the requirement is for either 1.5 or 2 stop bits between characters to provide an acceptable

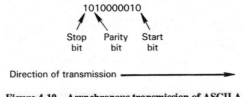

Figure 4-10   Asynchronous transmission of ASCII A.

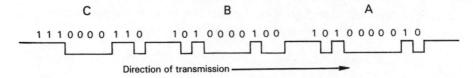

Figure 4-11   Asynchronous transmission of ASCII ABC.

minimum intercharacter spacing. Remember, however, that there is no maximum time between characters; theoretically, it could be either a tenth of a second or ten hours before the next character arrives.

All the transmitted bits, whether they are start, stop, data, or idle bits, will be transmitted at a previously agreed on rate of speed. The most common speeds used for asynchronous data on telephone lines are 300, 1200, and 2400 bits per second. In local environments (where there are no telephone lines involved), some devices transmit asynchronously at much higher rates of 19,200 or 38,400 bps.

The hardware required to implement asynchronous transmission is fairly simple since the task of sending a start bit, transmitting the data bits, generating a parity bit, and then sending a stop bit is not difficult. Consequently, asynchronous transmission hardware is relatively inexpensive and is often the first communications capability offered on smaller computers, and it may be the only capability offered on many inexpensive terminals.

Synchronous Transmission

Synchronous transmission is also called *block mode* transmission because data characters are collected into blocks and transmitted as a group rather than being transmitted individually as they are generated. While asynchronous transmission is well suited to traffic generated by humans typing at keyboards, synchronous transmission evolved when machines began to talk to other machines. Typically, each computer had more than one character available for transmission at one time or, at the least, it was able to generate the characters at a speed that was faster than the line could transmit them, so it always appeared to the line that characters were generated in blocks. With a backlog of characters available, it was very inefficient to package each character separately with a start and stop bit, so a more efficient technique was developed for synchronous transmission.

Synchronous packaging requires a special character, called a *sync character*, to be placed at the beginning of each block of data to signal the start of the new block. In actual practice, two or more sync characters are usually placed at the beginning of each block so that the receiver will recognize the start of the data even if one of the sync characters happens to get lost or is corrupted by noise on the line.

The sync character itself is nothing more than a bit pattern that is reserved specifically for this purpose. Refer to ASCII character 16 and EBCDIC character 32 in **Figures 2-2** and **2-5**, respectively, to find the SYN character.

Once the transmitter has begun to send data, it must transmit data continuously until the block is finished. After seeing the sync character(s), the receiving device extracts bits from the line at a precise rate, defined in advance, so the transmitter must ensure that every bit of every character is sent at the correct instant; there can be no gaps in transmission. It is from this fixed time relationship that the synchronous transmission mode derives its name.

Although the sync character serves a similar purpose to the start bit, there is no synchronous counterpart to the async stop bit. Most communication protocols that use synchronous transmission also employ a special character or bit pattern to signal the end of a block of data, as you will see in Chapters 6 and 7. After the end of block indication, the line is returned to the idle mode, which is the same all ones bit pattern that is used for asynchronous lines.

By way of summary, asynchronous transmission relies on cheap hardware that packages each data character between a start and a stop bit; the interval between characters is irrelevant. Synchronous transmission requires relatively more sophisticated hardware that precedes an entire block of data with several sync characters and must transmit continuously and precisely until the block is complete.

Relative Transmission Efficiency

The use of either start-stop transmission or synchronous transmission has several implications on the overall efficiency of a circuit. **Figure 4-12** contains several examples of the relative efficiency of each technique. All examples assume the use of 8 bits per data character, and the term overhead refers to the bits that are part of the packaging and that do not, therefore, carry any information for the end user.

As you can see from **Figure 4-12**, the use of synchronous transmission can be dramatically more efficient than the use of asynchronous techniques,

Number of 8-Bit Characters to be Transmitted	Technique	Total bits Overhead[c]	Total Bits of Data	Ratio of Overhead/Data
5	Async[a]	10	40	1/4
	Sync[b]	16	40	1/2.5
50	Async[a]	100	400	1/4
	Sync[b]	16	400	1/25
500	Async[a]	1000	4000	1/4
	Sync[b]	16	4000	1/250

[a] Assumes one start bit and one stop bit per character.
[b] Assumes two sync characters before each block.
[c] Overhead is the portion of the character or block that does not carry user data; that is, it is present only to allow the data to be transmited. This example compares only the overhead of the asynchronous and synchronous transmission itself and ignores any additional overhead associated with a communications protocol.

Figure 4-12   Relative efficiency of asynchronous versus synchronous transmission.

especially when there are more than eight or ten characters to be sent at one time. Why then, doesn't everyone use synchronous transmission? There are two primary reasons. First, the hardware required to implement synchronous communications is often more expensive due to the increased complexity of sending and receiving data in this manner, although with the availability of integrated circuit chip sets for synchronous communication, this is less of a consideration now than it once was. Second, this method of transmission is most efficient when there are multiple characters to be sent at one time, so configurations that generate only a few characters at a time may still be handled more efficiently with asynchronous transmission. As was the case in the discussion of half-duplex and full-duplex transmission, it is the equipment on each end of the line and not the line itself that determines the transmission mode to be used on a circuit.

As a concluding note about asynchronous and synchronous transmission, be aware that bisync is not a third transmission mode comparable to asynchronous and synchronous modes. Instead, bisync is the short name for a family of communications protocols developed by IBM, which will be discussed in Chapters 6 and 7.

RECAP

- Bandwidth is a measure of the carrying capacity of a circuit and is usually expressed either in bits per second or hertz.
- Circuits may be used in simplex, half-duplex, or full-duplex mode.
- All electrical signals are subject to attenuation, noise, and other transmission impairments.
- Analog signals have continuously variable amplitudes and are very susceptible to corruption by noise and attenuation.
- Digital signals have discrete amplitudes and are quite resistant to corruption from noise and attenuation.
- Analog circuits are readily available to data communication users in the form of telephone lines; digital circuits are increasingly available.
- Asynchronous transmission frames each character between a start and a stop bit; there is no fixed time relationship between characters.
- Synchronous transmission groups characters into blocks for transmission; time relationships between characters in each block are critical.

Part II

COMPUTERS
AND NETWORK
ARCHITECTURES

Part II focuses on those aspects of the computers and terminals in a network that are responsible for data communications and on the ways that complex data communications functions are organized into network architectures.

Chapter 5 describes the concepts and purposes of layered network architectures for implementing data communication networks. The layers of the Open Systems Interconnection Reference Model are described, followed by a brief discussion of vendor network architectures, including SNA.

Chapter 6 introduces the subject of communication protocols and presents the characteristics of five classes of data link protocols.

Chapter 7 provides detailed information about two data link protocols, bisync and HDLC. This chapter also discusses protocol converters and emulators that are used for connecting devices that do not share a common protocol.

Chapter 8 describes the services provided by the layers above the data link layer in the OSI Reference Model. Brief examples of ISO and CCITT protocol standards for these layers are discussed.

Chapter 9 describes some of the communication standards that have been created by organizations other than ISO and CCITT, such as IEEE and the Department of Defense.

NETWORK ARCHITECTURES

THE NEED FOR NETWORK ARCHITECTURES

It will become increasingly clear as we proceed through this book that the tasks involved with data communications are many and complex. Over the years, every vendor of computer products has chosen a different path to implement communications capabilities for their products, resulting in significant incompatibilities among vendors' products. The problem is worse than that in many cases, because two communication products from the same vendor may not even be compatible.

There are specific market niches where one vendor was sufficiently dominant that its communications protocol became a *de facto standard*, that is, an unofficial standard that other vendors had to meet in order to compete, but the effects of the standard were not generally felt outside that market segment. In the general computing market, no one vendor has had sufficient penetration to create de facto standards across the board, with the notable exception of IBM. And even though IBM has had the market clout to set de facto standards for many years, the company had a practice of introducing an entirely new, or significantly revised, set of protocols for each new communications product or family.

The middle 1970s saw the first attempts to bring order to this chaos by creating an overall framework, or *network architecture*, in which an entire set of communications products could operate. Fairly early in this process, two distinct approaches emerged.

Standards Approach

The first approach was for a group of experts in a particular subject area to assemble under the auspices of an international standards body, such as the *International Organization for Standardization (ISO)*, in order to define a networking architecture, propose it as an international standard, and encourage vendors to adopt and build products in conformance to this architecture. The most notable example in this category is the ISO *Basic Reference Model for Open System Interconnection (OSI)*[ISO 7498], commonly called the *OSI reference model*, the *OSI seven layer model*, or just the *OSI model*. (Note that ISO is the name of the organization, and OSI is the name of the reference model, although people are frequently careless and use OSI model and ISO model interchangeably.) The OSI model has also been adopted by the *Consultative Committee on International Telegraphy and Telephony (CCITT)* as [CCITT *X.200*].

ISO and CCITT are two of the primary international organizations involved in defining communications standards, although they are by no means the only ones. Members of ISO tend to be user and vendor companies with interests in data processing and data communications, while CCITT members tend to be part of the telephony industry, with strong representation from North American telephone companies and the *Postal Telephone and Telegraph (PTT)* authorities from other countries.

Vendor Approach

The second approach to a standardized framework was for a computer vendor to define a network architecture that encompassed all of that vendor's communications products. Other vendors could interconnect their products with the first vendor's network if they met all the specifications of the architecture and its varied protocols. The most notable example of this plan is IBM's *Systems Network Architecture (SNA)*, which has become a widely-implemented de facto standard and which will be discussed later in this chapter.

OSI CONCEPTS

Layering and Encapsulation

The OSI model breaks the immense task of computer communications into distinct layers that are conceptualized as a vertical *stack* of protocols in a computer system, as shown in **Figure 5-1**. The protocol stack exists to support a user application, which is also shown in **Figure 5-1**.

Each layer in the stack has a clearly defined set of functions that is distinct from and nonoverlapping with the functions of the adjacent layers. By that definition, no one layer can perform all the work required to communicate with another system, so the model defines an *interface* between each pair of adjacent layers. Each layer receives requests for its services across the interface from the next higher layer and, in turn, requests services from the next lower layer across another interface.

The interface between layers is deliberately kept as simple as possible to minimize the impact of changes in one layer on the adjacent layers. Layer independence is a key concept of the OSI model, and indeed of any layered architecture, as it allows substitution of an alternative layer implementation (but one that provides equivalent functions) without any effect on the overall communication system.

For example, **Figure 5-2** shows a computer that is capable of delivering electronic mail messages to systems on two different types of networks. On the left, it communicates using X.25 protocols to talk to systems across a wide area network (see Chapters 8 and 15 for a description of X.25). On the right, it uses 802.3 protocols to talk to systems on a local area network (see Chapters 9 and 17 for a description of 802.3). The upper layers are exactly the same in both cases and are not concerned with the nature of the delivery network.

The layering of the communications functions in a network architecture is not unlike the layering of functions in a typical corporation. Each "layer"

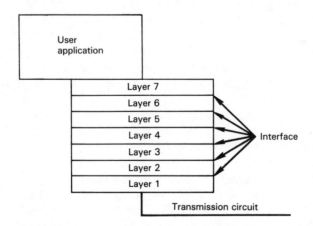

Figure 5-1   Protocol stack. In a layered network architecture, each layer has a function to perform and does so by means of a layer-specific protocol. The collection of layers is often referred to as a protocol stack. The entire stack exists to support the user application process shown on top in this figure.

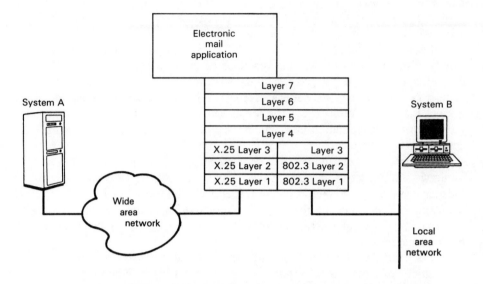

Figure 5-2 Layer independence. The electronic mail application and the upper layers of the protocol stack in this figure operate independently of the lower layers. This allows the electronic mail software to send messages to other systems connected either to the wide area network on the left or to the local area network on the right, with no changes whatsoever. It is the responsibility of the X.25 and 802.3 lower layers to deal with the specifics of their networks. The X.25 and 802.3 protocols in this figure are described in subsequent chapters.

of people in the company structure performs a set of functions, often at the request of people in "higher layers," and frequently accomplishes the assigned tasks with assistance from people in the next lower level in the hierarchy. Just as in the OSI model, there is some layer independence since the people at one "layer" in the organization are generally free to change the method by which they accomplish their job, as long as they continue to provide the same service to the "layer" above.

In a network architecture, the real purpose of each layer is not to talk to the higher or lower layers in the same system; that is just a means to an end. The real intent is to communicate with the corresponding layer, or *peer layer*, in another system. This is accomplished by means of a *layer protocol* that is different for each layer in the architecture based on its function. Keep in mind, of course, that the ultimate purpose for all the layers is to allow the user application processes to exchange meaningful information.

Layer protocols support the exchange of *protocol data units* (*PDUs*). The PDU for any one layer consists of the data that were passed to it from the next higher layer, plus the information needed by this layer to talk to its peer layer

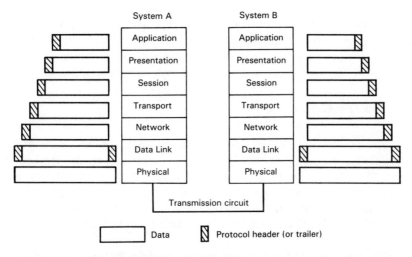

Figure 5-3   PDU encapsulation in OSI communication. Each layer in the protocol stack on system A encapsulates a PDU from the next higher layer by adding its own layer-specific header. The header from the upper layer is treated merely as data by the lower layer; the contents of a layer header are only examined by the peer layer on the receiving system. The opposite process occurs on system B, where each layer examines its layer-specific header, performs its function, removes the header, and passes the resultant PDU to the next higher layer.

in another system. The layer-specific information is placed into the *protocol header* before passing the new PDU across the interface to the next lower layer. The process of creating a new PDU by packaging a higher-layer PDU with a new header is called *encapsulation* or *enveloping* and is illustrated in **Figure 5-3**.

After the data have traveled across the physical medium to another system, each successive layer there examines its PDU header, performs its layer function, removes the header, and passes the resultant, smaller PDU across the interface to the next higher layer. This process continues until the top layer delivers the final PDU to the user application that was the target of this entire process.

How Many Layers?

The choice of the number of layers and the functions of each are essentially arbitrary, but the ISO settled on seven layers as a workable number. With seven layers, they were able to divide the total set of communications functions into meaningful units without having so many layers that it is difficult to determine which layer has which responsibility, and without having so few that the functions of any one layer become indistinct.

[Stallings1] provides a synopsis of the principles used by ISO in establishing the layers and their functions. For readers interested in going to the source, the OSI reference model is contained in [ISO 7498] and is quite readable (a statement that cannot be made about all international standards).

The OSI Model

The reference model defines seven layers, from bottom to top, as the physical, data link, network, transport, session, presentation, and application layers. The physical layer is closest to the actual transmission medium, and the application layer is closest to the end user function (for example, payroll processing or credit card purchase authorization). A system that performs its communications functions using the layered concepts of the OSI model is called an *open system*.

The remainder of this section contains a brief description of the functions defined for each of the seven layers. You will find more detailed descriptions of each layer, along with specific service and protocol examples, in the chapters that follow.

Physical layer. The primary job of the physical layer is to move bits across the transmission medium. It provides no error control or sequencing of data. This layer is concerned with the physical interface between the hardware of the open system and the transmission medium, and with the physical and electrical characteristics of the medium.

Data link layer. This layer transforms the physical layer into a reliable delivery mechanism by adding error detection and recovery procedures. It also allows for the transmission of both user data and control information in order to establish, maintain, and terminate logical connections over the physical link.

Network layer. The network layer provides the interface between an open system and the communications network. It knows enough about the underlying network to select routes and to establish logical connections between the open system and the network, as well as to relay incoming PDUs that are destined for a different open system.

Transport layer. The transport layer is the lowest layer that is concerned with end-to-end connections through the network, that is, connections from one end open system to another. It is responsible for such things as providing the higher layers with reliable connections over varying quality networks and with correct sequencing of PDUs if that service is not provided by the network itself.

It is not concerned with keeping PDUs from multiple sessions separate (that is up to the session layer), nor is it concerned with the topology of the network or the route that data will travel between open systems (those are lower-layer functions). The transport layer serves to shield the higher layers from the physical reality of the network.

Session layer. The session layer is responsible for establishing, maintaining, and terminating sessions between presentation entities on behalf of applications on two open systems. For example, a user at a terminal may ask to be connected to the payroll application in another system. The session layer builds a session PDU to describe the requested session parameters and once that session PDU has been delivered to the correct open system, this layer maintains the session on behalf of the application.

Presentation layer. This layer is concerned with the transformations that are required to get data from the format acceptable to one application into the presentation format acceptable to another application. Typical examples might include ASCII to EBCDIC conversion, reformatting of data intended for a IBM 3278 display screen into a form acceptable to a simple ASCII workstation, and conversion of data structures from those recognized by one computer language into those recognized by another.

Application layer. The top layer in the model, the application layer, is closest to the user of the open system and provides that user with the full range of OSI services. The application layer utilizes the entire stack of OSI protocols so that an application in one open system can exchange meaningful information with an application in another open system.

Null Layers and Sublayers

The OSI model requires that every layer be present in every OSI implementation. Null layers are not permitted, even when the normal functions of a particular layer are not necessary, such as when the network provides a fully reliable, sequenced delivery mechanism, obviating the need for a transport layer.

The layers of a network architecture are often broken into sublayers when the functions of the layer can be more precisely defined by breaking them into smaller pieces. For example, a layer may be divided into three sublayers as shown in **Figure 5-4**. The upper sublayer manages the services provided to the layer above, the middle sublayer implements the layer protocol, and the lower sublayer manages the interface to the next lower layer. Other sublayerings are used when needed for clarity.

Upper sublayer
Middle sublayer
Lower sublayer

Figure 5-4   Sublayering. The layers in the OSI reference model are often divided into three sublayers as pictured here. The upper sublayer is responsible for communicating with the next higher layer; the middle sublayer implements the layer protocol functions; the lower sublayer is responsible for communicating with the next lower layer. Sublayering allows clearer definition of the functions within the overall layer.

Connection-Oriented and Connectionless Services

Originally, the OSI model specified only *connection-oriented* services, also called virtual-circuit services, on the assumption that data transfer would always take place over previously established logical connections between open systems. Subsequent work by ISO led to the development of Addendum 1 to the OSI model which defines *connectionless* services for data transfer when a logical connection has not been previously established. The connectionless service concept is being factored into the definitions of most of the upper layers of the OSI model.

[Tanenbaum] and others have used the analogy of a telephone call for connection-oriented service, in that each call is established, used for transmission, and then cleared. For the duration of the call, the virtual circuit appears to be a dedicated pipeline for a given pair of users, and all data entered into one end of the pipe comes out the other, in the same sequence.

The analogy for connectionless service is the postal system. Individual items, each containing the address of the intended recipient, are sent into the network and will probably be delivered to the intended party, although there is no guarantee. Furthermore, each letter (or PDU) may travel by a separate route with different handling delays, so no claims are made for the timing or sequence of delivery.

Summary of the OSI Model

The lower three layers are responsible for the connection of an open system to the network. The upper three layers are concerned with the logical connections between applications in one open system and other open systems, and the transport layer acts as the glue between the upper and lower layers. In this way, the upper layers are insulated from changes in the network and the lower layers are separated from application processing requirements, allowing the information-processing functions of the open system to remain independent of the network itself, and vice versa.

Open System Data Flow Example

Refer to **Figure 5-3** to see the communication flow between two open systems. For the example that follows, our objective is to send a database inquiry from system A to system B. The application layer packages the inquiry in an application PDU and passes it to the presentation layer. A presentation PDU is passed to the session layer, where the session layer encapsulates the presentation PDU to create a session PDU. The transport layer on system A accepts the session layer PDU across the session-transport interface and then adds its own transport header to create a transport PDU before passing the data on to the network layer.

After subsequent processing by the lower layers in system A, the data link frame is moved to system B. The lower layers in system B provide their services as they pass the PDU upward until the transport layer in system B receives a transport PDU from its network layer. The transport layer examines the contents of the transport header, performs its set of functions on the remainder of the PDU, removes the header, and passes the balance of the data to the session layer. The information in the transport header that was meaningful to the transport layer was ignored by the network layer and all lower layers within system A, as well as by the lower layers in system B; it is decoded into meaningful information only by the receiving transport layer. In this manner, successive envelopes are stripped away at each layer until the system B presentation layer passes an application PDU to the application layer, which passes our database inquiry to the database application itself.

The logical communication in this example is from an application process in system A to an application process in system B using an application protocol; but since the application layer cannot deliver anything directly, it must rely on the services of the lower layers, as described above.

In this example, we did not actually describe what functions are performed at each layer of the model. The important point here is that you understand the data flow that is necessary to enable an application in system A to talk to an application in system B using OSI concepts. A more complete description of the functions of each layer is contained in Chapter 8.

Standards Based on the OSI Model

The reference model defines this scheme of layer services, interfaces between layers within a system, and protocols between peer layers in different systems in order to accomplish communication between open systems. The reference model does not define the specific protocols that are to be used at each layer. As the name suggests, it merely provides the model against which protocols may be defined.

However, the existence of the model has allowed the creation of vendor-independent service and protocol standards based on the layer definitions provided by ISO. Among the earliest efforts was the X.25 recommendation drafted by CCITT, which is discussed in detail in Chapter 15. Additional standards for the other layers of the model are also covered in later chapters.

Implementation and Protocol Testing

International standards from CCITT, ISO, and similar organizations are written by committees of people with common interests. A final standard represents the concensus of a group of experts but there are likely to be a few topics on which the group could not agree. As a result, any standard is likely to have some unanswered questions and some ambiguities, despite the best intentions of the committee.

In addition, the OSI model and attendant layer standards do not specify anything about implementation techniques, leaving the choice up to each vendor of how it will build a product that conforms to a particular standard. While this is good in that it does not arbitrarily limit vendor freedom, it does give rise to potential compatibility problems. Each vendor may interpret the standards slightly differently and may make different assumptions about gray areas in the documents, leading to incompatibilities between multiple vendor implementations of the same suite of protocols. Furthermore, many standards contain options which a vendor may choose to implement or ignore.

To alleviate this problem, organizations such as the *National Institute of Standards and Technology (NIST)* in the United States (known as the *National Bureau of Standards (NBS)* until late 1988), and the *Standards Promotion and Application Group (SPAG)* in Europe have formed committees to write implementors' agreements. These agreements are intended to resolve ambiguities and answer questions in the standards documents, as well as to define functional profiles for the implementors. In principle, an implementors' agreement, in conjunction with the base standard(s), should allow a vendor to build a product that complies with the standard and interoperates with another vendor's product that is built in the same manner. In practice, one or more additional steps may be necessary before complete multivendor compatibility is achieved.

Another group of organizations, such as the *Corporation for Open Systems (COS)* in the United States, and *SPAG Services* in Europe, has emerged to handle the next step by providing conformance testing for standards-based products. Their premise is that, if several vendors build products based on the same implementors' agreements and standards, and if those products are certified by an organization such as COS or SPAG Services, then the likelihood that the products will be able to communicate correctly with each other in a multivendor network is significantly improved.

Even certification is not a guarantee that OSI products from multiple vendors will interoperate or communicate with each other 100% correctly. Frequently, separate *interoperability testing*, in which the vendors directly connect their products to each other, is still necessary to ensure that true compatibility has been achieved.

The goal of implementors' agreements and certification is to eliminate the need for interoperability testing but the latter is likely to remain a fact of life for most standards until they are sufficiently mature that all of the loopholes and gray areas have been eliminated.

VENDOR NETWORK ARCHITECTURES

IBM's Systems Network Architecture

IBM introduced many different communications products and protocols over the years and was left with a profusion of incompatible offerings by the middle 1970s. Systems Network Architecture was their corporate attempt to gain control of the problem and to promote an overall architecture that could apply throughout their product line. [Tanenbaum] describes the problem that existed in this way:

> Prior to SNA, IBM had several hundred communication products, using three dozen teleprocessing access methods, with more than a dozen data link protocols alone. The idea behind SNA was to eliminate this chaos and to provide a coherent framework for loosely coupled distributed processing.*

The introduction of SNA was not an overnight success, in large part because of the relatively high cost and perceived lack of flexibility in the initial versions of the architecture. The early versions of SNA were centered on mainframe computers and did not provide for the distributed communication among peer systems that is a basic tenet of the OSI environment. This host-terminal approach reflected IBM's view of the world at the time, however.

In the years since its introduction, SNA has evolved in many significant ways and today is the most widely implemented network architecture in the world. According to a Gartner Group report [Gartner], it forms the basis for

---

*Andrew S. Tanenbaum, *Computer Networks* (Englewood Cliffs, N.J.: Prentice-Hall, Inc., 1988), p. 43.

more than 30,000 networks, even when those networks contain equipment and software from multiple vendors.

Networks even exist that use SNA as their architecture despite an almost total lack of IBM equipment in the network. The Department of Social Security in Australia maintains a nationwide network of this type. As described in [Korzeniowski], the department's SNA network contains 8 Amdahl mainframes with Amdahl front-end processors, more than 200 Wang VS computers used as IBM 3274 cluster controller replacements, and over 5000 Wang color workstations that provide access to both the VS computers and any of the mainframes in the country. Virtually the only IBM products in the network are the software products running on the plug-compatible Amdahl mainframes, yet SNA is the network architecture of choice.

IBM product announcements in the middle 1980s have demonstrated that SNA is moving in the direction of peer communications. It is now possible to have two nonhost computers in an SNA network talk to each other directly, without first establishing sessions with an intermediate host. IBM also provides support for selected OSI and CCITT protocols in response to market demand, but SNA remains the company's primary network architecture.

The Layers of SNA

SNA is a layered architecture for most of the same reasons that we discussed for the OSI model. Although the names and functions of the SNA layers differ somewhat from the OSI layers, the concept is exactly the same, that is, to separate the overall communication functions into discrete, manageable sets.

Figure 5-5 shows the layers of SNA with a brief description of the functions provided by each layer. You will notice the similarity between the descriptions in this figure and the descriptions listed earlier in this chapter for the OSI model. The overall job to be done remains the same, so it should not be too surprising that many of the concepts in the two architectures are similar.

Both network architectures have evolved since their initial introduction, and both will continue to evolve. While they will never be identical, there has been considerable cross-fertilization between the two, and that process is likely to continue.

It is not my intent in this book to provide details about SNA since other authors have done that very well (for example, [Meijer], [Cypser], and [Gurugé]). SNA is the dominant vendor architecture as well as a de facto industry standard and, therefore, it warrants at least a brief description in this book.

Other Vendor Architectures

SNA is not the only vendor-sponsored network architecture. Most mainframe and minicomputer vendors offer an architecture to tie their product lines together; however, none has achieved the prominence of SNA. [Meijer] examines the architectures from DEC, Unisys (Burroughs), ICL, Honeywell, and others.

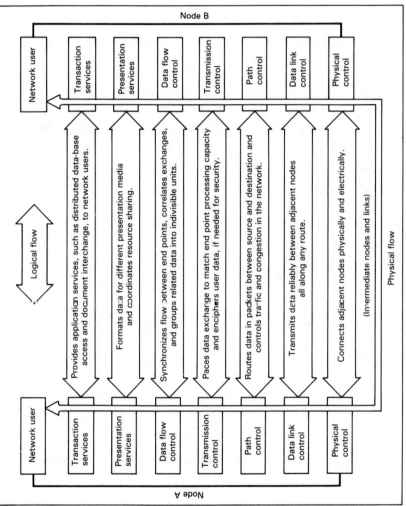

Figure 5-5 Layering of SNA. IBM's Systems Network Architecture (SNA) is a layered architecture, and while the purpose behind the layering and the overall set of functions to be performed are similar, the layering is different from the OSI model. [Source: Kathy Chin, "Users Laud, Criticize IBM NetView Software," *Communications Week*, vol. 102 (July 28, 1986), p. 52.]

49

R E C A P

- Network architectures provide a framework for the development and implementation of communication protocols.

- Each layer of an architecture provides a set of services to the next higher layer, performs a set of well-defined functions, and requests services of a lower layer.

- Peer layers communicate by means of layer-specific protocols.

- The OSI reference model contains seven layers: physical, data link, network, transport, session, presentation, and application.

- SNA is IBM's layered network architecture and is the most widely installed network architecture in the world.

DATA LINK PROTOCOLS: INTRODUCTION

Many factors must be agreed on in advance whenever computers are to communicate, just as two people must agree on certain language conventions. If I speak to you in French and you don't understand French, we will not communicate. Even if you do speak French, that may not be entirely sufficient as there may be syntax differences or regional idioms that can still cause us to misunderstand each other occasionally. For example, Parisian French and French Canadian are essentially the same language, but they are sufficiently different that a Parisian and a Montrealer may have some difficulty in exchanging ideas.

THE NEED FOR PROTOCOLS

Computers have an even greater requirement than humans do for exactness of definition in the rules of communication. The protocol to be used by two computers when they communicate must be specified very precisely if the exchange of information is to be successful.

In practice, a number of protocols are required for two systems to communicate since each layer in a network architecture uses its own set of rules to communicate with its peer layers in other systems. This chapter and Chapter 7 focus on the data link layer protocols. Many data link protocols existed before layered architecture models since the need to establish a connection across a link was always evident, whereas the need for higher-layer protocols emerged over time. Two subsequent chapters describe selected protocols for higher layers of the OSI reference model.

Proliferation of Data Link Protocols

The process of getting computers to communicate with each other would be considerably simpler if there were only one or two protocols from which to choose. However, computer manufacturers have had a habit of defining new communication protocols whenever they introduced a new computer or a new family of terminals. By doing so, they hoped that the new protocol would provide a better technical solution or that it would give them an edge over their competition, or both, but in any case that it would help them to sell more equipment. This problem was not limited to competing protocols from different manufacturers; [Tanenbaum] reports that, as of 1974, IBM offered at least 12 separate data link protocols. For the user community, the unfortunate result was the existence of dozens of data link protocols from which to choose.

In the last ten years, two factors have caused the proliferation of protocols to slow considerably, vendor protocol standards and international protocol standards.

Vendor Protocol Standards

First, certain protocols have gained sufficiently widespread acceptance that they have become dominant. Other computer vendors, in striving to offer compatibility with the dominant vendor's protocol, choose to do so by implementing that vendor's protocol on their machines.

The primary example of a de facto data link protocol standard is the bisync protocol from IBM. Implementations of bisync are available on the computers of every major and most minor vendors' systems due to the sheer market presence of IBM and the concomitant desire of other vendors to allow their machines to talk to IBM equipment.

It is not even unusual to find brand X and brand Y computers talking to each other using bisync protocol with no IBM equipment present. In a situation like this, product planners for both company X and company Y chose to implement IBM communications for competitive reasons, but did not find it advantageous to emulate each others' protocols.

Specific information on bisync protocol is contained in Chapter 7.

International Protocol Standards

The second significant trend is the development of international standards for data communications. An increasing number of computer users are requiring that their communications networks be built in conformance with international standards. The expected payoff for users is the interoperability of communication products from multiple vendors. The greater the number of layers that are implemented by computer vendors according to standards, the greater the likelihood that two application processes running on different types of systems can communicate with each other without special knowledge of the intervening system(s) or network(s).

The payoff for vendors is that products built to widely accepted standards should be marketable to a larger number of customers than a proprietary product. The net result is that vendors who wish to compete in the international market are being forced to offer products that implement the standards.

DATA LINK PROTOCOL CONSIDERATIONS

The questions in the following categories are typical of those that must be answered in a link layer protocol definition prior to establishing communications:

1. Framing: How do we know where the data start and stop? That is, how will the information be packaged?

2. Sequencing: Who transmits first? What happens next? What happens after that?

3. Contention: What happens if both of us try to transmit at the same time? Do I always win? Do you? Is there some other rule we use to determine who wins?

4. Acknowledgment: Do I acknowledge every message that you send to me? If so, do I acknowledge each message immediately or do I acknowledge messages in groups?

5. Error detection: How can I be reasonably sure that the information that I received is the same as what you sent? How important is it to be sure?

6. Timing: If I am expecting to hear from you and I do not, how long do I wait before I give up? Do I wait the same amount of time in all cases or are there variations?

7. Error recovery: If I suspect that I have received incorrect data, what do I do? If a timeout has occurred, how do we reestablish communications? Do we start again at the beginning or at some intermediate point? Do I send you a message to let you know? Do you assume that you should retransmit the data if you don't hear from me?

These are by no means the only questions that need to be considered in defining a data link protocol, but they are certainly representative. The next section of this chapter examines how several categories of protocols have been designed around some of these considerations.

CONTROL MECHANISMS

Protocols are differentiated by the method that they use to control the flow of data on the communications link.

Polling Protocols

Polling protocols assume the presence of a master station that can send messages at any time and the presence of one or more secondary, or slave, stations that can only transmit when they are specifically given permission to do so. A *poll* is a means for the master to ask each secondary, in turn, whether it has data to send back to the master. The slave device responds with either a "No thank you" message or with a message containing data.

In normal operation, the master device sends a poll to each secondary station using a predefined list containing the order of polling. If there are five stations, called A, B, C, D, and E, for example, the poll list may be a simple list of the five stations:

A B C D E

However, the list may be built to favor one or more devices over the remainder. If we want to favor device A to give it more frequent opportunities to transmit (perhaps it sits on the desk of the company president), we might build a polling list that looks like this:

A B A C A D A E

For a more complex case in which there are many stations and there is an important subset that we want to favor, the poll list may become very complicated; however, the concept of polling is based on two simple principles. First, we poll the stations in accordance with a predetermined list and, second, no secondary station can transmit until it receives a poll.

Polling allows us to solicit data from remote terminals, but we still need a method to send data to remote devices in an organized manner. A *select* message is sent to a particular secondary to ask whether it is able to receive a message from the master. The slave will either respond with a "Yes I can" message, or it will respond with a "No I cannot" message if, for example, it has a temporary shortage of buffer space in which to store an incoming message or if it is sending a message and cannot receive at the same time. If a secondary responds "No" to a select, the master will retain the outbound message for that device and will select that slave again later. In the meantime, the master will proceed to poll or select other devices on the link. See **Figure 6-1** for an example of several typical interchanges on a link that is controlled with a polling protocol.

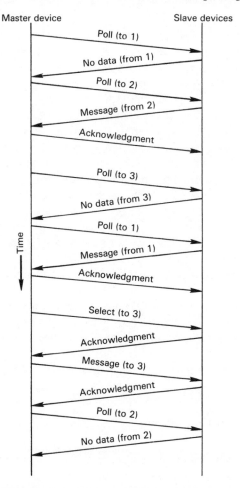

Figure 6-1 Stylized example of polling and selecting. This figure shows a stylized exchange between a master device on the left and several slave devices on the right. Each poll from the master is answered with either a "no data" response or with an actual data message. In the latter case, the master sends an acknowledgment upon receipt of the message. Each select from the master is answered by a "don't send now" message or by an acknowledgment from the slave. An acknowledgment causes the host to send the data message, which the slave answers with its own acknowledgment.

The actual format of a poll or select message varies from vendor to vendor, but the purpose is always the same. The poll message allows data to move from the secondaries to the master in a controlled manner, and the select allows the master to send data to the slaves.

Contention Protocols

The process of polling can impose a considerable extra burden on the master device, especially when there are a large number of secondary devices. On a circuit where there are a small number of devices or where most of the stations spend a considerable percentage of the time responding "No thank you" to polls, a *contention protocol* may be employed.

Contention is an alternative control procedure to polling in which there is no master-slave relationship among the devices on the link. In a contention environment, all devices are considered to be equal, so any device that wishes to transmit may do so without first waiting to be granted permission. The underlying assumption is that the link will be idle much of the time and that the devices will, therefore, be able to transmit successfully whenever they choose to do so.

It should be obvious, however, that this will not always be the case. Consequently, there must be rules for how to resolve the resultant collisions when two devices try to send data at the same time. Frequently, this is accomplished by temporarily giving one device a higher priority than the others.

A contention protocol remains efficient until the number of collisions and retransmissions rises too high. When this occurs frequently, the additional order that is imposed by a polling protocol may actually increase the efficiency on the line by eliminating the retransmissions that result from collisions in contention mode.

All the protocol types described later in this chapter have the potential to be used in either polling or contention environments.

Data Acknowledgments

Most protocols require some form of *acknowledgment* for transmitted data. The acknowledgment, also called an *ACK,* informs the transmitter that the receiver got the data. Some protocols require an ACK for every message or block (see half-duplex protocols below); others use a mechanism that allows one acknowledgment to cover multiple previous messages.

Protocols also use some form of *negative acknowledgment (NAK)* to inform the transmitter of errors in the received data. Chapter 7 examines the use of ACKs and NAKs for two sample protocols.

Full Duplex versus Half Duplex

A *full-duplex protocol* is one that allows data to flow in both directions simultaneously. A *half-duplex protocol* requires an acknowledgment for every block of data before the next block can be transmitted, so data will never be moving in both directions at the same time.

You will note the similarity between this usage of the terms full and half duplex and the description of full- and half-duplex circuits in Chapter 4, but the meaning is not exactly the same. A full-duplex circuit can support either a full- or half-duplex protocol, but the full-duplex protocol will be much more efficient since it allows transmission in both directions at the same time. Although a half-duplex circuit can also support either type of protocol, the fact that data cannot flow in both directions on the circuit will prevent a full-duplex protocol from operating at maximum efficiency on that type of line.

Half-duplex protocols have a significant disadvantage over full-duplex protocols on any circuit with a long delivery time. Chapter 7 provides an example of this problem on a satellite link.

ERROR-DETECTION TECHNIQUES

Parity

Parity checking is a simple scheme for detecting errors in received data. It is by no means foolproof, as we shall see in the examples that follow, but it does provide the receiver with some assurance that the character received is the same as the one that was transmitted.

Parity is usually used with asynchronous protocols and relies on adding an extra bit to each transmitted character so that the total number of one bits in the character is either an even number or an odd number, resulting in the terms *even parity* and *odd parity*. Even parity is more commonly implemented and will be used in the examples in this chapter; however, the same techniques apply to odd parity.

The hardware of the transmitter counts the bits in each character to be sent and either turns the parity bit on or off before shipping the character out so that the correct parity is maintained. For example, the letter A in ASCII consists of the 7 bits 100 0001 (refer to the ASCII chart in Figure 2-2). The transmitter counts the one bits and finds two, which is an even number, so it sets the parity bit to 0. The actual 8 bits that are transmitted are 0100 0001. As a further example, **Figure 6-2** shows characters that make up the word ATOM before and after insertion of parity bits.

When the hardware on the other end of the circuit receives each of these characters, it counts the number of one bits and determines whether the total

ASCII Character	Bit Pattern of Character	Number of 1 Bits	Transmitted Character (with parity bit underlined)
A	_100 0001	2	0100 0001
T	_101 0100	3	1101 0100
O	_100 1111	5	1100 1111
M	_100 1101	4	0100 1101

Figure 6-2 ASCII characters with even parity. For even parity, the transmitter ensures that the total number of bits in the character is an even number. The parity bit is set to 1 if the total number of data bits is odd; it is set to 0 if the number of data bits is already an even number.

is even or odd. If it is even, then it assumes that the received character is the same as the one that was transmitted. If the total is odd, a *parity error* has occurred and the received character is rejected. Because parity relies on a simple counting mechanism, it is relatively easy for multiple-bit errors, specifically an error affecting an even number of bits, to go undetected. For example, if the character A is transmitted as described above, using even parity, it will be sent as 0100 0001. If, due to a transmission error, it arrives as 0100 1101, the receiver will count the one bits and determine that the total is an even number and can only assume that this character is correct.

Longitudinal parity is an attempt to improve the odds against letting flawed characters slip through by adding an extra character periodically, usually at some logical point such as the end of a block of characters. Generally, the same parity rule, either even or odd, applies to setting the bits in the extra character as for setting the parity bit within each character. For the longitudinal parity character, however, each bit is set based on the number of one bits in that bit position within the entire block, rather than on the bit counts within one character. Longitudinal parity is also referred to as a *longitudinal redundancy check (LRC)*.

Repeating the previous example using the word ATOM, the LRC character that is added to the block is shown at the bottom of **Figure 6-3a**. Note that each column and row has an even number of bits.

Longitudinal parity will detect double-bit errors that would slip past a simple character parity check. **Figure 6-3b** shows the results of a double-bit error in the letter T. The parity bit for the letter T in **Figure 6-3b** will still be correct when this block is received, but the LRC will not match in the last two columns, allowing the receiver to reject this block.

Even longitudinal parity is not foolproof since an even number of altered bits in any given row or column will not be detected. **Figure 6-3c** shows the results of multiple-bit errors with an even number of errors in the affected rows and columns. In this example, everything looks fine to the receiver since the parity bits are correct; however, the actual bits received in the right side of **Figure 6-3c** are the letters tTIM instead of ATOM.

ASCII Character	Bit Pattern of Character	Number of 1 Bits	Transmitted Character (with Parity Bit)
A	_100 0001	2	0100 0001
T	_101 0100	3	1101 0100
O	_100 1111	5	1100 1111
M	_100 1101	4	0100 1101
LRC character			0001 0111

(a) Addition of LRC character

ASCII Character	Bit Pattern of Character	Number of 1 Bits	Transmitted Bit Pattern	Received Bit Pattern	Received ASCII Character
A	_100 0001	2	0100 0001	0100 0001	A
T	_101 0100	3	1101 0100	1101 01*11*	W error
O	_100 1111	5	1100 1111	1100 1111	O
M	_100 1101	4	0100 1101	0100 1101	M
LRC character			0001 0111	0001 0111	error

(b) Detected 2-bit error

ASCII Character	Bit Pattern of Character	Number of 1 Bits	Transmitted Bit Pattern	Received Bit Pattern	Received ASCII Character
A	_100 0001	2	0100 0001	0100 0*11*1	t error
T	_101 0100	3	1101 0100	1101 0100	T
O	_100 1111	5	1100 1111	1100 1*00*1	I error
M	_100 1101	4	0100 1101	0100 1101	M
LRC character			0001 0111	0001 0111	

(c) Undetected multiple-bit errors

The underlined bits are the added parity bits. The bold italic bits in parts b and c are the bits that were altered during transmission.

Figure 6-3   **Longitudinal parity.** Longitudinal parity consists of an extra character that is added to the end of a group of characters. Generally, the same rules used to set the parity bit in each character are used to set each bit in the LRC character.

Cyclic Redundancy Check

Most protocols other than async protocols use a more sophisticated error-detection scheme to provide a greater level of confidence that all received data are identical to what was transmitted. A *cyclic redundancy check (CRC)* is a mathematical value that is calculated for this purpose by the transmitting hardware. The CRC is generated by the hardware as it figures each new byte of transmitted data into the formula. The resultant value, also known as a *check digit,* is then transmitted at the end of the actual data.

The receiving system performs the identical calculation on the data that arrive on the line and compares its result with the CRC that was transmitted. If the values match, there is a very significant probability that the original data arrived correctly. If they do not match, the rules of the protocol should specify how the error is to be corrected; this is very often done by having the receiver request retransmission of the bad block from the sender.

Several different algorithms are used for CRC computation, the most common being the CRC-16 and the CRC-CCITT, each of which generates a 16-bit value after processing 8-bit data characters. Refer to [Stallings1] for a mathematical presentation that defines the actual algorithm used for several CRC schemes and discusses the probability of an undetected error for different error-detection mechanisms.

Forward Error Correction

Forward error correction (FEC), as the name implies, is a method that goes beyond mere error detection and provides a means to correct certain types of errors in received data. FEC works by performing a type of CRC calculation that generates a much larger number of error-detection bits. The extra bits actually allow the receiver to re-create the original data if errors do occur. The number of additional bits added for FEC may be considerable, perhaps as many bits as are in the original data. Consequently, FEC is used in situations where sending more data bits in the original transmission is likely to be more efficient than retransmitting data blocks received with errors.

Manufacturers of very high speed modems often build FEC into their products to improve overall throughput. Their underlying assumption is that, because the probability of errors and retransmissions is sufficiently great when attempting to transmit at very high speeds over noisy telephone lines, eliminating retransmissions will more than compensate for the added bits required by the FEC.

Applications that require near real-time transmission of data, such as process control functions in a factory or digitized voice transmission, may not be able to tolerate the delays that result from retransmissions due to errors and may use FEC. Transmissions from a space probe on its way to another planet, where transmission times are measured in days or weeks, are a prime application for FEC since retransmissions would also take days or weeks.

DATA LINK PROTOCOL CLASSES

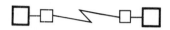

Data link protocols can be divided into five classes based on the framing, or the manner in which the characters of data are packaged for transmission.

Asynchronous Protocols

Async protocols are so named because they always function over asynchronous communications lines. Compared to the rules for the other classes of protocols described in this chapter, this category of protocol barely qualifies as a protocol; the rules are so simple as to be almost nonexistent. There is no requirement for the receiver to acknowledge data, and error checking is minimal or nonexistent and often results in the transmitter sending data and merely hoping for the best. If an error-detection method is employed, it usually consists of character parity alone or with longitudinal parity.

As a result of its simplicity, an async protocol is generally inexpensive to implement and is used in situations where cost is a major factor and where either there is assumed to be a high probability of successful transmission or where an occasional error is not significant. Async protocols are also called *teletype* or *TTY protocols*, a name that refers to the earliest devices that employed this type of communication.

Figure 6-4 depicts a typical data exchange using async protocol. Characters are transmitted one by one, with no packaging other than the start and stop bits. If parity is used and the receiver detects an error, it usually discards or ignores the flawed data.

While simplicity may be the greatest advantage of an async protocol, it also provides the biggest drawback, the lack of reliability. Since there is only minimal error checking, undetected errors will slip through. Nevertheless, millions of characters of data are transmitted daily using TTY protocols.

Character-Oriented Protocols

In a *character-oriented protocol,* also known as a *byte-oriented protocol,* data characters are packaged into logical groups called *blocks,* which are delimited by control characters. The control characters provide a way to define the beginning and end of a block of data, as shown in **Figure 6-5**. There are many variations on this general format, but all begin with this basic template.

Each control character in **Figure 6-5** (for example, STX and ETX) consists of a specific bit pattern that has been reserved for this purpose; see the ASCII and EBCDIC charts to locate these special characters. Other control characters

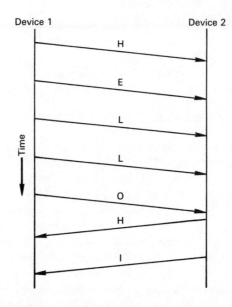

Figure 6-4 Async protocol data exchange. The rules for an async protocol are usually as simple as transmit and hope for the best. Error checking, if used at all, consists of character parity and, perhaps, longitudinal parity.

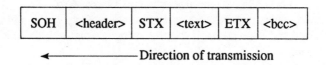

←————————— Direction of transmission

where

SOH	is a special character meaning Start of Header, which is only present if the <header> is present
<header>	is used for administrative purposes (not for user data) and is optional
STX	is a special character meaning Start of Text
<text>	is the user's data
ETX	is a special character meaning End of Text
<bcc>	is the block check character; it is the result of a calculation based on the preceding characters and is used for error detection

Figure 6-5 Block format for character-oriented protocols.

provide a mechanism for the sender and the receiver to talk about and control the flow of data.

The most common character-oriented protocol is IBM's bisync, which will be discussed in Chapter 7. In addition, dozens of other character-oriented protocols are in use on computers all over the world.

Transparency.   Character-oriented protocols provide considerable flexibility because there are control characters defined to handle a wide variety of situations. One drawback of these protocols, however, stems from their very use of control characters. If the <text> portion of the message in **Figure 6-5** happens to contain a bit pattern that is the same as one of the control characters, the receiver of the message will be unable to process the message successfully, because it cannot distinguish the real control characters from the imposters.

Consequently, many character-oriented protocols require fairly cumbersome software schemes to achieve *transparency,* which is the ability to transmit any data stream without affecting the operation of the protocol itself. Most transparency procedures for character-oriented protocols require the insertion of extra characters into the transmitted data stream. Chapter 7 provides details of transparent mode operation in bisync.

Bit-Oriented Protocols

Bit-oriented protocols transmit the user's data in a consistently formatted, variable-length package called a *frame.* Each frame begins and ends with a unique bit pattern called a *flag,* which is the only reserved bit pattern used by bit-oriented protocols. Instead of requiring a long list of special control characters, bit-oriented protocols use individual bit settings within the frame header to allow the sender and receiver to control the flow of data on the link.

The most commonly used bit-oriented protocols are *Synchronous Data Link Control (SDLC)* and the *High-level Data Link Control (HDLC).* The former is a protocol that was developed by IBM; the latter is a superset of SDLC that was developed by ISO. Chapter 7 examines HDLC in considerable detail as the primary example of a bit-oriented protocol.

The general format of a bit-oriented protocol frame is shown in **Figure 6-6.** The details of each of these fields will be discussed in the section on HDLC in Chapter 7. Descriptions of bit-oriented protocols use the term *octet* to refer to a group of 8 bits, since the word byte can refer to a different number of bits in some cases. Consequently, you will see references to the control octet, for example, meaning the 8-bit control field within the HDLC frame. You will often hear frame lengths referred to in terms of the number of octets. (While it might be logical to assume that half of an octet is called a quartet, for some perverse reason it is called a *semi-octet.*)

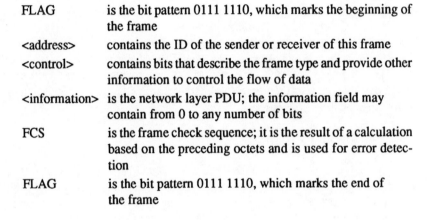

where

FLAG	is the bit pattern 0111 1110, which marks the beginning of the frame
\<address\>	contains the ID of the sender or receiver of this frame
\<control\>	contains bits that describe the frame type and provide other information to control the flow of data
\<information\>	is the network layer PDU; the information field may contain from 0 to any number of bits
FCS	is the frame check sequence; it is the result of a calculation based on the preceding octets and is used for error detection
FLAG	is the bit pattern 0111 1110, which marks the end of the frame

Figure 6-6   Frame format for bit-oriented protocols.

Bit stuffing for transparency.   Bit-oriented protocols have the considerable advantage that there are no control characters, so data transparency is almost automatic. The only requirement is to ensure that the flag pattern does not inadvertently appear in the address, control, information, or FCS fields. This is accomplished by implementing a technique called *bit stuffing* in the transmitting and receiving hardware. The basis for bit stuffing is simple: There cannot be more than 5 one bits in a row, except in the opening or closing flag. For the transmitter the rules are as follows:

- Transmit the opening flag.
- For all fields prior to the closing flag, count the number of one bits, resetting the counter whenever a zero bit is transmitted.

- If there are 5 one bits in a row, insert a zero bit.
- Continue until the FCS has been transmitted.
- Transmit the closing flag.

The receiver's rules are as follows:

- Count the number of one bits in the received bit stream, resetting the counter whenever a zero bit is received.
- If there are 5 one bits and the next bit is a zero, discard the zero bit and reset the counter.
- If there are 5 one bits and the next bit is a one, then check the seventh bit; a zero in this position means this is a flag.
- Repeat until the closing flag is found.

To confirm that this simple yet elegant technique does work, you should work through the examples in **Figure 6-7.**

Original data:	...0111	1011	1111	1011	0001...
As transmitted:	...0111	1011	111<u>0</u>	1101	1000 1 ...
After unstuffing:	...0111	1011	1111	1011	0001...

◄─────── Direction of transmission

(a) Example 1

Original data:	...1010	0111	1110	1111	1011...
As transmitted:	...1010	0111	11<u>0</u>1	0111	11<u>0</u>0 11...
After unstuffing:	...1010	0111	1110	1111	1011...

◄─────── Direction of transmission

(b) Example 2

Underlined zero bits are the inserted bits.

Figure 6-7 HDLC bit stuffing. The transmitter and receiver hardware used for HDLC provide built-in transparency with a technique called bit stuffing. The transmitter inserts additional zero bits to prevent more than five 1 bits from being transmitted anywhere other than in the opening and closing flags of the frame. The receiver removes the added bits before passing the data to HDLC for handling. The rules for bit stuffing are explained in the text.

The only condition other than a flag in which there will be more than five consecutive one bits is an abort sequence. The transmitter uses the abort sequence, which consists of at least 7 one bits in a row, to indicate that there is a fatal error on the link and that the entire link must be reset for communication to continue.

Protected Asynchronous Protocols

A new breed of hybrid protocol has emerged to take advantage of the low cost of asynchronous communications, but, at the same time, to provide the improved reliability of bit-oriented protocols. These protocols, which are called *protected async protocols* or *blocked async protocols*, often use the framing techniques of bit-oriented protocols, but still transmit data as separate async characters with a start bit and stop bit around each character.

Protected async protocols are frequently used for PC communications because their ability to use low-cost async hardware and modems reduces capital outlay for the PC owner. Several of these protocols, such as Kermit and XModem, are in the public domain. PC owners can obtain free protocol software, typically by dialing into various electronic bulletin boards. There are also commercial products that incorporate Kermit, XModem, or proprietary protected async protocols such as MNP. [daCruz] contains a good summary of this class of protocol.

Byte Count Protocols

The final class of protocols is the *byte count protocol*. The user's data in a byte count protocol is packaged in a variable-length frame that is similar in concept to the frame used for a bit-oriented protocol. The primary difference is that the length of each frame is actually stored in a count field contained within the frame header. Bits set in other fields in the frame allow similar communication between sender and receiver as in bit-oriented protocols.

Byte count protocols provide built-in transparency because the receiver is not required to search for the end of the frame or to examine every incoming character to determine whether it is a control character. Instead, the receiver knows where the end of the frame will be based on the count field in the frame header.

The only widely implemented example of a byte count protocol is Digital Data Communications Message Protocol (DDCMP), which is used by Digital Equipment Corporation as part of their DECnet communications architecture. For additional information on DDCMP, refer to [McNamara].

RECAP

- A small number of protocols are becoming widespread due to two factors: vendor dominance and international standards.

- Protocols usually employ one of two control mechanisms: polling or contention.

- Half-duplex protocols require the transmitter to stop after each block to wait for an acknowledgment.

- Full-duplex protocols allow simultaneous two-way data flow because each block does not require an immediate acknowledgment.

- Common error-detection techniques include parity, cyclic redundancy checks, and forward error correction.

- Protocols can be divided into five classes: asynchronous, character oriented, bit oriented, protected asynchronous, and byte count.

DATA LINK PROTOCOLS: EXAMPLES

This chapter describes two of the most widely implemented data link protocols, IBM's bisync and HDLC. It also discusses protocol emulators and converters for computers that do not share a common data link protocol that need to communicate with each other.

CHARACTER-ORIENTED PROTOCOL EXAMPLE: BISYNC

IBM's binary synchronous protocol, also called *bisync* or *BSC*, was the most widely implemented protocol in the world for many years due to the widespread use of IBM equipment. While its dominance has receded in favor of bit-oriented protocols like SDLC and HDLC, thousands of bisync lines are still in use in the world. BSC is actually a family of related protocols that share many common characteristics. While this chapter will mention a few of the variations, IBM offers several publications that document all the vagaries of the bisync family.

Bisync Formats and Procedures

Some character-oriented protocols (for example, Unisys Poll/Select) may be used on either asynchronous or synchronous circuits, but bisync specifies the use of synchronous communication lines. As a result, the general format for a bisync data block is the same as in **Figure 6-2**, but always includes two

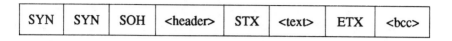

| SYN | SYN | SOH | <header> | STX | <text> | ETX | <bcc> |

◄─────────────── Direction of transmission

Figure 7-1 **Format of bisync data block.** Bisync uses the basic block format for character-oriented protocols that is shown in Figure 6-2. Because bisync requires synchronous transmission facilities, there will always be two or more SYN characters at the beginning of each block. The start of header (SOH) character and the <header> portion of the message block are optional because some BSC variations use it while others do not.

or more sync characters before the data block. **Figure 7-1** shows a bisync block including the sync characters.

If we are using one of the bisync variations that does not use the message header, the following string of characters

ABCDEF123456

would be transmitted as

SYN SYN STX A B C D E F 1 2 3 4 5 6 ETX <bcc>

where the block check character would be calculated at the time of transmission.

In addition to the control characters shown in **Figure 7 1**, BSC relies on numerous other control characters to regulate the flow of data on a line. Some characters, such as the enquiry (ENQ) and *end of transmission (EOT)* are used to establish, control, and terminate the flow of data between two or more bisync devices. Others, such as end of text block (ETB) and intermediate text block (ITB), allow for special handling of long messages.

The *data link escape (DLE)* control character is used for two purposes, one of which is to be the first character of a two-character sequence for acknowledgment of data blocks. *ACK0* and *ACK1* are used to acknowledge even- and odd-numbered blocks, respectively. The use of two different acknowledgments helps to reduce the probability of missing or duplicate blocks.

Figure 7-2a shows a normal exchange of several bisync data blocks with alternating ACK types. In **Figure 7-2b**, however, message block 2 is corrupted en route (for example, due to noise on the line) and it cannot be recognized by system B as a valid data block. Consequently, system B does not issue an acknowledgment.

When it does not receive a reply, system A waits the amount of time prescribed by bisync rules, usually 3 seconds, before it issues an ENQ to prompt B into responding. In effect, the ENQ says to system B, "Are you still alive? If so, retransmit the last block you sent to me."

When system A now receives an ACK1 instead of an ACK0 from system B, it knows that block 2 never arrived at system B and must be resent before it can continue to send other blocks, as shown in the remainder of **Figure 7-2b.**

Compare **Figure 7-2b** with **7-2c** in which data block 2 does arrive correctly, but the corresponding ACK0 does not make it across to A. In this example, when B replies to the ENQ with ACK0 (the last thing it transmitted), system A knows that block 2 did arrive correctly, so it can proceed to transmit block 3. (If B had transmitted an ACK1 in response to the ENQ, system A would have needed to resend block 2.)

Data Transparency

DLE is also used to implement transparent mode in bisync. There would be no need for transparent mode transmission if the <text> portion of all messages consisted of the letters A to Z, the numerals 0 to 9, and a few special print characters like $, +, and =. However, the <text> to be sent may consist of the contents of a file or the executable object code for a program and may, therefore, contain bit patterns that are the same as the control characters that bisync uses to maintain order on the line. You can imagine the confusion if the <text>

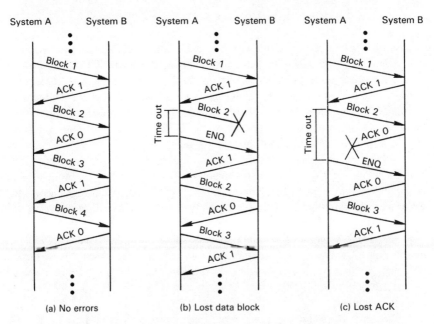

(a) No errors   (b) Lost data block   (c) Lost ACK

Figure 7-2 Bisync use of two acknowledgment types. Bisync protocol uses ACK0 and ACK1 to reduce the probability of lost or duplicated message blocks.

portion of the message happened to contain the bit pattern that means ETX; the receiver of the block would only be able to assume that the block had ended, and we would not have successfully communicated between the two systems.

Bisync implements transparency by means of character insertion; that is, the character DLE is inserted according to a set of rules that allow data to become "invisible" to the protocol. The sequence DLE STX, instead of just STX, is used to signal the start of transparent mode <text> transmission. When the end of block is sent, the transmitter must send a DLE ETX (or DLE ETB, or DLE ITB if this is the middle of a long message) to "wake up" the receiver.

This solution does present a problem, however, since the data could coincidentally, but legitimately, contain any of these two-character end of block sequences. Bisync solves this problem by requiring any DLE that is actually data to be preceded by another DLE. Upon receiving two consecutive DLEs, the receiver always discards the first and keeps the second.

Consider the case in which the user data happens to consist of the following sequence of EBCDIC characters:

A B C STX D E F ETX 1 2 3 DLE 4 5 6

where the STX, ETX, and DLE are merely data. These data could not be sent in normal (nontransparent) mode since the character that has the same bit patterns as the ETX would cause the data block to be misinterpreted. Therefore, this data block, when sent in bisync transparent mode, would appear on the communication line as

SYN SYN DLE STX A B C STX D E F ETX 1 2 3 DLE DLE 4 5 6 DLE ETX

Because the transmitting system has said "Enter transparent mode" by using DLE STX instead of STX to start the block, the action of the receiver is to look at each arriving character and compare it to the DLE character:

- If the received character is not a DLE, the 8 bits are accepted without further examination.
- If the received character is a DLE and the next character is also a DLE, the first one is discarded and the second is retained as user data.
- If the received character is a DLE and the next character is an ETX, ETB, or ITB, the two-character sequence is a legitimate end of block indication.

Most character-oriented protocols would be very simple if transparent mode transmission was not required. Implementing transparency in this type of protocol is cumbersome at best, but is usually necessary since we want to be able to transmit <text> that consists of any bit patterns at all, not merely A to Z and 0 to 9. As we will see later in this chapter, other types of protocols are designed

with built-in transparency and do not suffer from the added complexity required
to obtain transparency in a character-oriented protocol.

Code Sets and Error Checking

BSC allows the use of ASCII, EBCDIC, or 6-bit Trancode (a pre-EBCDIC
IBM code set) data within its message blocks. For error checking of EBCDIC
and 6-bit Trancode data, bisync specifies a two-byte CRC that is inserted
immediately after the ETX in each data block, as shown in **Figure 7-1**. Error
checking of ASCII data is accomplished by using a parity bit within each character
and by adding an LRC character to the end of the data block.

Bisync Subsets

The bisync family of protocols consists of several well-known subsets that
are based on specific IBM device types. BSC 3270, for example, is a version
of the protocol for interactive terminals and uses the basic BSC block format.
In addition, it employs the optional message header to contain a device address
so that each message can be sent to a specific remote device. BSC 3270 is
a polling protocol, and it uses special message formats to send poll and select
messages in order to control the flow of communications on a line.

BSC 2780 is a subset that is designed for use with the IBM 2780 family
of remote job entry (RJE) stations. Typically, the RJE station has a file of
information that is to be transmitted to another system for processing, after which
the other system returns a file containing the results of the processing. The
requirements for batch processing like this are different from an interactive
environment such as 3270, so there are some variations in the bisync protocol
to accommodate these needs; however, the basic block format remains the same
as shown in **Figure 7-1**. A later-model RJE device introduced by IBM, the
3780, also spawned a new variation of batch protocol for the bisync family.

Bisync Limitations

Bisync protocol was developed in the late 1960s when the primary
communications environment consisted of relatively low speed *terrestrial* telephone
circuits (also called *land lines*). While bisync dominated this environment for
years due to the massive numbers of IBM 3270 and 2780/3780 devices, it has
one major drawback that limits its use in many modern communications environments. Bisync is a half-duplex protocol, which makes it especially inappropriate
on circuits that have potentially long delivery delays, such as satellite links or
links that pass through multiple intermediate nodes before reaching the destination computer.

Do not confuse this use of the term half duplex with the description of half-duplex transmission in Chapter 4, although the meanings are very similar. A half-duplex circuit is one on which data can flow in both directions, but not at the same time. A half-duplex protocol is one in which the rules for acknowledgment of data blocks prevent the flow of communication in both directions simultaneously, because every block must be acknowledged before the next block can be sent. As a result, even if bisync protocol is used on a full-duplex circuit, there will never be data moving in both directions at the same time.

Figure 7-3 illustrates the timing problems that a half-duplex protocol introduces on a satellite circuit. Because the satellite is located approximately 22,300 miles above the earth, the minimum distance that a signal must travel to get from system A to system B is approximately 45,000 miles. At the speed of light, it will therefore take approximately 1/4 second (45,000 miles/186,000 miles per second) for one block of data to travel from computer A in Los Angeles to computer B in New York.

Using the bisync protocol, B must now acknowledge the received block of data before A will be allowed to transmit another block. The acknowledgment will require another 1/4 second to travel from B to A; consequently, the total time required for each block of data and its return acknowledgment is almost 1/2 second; compare this with a total of approximately 1/30 second for a New York to Los Angeles telephone line that is 3000 miles long (3000 miles/186,000 miles per second * 2).

Realize, too, that the satellite distance and the travel time remain relatively constant regardless of the locations of the earth stations, so for shorter land distances, say Boston to New York, the disparity between satellite transmission

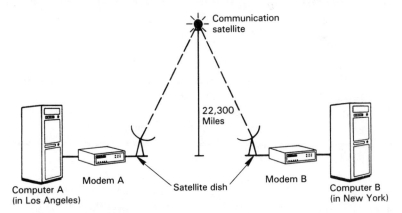

Figure 7-3   HDX protocol timing problems on satellite link. Half-duplex protocols exhibit severe degradation on any link with a long delivery delay, such as the satellite link pictured here, because the transmitter must stop and wait for an acknowledgment after sending each block of data.

time and land line time is even greater. As we will see in the next section, a full-duplex protocol is significantly more efficient on a satellite circuit.

BIT-ORIENTED PROTOCOL EXAMPLE: HDLC

[Tanenbaum] describes the evolution of bit-oriented protocols by indicating that

> They are all derived from the data link protocol used in SNA, called SDLC (Synchronous Data Link Control protocol). After developing SDLC, IBM submitted it to ANSI and ISO for acceptance as U.S. and international standards, respectively. ANSI modified it to become *ADCCP (Advanced Data Communication Control Procedure)*, and ISO modified it to become HDLC (High-level Data Link Control). CCITT then adopted and modified HDLC for its *LAP (Link Access Procedure)* as part of the X.25 network interface standard, but later modified it again to LAPB, to make it more compatible with a later version of HDLC. The nice thing about standards is that you have so many to choose from. Furthermore, if you do not like any of them, you can just wait for next year's model.* [Italics added]

Considering the number of organizations that have been involved with the specification of bit-oriented protocols, it is perhaps surprising that they have evolved into very similar forms. In this section we will discuss HDLC, but the concepts and formats are very much the same as for SDLC and the others. Chapter 15 describes the LAPB subset of HDLC as used in X.25. Refer to [Brodd] for an article describing the differences between HDLC, SDLC, and ADCCP.

HDLC Station Types

HDLC defines three station types: primary, secondary, and combined. A *primary station* is the controlling station on a link and it issues commands to the other station(s) on the link. A *secondary station* operates under the control of a primary and can only send responses to commands from the primary. *Combined stations* can issue either commands or responses.

HDLC Frame Format

HDLC defines three frame types: *information frames (I-frames)* that actually carry data, *supervisory frames (S-frames)* that are used to control the flow of information frames, and *unnumbered frames (U-frames)* that are used in establishing and terminating connections across a physical link. All three frame types

*Andrew S. Tanenbaum, *Computer Networks* (Englewood Cliffs, N.J.: Prentice-Hall, Inc., 1988), p. 254.

have the same basic format that was illustrated in Figure 6-3 and are differentiated by the contents of the control field. **Figure 7-4** contains a list of all the HDLC frame types.

Fields in an HDLC Frame

Address field. The *address field* in HDLC contains 8 bits that are used to uniquely identify the intended receiver, or in some cases the sender, of the frame. The address bits are usually assigned so that each device has a unique bit pattern. Certain address bit patterns may be set aside to define groups of devices, including the all ones pattern that indicates a broadcast message intended for all stations.

An 8-bit address field allows 256 unique addresses; however, in a large network this may not be sufficient. Therefore, HDLC allows for an extended address field that contains 16 bits and supports 65,535 unique addresses.

Frame Type		Command		Response
Information	I	Information	I	Information
Supervisory	RR	Receive ready	RR	Receive ready
	REJ	Reject	REJ	Reject
	RNR	Receive not ready	RNR	Receive not ready
	SREJ	Selective reject	SREJ	Selective reject
Unnumbered	UI	Unnumbered information	UI	Unnumbered information
	SNRM	Set normal response mode		
	DISC	Disconnect	RD	Request disconnect
	UP	Unnumbered poll		
			UA	Unnumbered acknowledgment
	TEST	Data link test	TEST	Data link test
	SIM	Set initialization mode	RIM	Request initialization mode
			FRMR	Frame reject
	SARM	Set async response mode	DM	Disconnect mode
	RSET	Reset		
	SARME	Set ARM extended mode		
	SNRME	Set NRM extended mode		
	SABM	Set async balanced mode		
	XID	Exchange identification	XID	Exchange identification
	SABME	Set ABM extended mode		

Figure 7-4   HDLC command/response types.

Control field. **Figure 7-5** shows the format of the control field for each of the three frame types. Note that only the first 2 bits of the control field are needed to define the frame type. If the first bit is a zero, the frame is an I-frame. If the first bit is a one, then the second bit indicates whether the frame is a supervisory or unnumbered frame.

In all three frame types, bit 5 is the *poll/final bit*. Although the poll/final bit is only 1 bit, it actually has four meanings based on the context in which it is used. It has the poll significance in a command and can either be set ON or OFF. In a response, it has the meaning of "final" and can also be set ON or OFF.

One use of the poll/final bit is to demand a response. For example, the poll bit can be set ON when one station has not heard from its peer station in

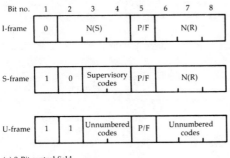

(a) 8-Bit control field

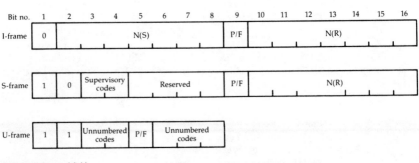

(b) Extended control field

N(S)   Send sequence number
N(R)   Receive sequence number
P/F   Poll/final bit
Supervisory codes   Bits used to identify the specific supervisory frame
Unnumbered codes   Bits used to identify the specific unnumbered frame

Figure 7-5   HDLC control field formats.

a while and wants to determine whether the other station is still alive and well. Use of the poll bit demands an immediate response, before transmission of any other pending frames, and the response frame must have the final bit set ON. See **Figure 7-6.**

The poll bit is also used by the master station on a multipoint link to grant permission to a specific secondary station to transmit. If the secondary has no data to send, it replies with a supervisory frame with the final bit set. If it does have data to send, it replies with one or more I-frames in response to the poll and turns the final bit ON in the last (or only) frame of the sequence. Refer to **Figure 7-7.**

Information field. The *information field* contains the user data and may be any length from 0 bits to infinity. In practice, a more practical upper limit

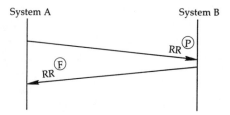

Figure 7-6 Use of HDLC poll bit to demand a response. The poll bit can be set in an HDLC command to demand an immediate response. To signify that it is answering a poll, the other station must set the final bit.

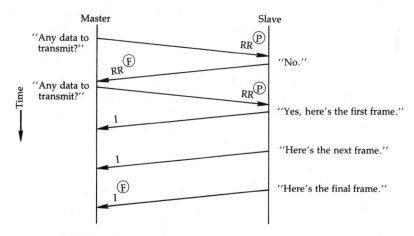

Figure 7-7 Use of HDLC poll/final bit on a multipoint link. On a multipoint link, the poll bit is set in a command from the master device to signify that it is polling the device whose address is in the address field. The polled station either responds with a "no data" indication or responds with one or more information frames. In either case, the last (or only) frame of the sequence must have the final bit set.

is used, such as 1000 or 2000 octets. Although HDLC does not specifically require that the information field be a multiple of 8 bits, many HDLC implementations do mandate an integral number of octets for the information field.

Frame check sequence. Error detection is provided by means of a cyclic redundancy check called the *frame check sequence* *(FCS)*. The FCS is a 16-bit calculated result, very similar to the CRC described earlier, that allows the receiver of a frame to verify its integrity. The hardware of the sending device uses a formula to calculate the value of the FCS based on the contents of the address, control, and information fields in the frame. It places the result into the FCS field just before putting the closing flag onto the frame. The receiving hardware performs the same calculation on the same fields in the frame that it receives, and when it detects the final flag it examines the previous 16 bits, which are always the FCS, and compares its calculated result with the received value. If they match, there is a high probability (although not an absolute certainty) that the frame received is exactly the same as the frame that was sent. If the FCS values are not equal, the receiver will use one of the supervisory frames described later to let the sender know about the problem.

HDLC Procedures

Information frames. The key factor that separates bit-oriented protocols from async and byte-oriented protocols is the use of sequence numbers for each frame of data that is transmitted. While bisync requires that each block of data be acknowledged before the next block can be sent (since there is no way to tell individual blocks of data apart), HDLC requires that a sequence number be assigned to each I-frame.

In this manner, the sender may transmit multiple frames without being required to stop and wait for an explicit acknowledgment for each. And because each frame is numbered, it is a simple matter for the recipient to know whether it has gotten every frame in the sequence. The receiver is only required to acknowledge on a periodic basis by indicating the sequence number of the next frame it expects to receive, which provides an implicit acknowledgment of all lower-numbered frames.

The control field of every information frame actually contains two sequence numbers, as can be seen in **Figure 7-5**, the *send sequence number* (N_S) and the *receive sequence number* (N_R). The transmitter must increment the send sequence number with every transmitted I-frame, and it must also place the number of the next I-frame that it expects to receive into the receive sequence number field. Thus, every I-frame contains its own send sequence number, as well as a receive sequence number that acknowledges frames received from the other end. With this simple technique, HDLC allows an acknowledgment to be piggybacked onto a frame containing data that are traveling in the reverse direction; consequently, the receiver does not even need to interrupt its own data transmission to send an acknowledgment.

The sequence numbers in the control field in **Figure 7-5** are each 3 bits long. Since the largest number that can be represented using 3 bits is 7, the transmitter of I-frames must reset the sequence number after sending a frame with the number 7 in the send field (that is, frame number 0 follows frame number 7). Counting in circular fashion like this is called *modulo arithmetic*. HDLC uses modulo 8 counting since there are 8 unique sequence numbers available using all combinations of the 3 bits in the sequence number field.

Modulo 8 sequencing also leads to another important point regarding the frame-numbering process. A transmitter must never have two unacknowledged frames in transit that contain the same sequence number or the entire acknowledgment mechanism breaks down. Therefore, the sender must stop and wait for an acknowledgment so that it does not repeat a sequence number prematurely. For convenience, the maximum number of unacknowledged frames allowed is usually one less than the modulus. Consequently, if seven frames have been sent and no acknowledgment has been received, the transmitter must stop and wait for an acknowledgment.

The maximum number of outstanding frames is called the *window size* for the protocol. Although seven unacknowledged frames are a vast improvement over a half-duplex protocol with a window size of one, even seven may not be a sufficiently large window for circuits with long delivery times. HDLC allows for extended frame numbering using a 16-bit control field that provides 7 bits each for the send and receive sequence numbers. The format of the three frame types using the extended control field is shown in **Figure 7-5b**.

Consider the advantage of this approach on the satellite link described in **Figure 7-3**: the travel times have not changed, but the sender may now transmit multiple frames, one right after the other, during which time an acknowledgment from the other end will probably arrive. In the worst case, the sender will transmit the maximum number of unacknowledged frames and will be required to stop and wait for a reply; however, it will have transmitted multiple frames before stopping, rather than having transmitted only one frame as in the bisync case.

The receive sequence number in the control field of an I-frame makes the process of sending acknowledgments very simple, since the acknowledgment can be piggybacked onto data that the recipient was going to send anyway; that is, the receiver is not required to generate a special frame type if it was going to send an I-frame anyway.

Figure 7-8 is a typical half-duplex exchange between two devices using HDLC. **Figure 7-9** is slightly more complex to follow because it shows the type of full-duplex activity that is supported by HDLC. Each station is able to transmit continuously if it has frames to send and if its sequence number window has not closed.

NOTE

In the HDLC protocol diagrams that follow, time flows from top to bottom on the page; that is, any event drawn closer to the top of the page happened before anything below it. This time relationship is especially important in understanding the sequence numbering concepts of HDLC.

Another convention used is to depict sequence numbering of HDLC frames by using one or two subscripted numerals following the letter(s) designating the frame type. When there are two numbers, the first is the send sequence number and the second is the receive sequence number. For example, $I_{2,6}$ represents an I-frame with a send sequence number of 2 and a receive sequence number of 6. For these diagrams, this provides an easy way to show the transmitter saying "Here is my I-frame with a sequence number of 2, and the next I-frame I expect from you is number 6." (Remember that the receive sequence number is *always* the sequence number of the *next* I-frame you expect to receive.)

Whenever a single sequence number appears, it is the receive sequence number; check **Figure 7-5** to see that there are no frame types that have only a send sequence number.

If the poll/final bit is set, a superscripted P or F is used. For example, RR_3^P represents an RR frame with a receive sequence number of 3 and the poll bit set.

Supervisory frames. Supervisory frames are used to control the flow of information frames and the sequence of events on the data link. As shown in **Figure 7-5**, each supervisory frame contains a receive sequence number in the control field. The purposes of the primary supervisory frames are as follows:

RR   Receive ready: explicit acknowledgment of all frames prior to the specified frame and indicates that receiver is ready to receive beginning with the specified frame.

RNR   Receive not ready: explicit acknowledgment of all frames prior to the specified frame and indicates that receiver is *not* ready to receive additional frames.

REJ Reject: explicit acknowledgment of all frames prior to the specified frame and requests retransmission of all frames beginning with the specified one.

SREJ Selective reject: requests retransmission of only the specified frame.

The *RR frame* is used primarily to provide an acknowledgment when the receiver does not have any data to send across the link and an acknowledgment is needed, for example, when the sender's window is closed. RR frames are also transmitted intermittently during periods of inactivity to show that a station is alive and well but has no data to send. See **Figure 7-10** for an example.

RNR frames are used when a receiver needs to stop the flow of incoming frames temporarily. Because an RNR also carries a sequence number, it can

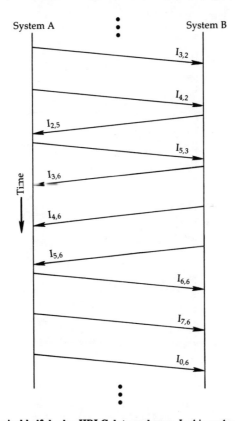

Figure 7-8 Typical half-duplex HDLC data exchange. In this exchange, all acknowledgments are transmitted via the receive sequence number in the control field of the I-frame. Note that the receive sequence number always reflects the NEXT sequence number that is expected.

still be used as an acknowledgment; but it does indicate that the receiver is not able to accept any more I-frames, perhaps because its buffers are full. When the receiver is once again able to accept I-frames, it generates an RR and sends it across the link. It is permissible for the original sender to ask periodically whether it can send more data yet, usually by sending an RR with the poll bit set on to demand a response. The appropriate answer from the busy receiver is either an RNR with the final bit set on (meaning NO) or an RR with the final bit set on (meaning YES). See **Figure 7-11**.

REJ frames are used in cases where a station receives an out of sequence frame or some other error condition that necessitates having the sender retransmit beginning at a specific frame number. Any frames that were transmitted after the specified frame must also be retransmitted. See **Figure 7-12a** for an example

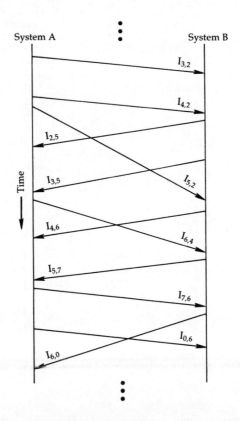

Figure 7-9   Typical full-duplex HDLC data exchange. HDLC allows full duplex data flow; therefore, I-frames can be moving in both directions at the same time. While it may appear at first that this would lead to confusion, you should be able to satisfy yourself that the process works if you follow through this and subsequent examples carefully.

of an REJ frame. The *SREJ frame* requests retransmission of exactly one frame, the one whose number is carried in the N_R field of the SREJ. The SREJ frame is not as commonly used as the REJ. See **Figure 7-12b** for an example.

Unnumbered frames. Among the unnumbered frames listed in **Figure 7-4**, the most commonly used are the mode-setting commands and the unnumbered acknowledgment. As an example, the *set asynchronous balanced mode*

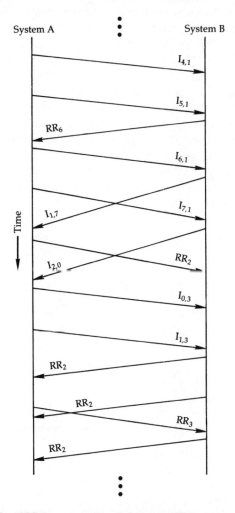

Figure 7-10   Use of RR frames as acknowledgments. RR frames are used as acknowledgments when a station has no I-frames ready to transmit but needs to issue an acknowledgment. Note that the use of the receive sequence number in the RR frame is identical to the I-frame; that is, it is the number of the NEXT frame that is expected.

(*SABM*) command is used to establish a logical connection between two combined stations, that is, to establish a link on which there is no master-slave relationship. Because both are combined stations, either can send the SABM and either can initiate commands and responses once the link has been established.

The appropriate positive response to a mode-setting command is an unnumbered acknowledgment (UA) indicating that the receiving station agrees to establish the connection in the requested mode. If the receiver does not wish to accept the command, the appropriate response is a disconnected mode (DM) frame. Other unnumbered frames are used to indicate errors in link operation, such as the frame reject (FRMR) that indicates a severe error, such as an invalid control field or an invalid receive count. A reset (RSET) command is used to tell the opposite station that the sending station is going to reset its sequence numbers to zero and that the receiver should do the same.

As the name implies, an unnumbered frame does not contain a sequence number. Consequently, the sender of an unnumbered frame cannot send a second unnumbered frame without first receiving a response. See **Figure 7-13** for examples of the use of unnumbered frames.

HDLC, and bit-oriented protocols in general, provide considerable advantages over character-oriented protocols in reliability, transparency, and both sophistication and simplicity.

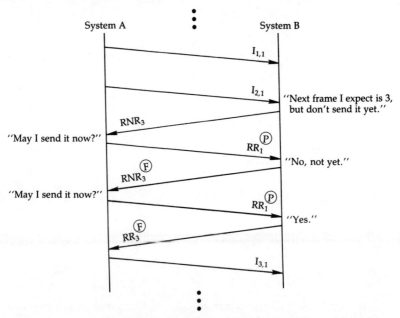

Figure 7-11 Use of RNR frame. System B sends an RNR frame to acknowledge previously received frames and to tell system A not to transmit any additional frames until system B sends an RR.

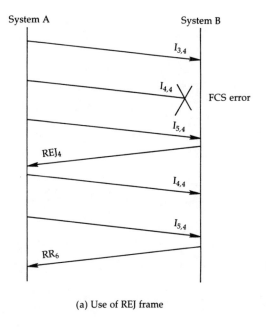

(a) Use of REJ frame

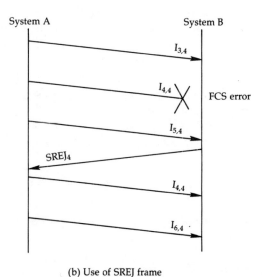

(b) Use of SREJ frame

Figure 7-12   Handling bad frames in HDLC. The REJ and SREJ frames tell the sender to retransmit I-frames because they were received with errors, perhaps due to line noise that resulted in FCS errors. The REJ frame instructs the transmitter to resend all unacknowledged frames beginning with the frame designated in the N_R field of the REJ frame. The SREJ instructs the transmitter to resend only the designated frame.

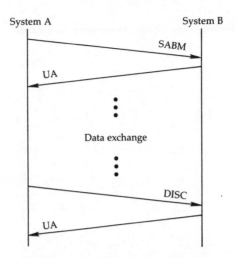

Figure 7-13 Use of SABM, UA, and DISC to establish and terminate logical link.

CONVERTERS AND EMULATORS

Because many different protocols are available and because, in the real world, there are very few totally homogeneous networks, the need frequently arises to connect two or more devices that do not share a common protocol. Two categories of products are available to assist in this situation: protocol converters and protocol emulators.

A *protocol converter* is usually a separate piece of hardware that has been designed and programmed to understand the rules of two different protocols so that it may be connected between two computers that could not ordinarily communicate. **Figure 7-14** shows a Unisys computer communicating with an

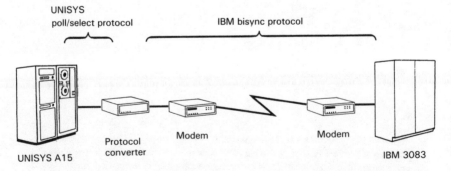

Figure 7-14 Protocol converter, computer to computer. Two computers that do not share a common communications protocol can communicate via a protocol converter that makes one computer behave as though it speaks the other's language.

IBM computer by means of a Unisys Poll/Select to IBM BSC converter. Each computer thinks it is talking to another device that speaks its language; however, the box in the middle is doing all the necessary conversions to allow the data exchange to take place.

Another common type of protocol converter allows a dumb terminal to talk to an IBM computer over bisync links. On one RS-232 interface, the converter "speaks" simple, async protocol, and on the second RS-232 interface, the box "speaks" fluent bisync. In **Figure 7-15**, the IBM computer operates as though it is connected to a 3270-type terminal, but the user is able to use an inexpensive, dumb terminal instead of a more expensive bisync device.

As a word of caution, the terminal to computer connection via a protocol converter is seldom as simple as inserting a protocol converter between the two devices. There are likely to be considerable differences between the keyboards and screen characteristics of the original terminal and the one that is connected to the protocol converter. The converter can probably handle some of the differences, but often the physical limitations of the substitute device cannot be overcome. For example, an equivalent key may not be available to substitute for a special function key on the original device, or there may not be any way to highlight data in the same way on the screen of the substitute terminal. Nonetheless, protocol converters can offer an effective way to communicate between otherwise incompatible devices.

Protocol emulators also allow incompatible devices to communicate but employ software and/or hardware inside one computer to make it look like another type of computer, rather than using an external protocol converter. **Figure 7-16** shows the same Unisys computer exchanging information with the IBM computer, as in **Figure 7-14**, but in this case the Unisys system has been programmed to emulate the IBM protocol. If the emulation software is written correctly, the IBM system will never know that the device on the other end of the line is not another IBM device. Most computer companies have built

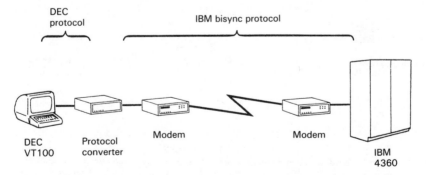

Figure 7-15   Protocol converter, terminal to computer. A computer and terminal that do not share a common communications protocol can communicate via a protocol converter that makes the terminal behave as though it speaks the computer's language.

emulators for one or more IBM protocols because of the significant presence of IBM computers in the business world.

Many personal computers have emulator packages for popular communications protocols. For example, an IBM PC can be made to look like an IBM 3278 terminal or a Wang PC may emulate a Unisys TD830. The software and hardware for these emulations are available from PC vendors and from third-party software companies. See **Figure 7-17** for a diagram of an emulator configuration that is similar to **Figure 7-15**.

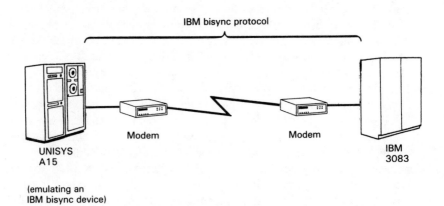

Figure 7-16 **Protocol emulator, computer to computer.** Two computers that do not share a common communications protocol can communicate if one of them has been programmed to emulate the protocol of the other.

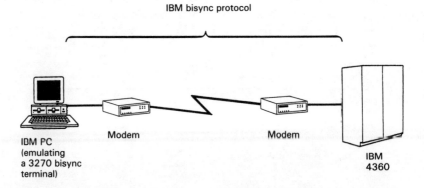

Figure 7-17 **Protocol emulator, terminal to computer.** A computer and a terminal that do not share a common communications protocol can communicate if the computer contains software to emulate the behavior of the terminal controller. Alternatively, the terminal could emulate the functions of the type of terminal that the computer understands.

RECAP

- Bisync was developed by IBM and is a family of extremely widely used, character-oriented, half-duplex protocols that implement data transparency through the use of character insertion.
- HDLC is a bit-oriented protocol that supports full-duplex operation and was developed by ISO.
- Protocol converters and emulators allow otherwise incompatible devices to communicate with each other.

ISO AND CCITT STANDARDS
ABOVE THE LINK LAYER

The underlying purpose of a protocol at layer 3 and above is identical to the base purpose of a protocol at layer 2: to establish a set of rules by which two peer layers may communicate. The data link layer protocols provide connections over physical links and ensure that groups of bits will be delivered correctly. The protocols at the higher layers place their emphasis on the logical uses of those links and on the integrity of the data and messages through the overall network, as well as such functions as data sequencing and flow control.

Chapter 5 introduced each layer of the OSI model. Chapters 6 and 7 described layer 2 in considerable detail. This chapter describes the services and protocols that ISO and CCITT have specified for layers 3 through 7. For some layers, the ISO and CCITT standards are very different and are described separately in the paragraphs that follow. For other layers, the two sets of recommendations are very similar and are described together. Even when they are similar, however, do not assume that the ISO and CCITT standards are identical. The two groups frequently work together to ensure commonality, but they are independent organizations with different constituencies.

NETWORK LAYER

Services

Network layer services are specified in [ISO 8348] and [CCITT X.213]. The primary network service is to provide a delivery mechanism to the transport layer. The network layer masks the routing and switching functions from the transport layer and prevents the upper layers from needing to know anything about the network topology or technology. The network layer provides both connection-oriented and connectionless services as described in Chapter 5.

The requirements for the network layer change depending on upper layer needs and the characteristics of the physical connection between open systems. When the physical connection is not a direct link, but is via an intermediate network, as shown in **Figure 8-1a**, the network layer behaves more like the data link layer in that it is concerned only with the connection from the DTE to the network node and not with end system to end system communications. In this situation, end-to-end protocols are the territory of the transport layer and above.

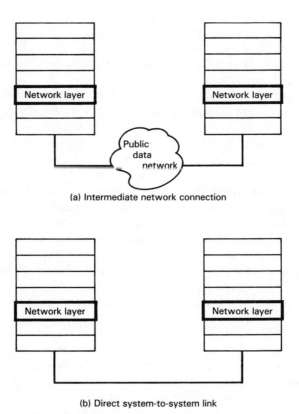

(a) Intermediate network connection

(b) Direct system-to-system link

Figure 8-1   OSI network layer. *(a)* Two open systems are connected via an intermediate network. *(b)* Two open systems are directly connected to each other. The services provided by the network layer will be more comprehensive in the first case because the connection is more complex.

When the physical layer is a direct link between the systems, however, as in **Figure 8-1b**, the network layer behaves more like the upper layers and communicates from end system to end system.

The amount of error checking and reliability provided by the network layer varies with the quality of the underlying data link and physical layers. Less work is required of the network layer when the reliability of the physical connection is higher, since it can rely on the data delivery and integrity services of the lower layers.

In addition to ISO 8348 and CCITT X.213 mentioned above, several other recommendations apply to network layer services, including [ISO 8648], which describes the internal organization and structure of the network layer, and [ISO 8878], which describes the use of X.25 to provide OSI connection-mode service.

Protocol Examples

X.25.   The network layer of the CCITT *X.25* recommendation is one of the more common network layer protocol standards. In the X.25 recommendation, the network layer is usually referred to as the *packet layer* and a network PDU is called a *packet*.

X.25 specifies two types of virtual circuit service, *switched virtual circuits (SVC)* and *permanent virtual circuits (PVC)*. SVCs are established on demand, like a dialup telephone connection, and PVCs provide the equivalent of a leased telephone line; that is, a PVC is always available whenever both DTEs are in service. X.25 also provides for multiple, simultaneous conversations over one link layer using a separate logical channel number for each conversation.

The X.25 protocol defines a specific header for every packet generated at layer 3. Among other data fields, the header contains a packet type identifier that is used to tell the receiving packet layer what type of packet is arriving. *Data packets* are used to carry PDUs received from the transport layer. *Control packets* are used to request and establish a connection through the network, to acknowledge receipt of data packets, to terminate a connection, and to recover from various error conditions.

See Chapter 15 for a detailed description of X.25. See also [CCITT X.25].

X.75.   CCITT recommendation *X.75* provides connections between multiple X.25 networks and gives the end-user nodes the appearance of a single virtual circuit through the total set of networks. In reality, the boundary node at the edge of each X.25 network terminates the virtual circuit through that network, but maintains enough information to link that virtual circuit to another one in the next network. This process is completely transparent to the DTE at each end of the linked virtual circuits. CCITT calls the boundary node the *signaling terminal (STE)*. See **Figure 8-2**.

X.75, which is also discussed in Chapter 15, uses almost the same network layer protocol as X.25, but contains several extensions to the packet header to provide for internetwork communications. See also [CCITT X.75].

X.21. The network layer of CCITT recommendation X.21 defines a means to establish, control, and terminate circuit-switched synchronous connections over a public data network. X.21 actually includes recommendations for all three lower layers of the seven layer model. [Stallings1] provides a complete description of X.21 in his Chapter 13; Chapter 10 of this text provides additional information on the physical layer of X.21. X.21 is used more widely in Europe than in North America.

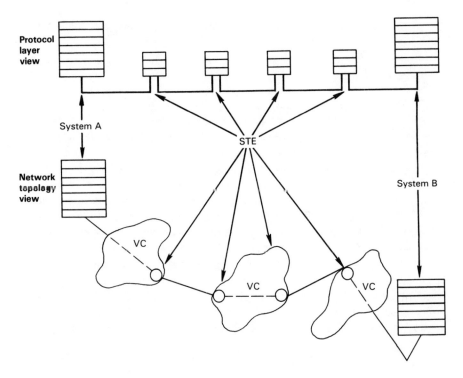

STE = signaling terminal
VC = virtual circuit

Figure 8-2   X.75 signaling terminal (STE). Each X.75 STE appears to its network to be just another X.25 host, yet it is able to use the information in the X.75 packet header to link a virtual circuit from its network to another STE in an adjacent network. The result is a set of linked virtual circuits spanning multiple networks, allowing freedom of interconnection among all DTEs on any of the networks.

TRANSPORT LAYER

Services*

Transport layer services are specified in [ISO 8072] and [CCITT X.214]. The primary service of the transport layer is to provide reliable end system to end system connections between session entities. The transport layer is not concerned with how the end systems are actually connected, since routing and switching functions are provided by the network layer.

[Stallings1] argues that the transport layer is the "keystone of the whole concept of computer-communications architecture." This is true, he suggests, because

- the lower layers are simpler and well understood and there are widely agreed upon standards, and
- the higher layers can actually be ignored if applications are written to call directly upon transport layer services.

He also points out that the complexity of any given transport layer implementation is inversely proportional to the sophistication of the network services that underlie it. A simple network service may require a complex transport protocol to compensate for network deficiencies, while a sophisticated network service may justify a rudimentary transport service.

For example, a network that only provides connectionless service will require a more sophisticated transport layer than if the network provides reliable, virtual circuit service. In the former case, it will be left up to the transport layer to provide sequencing and to check for missing or duplicate packets. In the latter case, the transport layer will have minimal responsibilities.

The transport layer is also responsible for controlling the quality of service requested by the session layer. Such characteristics as the maximum delay, security, and multiplexing of multiple sessions per transport connection can be requested by the session layer. The transport layer may also provide expedited data transfer to allow a higher-priority PDU to take precedence over a normal PDU.

[Stallings1] devotes an entire chapter just to transport protocols in order to support his claim for the importance of the transport layer.

Protocol Examples

ISO/CCITT have created multiple transport layer protocol definitions in [ISO 8073] and [CCITT X.224] because of the wide variability in the quality

---

*Ideas in this section adapted with permission of Macmillan Publishing Company from *Data and Computer Communications* by William Stallings. Copyright © 1985 by Macmillan Publishing Company.

Type A   Offers the *most reliable* network service by providing an acceptable level of residual errors and signaled errors to the transport layer. When operating over a type A network, the transport layer implementation can be fairly simple.

Type B   Provides a *moderate* network service level. It requires a somewhat more robust transport layer because, although the residual error rate is acceptable, the signaled error rate is unacceptable.

Type C   Network services are the *lowest quality* where both the residual error rate and the signaled error rate are unacceptable to the transport user. Consequently, the transport layer must be significantly more complex in order to render the transport service acceptable to the session layer.

Figure 8-3   ISO network types. The functions of the transport layer will vary based on the quality of the underlying network. ISO defines three network types in [ISO 8073].

of the underlying network services that exist. The specific transport protocol recommended for a given network depends on the network type as listed in **Figure 8-3**. ISO and CCITT have categorized networks based on the types of errors that they allow. A *signaled error* occurs when a lost or duplicated transport PDU cannot be recovered by the network service, but the transport layer is informed of the problem. A *residual error* occurs when the error cannot be corrected by the network service and the transport layer is not notified that the problem has occurred.

Figure 8-4 lists the five classes of transport protocols for use over the three network service types in **Figure 8-3**. **Figure 8-5** shows the acceptable combinations of network type and transport protocol class.

SESSION LAYER

Services

Session layer services are specified in [ISO 8326] and [CCITT X.215]. The session layer provides organization and synchronization of the data flow between two applications. When an application requests that a session be established, the session layer requests a transport connection. Once the transport connection exists, the session layer provides dialog management services to regulate the flow of data across the connection in one of several ways, based on application requirements:

- The session layer regulates the transfer of control from one application to another for applications that require alternating (half-duplex) communication.

Class 0   The *simple* class of transport protocols is used exclusively with type A networks, the most reliable type of network. Flow control is assumed to be provided by the network.

Class 1   The *basic error recovery* class is used with type B networks such as X.25 networks, and provides several features, such as, numbered transport PDUs and expedited data transfer, that are not found in class 0. Flow control is still provided by the network.

Class 2   The *multiplexing* class is used with type A networks, but, unlike class 0, provides for the multiplexing of several transport connections over a single network connection. Flow control may be provided by the transport layer for class 2 and is fairly complex since it must be implemented on a per transport connection basis if it is used at all.

Class 3   The *error recover and multiplexing* class is a combination of class 1 error recovery and class 2 multiplexing and flow control for use over type B networks.

Class 4   The *error detection and recovery* class is the only class of transport protocol usable over an unreliable, type C network. It employs checksums, timeouts, and a variety of other protocol devices to turn an unreliable network into an acceptable transport service.

Figure 8-4   ISO transport protocol types. The transport protocol types defined in [ISO 8073] provide varying services based on the underlying network type (see Figure 8-3).

	Transport Class				
	0	1	2	3	4
Network Service Type	Simple	Basic Error Recovery	Multiplexing	Recovery and Multiplexing	Detection and Recovery
A (reliable)	X		X		
B (moderate)		X		X	
C (unreliable)					X

X indicates an acceptable combination of transport class and network type.

Figure 8-5   ISO network type versus transport class.

- The session layer provides simultaneous, two-way data flow control for applications that require full-duplex communication.
- The session layer provides the means to insert synchronization points at intermediate points during a session. In this way, if the connection should fail for some reason, the session layer can recover from the most recent synchronization point, rather than restarting from the beginning of the session.

Protocol Examples

The session layer protocols defined in [ISO 8327] and [CCITT X.225] provide for session establishment, data transfer, and session release. Within a session, dialog is organized into activities, each of which may contain one or more synchronization points. The session protocol supports both major and minor synchronization points to facilitate session resynchronization in the event of connection failure.

PRESENTATION LAYER

Services

Presentation layer services are specified in [ISO 8822] and CCITT X.216. The presentation layer provides data transformation and formatting services to the application layer. The presentation layer is concerned with the structure of the data, called the syntax, but not with the meaning, referred to as the semantics. The interpretation of the data is the responsibility of the application layer.

Examples of transformations provided by this layer include code conversion (for example, from ASCII to EBCDIC), electronic mail structure conversions, and document format conversions when documents are transferred from one word-processing system to another.

Protocol Examples

Presentation protocols are defined in [ISO 8823] and CCITT X.226. They provide for the establishment of presentation connections, transfer of data, and release of connections. They also provide the means to establish a context for presentation services in case the same data value has different meanings in different contexts. The presentation protocol provides for confirmed services, in which the presentation and application layers exchange confirmation on completion of presentation layer transformations. Unconfirmed services assume that application layer entities validate the completion of the presentation services without explicit confirmation from the presentation layer.

Abstract Syntax Notation

[ISO 8822] and [ISO 8823] define the services and operation of the presentation layer, but ISO and CCITT both recognized a need for a notation to specify the syntax. ISO created two standards: [ISO 8824], which defines a language called Abstract Syntax Notation 1 (ASN.1), and [ISO 8825], which defines the encoding rules for ASN.1. CCITT, as part of its message handling services (MHS) standards set, created [CCITT X.409] to define the language used to specify presentation syntax for electronic mail systems. CCITT has since broken X.409 out into X.208 and X.209 in recognition of their broader applicability beyond MHS. X.208 and X.209 will probably be the technical equivalents of ISO 8824 and 8825, respectively.

APPLICATION LAYER

Services

The application layer provides the final set of functions that allows application processes to access the layered stack of protocols. The standards work has focused on defining service elements that are common to all applications, as well as service elements that are specific to groups of applications.

Protocol Examples

[CCITT X.400] is one of a family of recommendations for electronic mail and document interchange on multivendor computer networks. The X.400 series defines the protocols for the exchange of messages as well as defining the structure of the mail items.

[ISO 8571], *File Transfer, Access and Manipulation (FTAM)*, allows applications to access and transfer data located throughout a network without specific knowledge of how the data are stored on a host system.

The ISO *virtual terminal (VT)* protocol defines the characteristics of a universal terminal and the manner in which it will interact with an arbitrary host computer. Virtual terminals are vital to the concept of providing "open" communications, in this case, by giving a terminal access to any application on any host computer in the network. Without a VT protocol, one of three things happens: (1) terminals are confined to connections with hosts and applications for which they were specifically designed, (2) every type of terminal must be able to emulate every other terminal, or (3) every host must be able to emulate every other host. With the great diversity of hardware and software vendors producing terminals, computers, and applications, none of these solutions is very likely. Instead, a virtual terminal protocol can allow universal access since each host system can transform the standard VT protocol into its own internal protocol for handling terminals.

ISO and CCITT are continuing to work on application protocols for such other areas as transaction processing, job transfer and management, and remote database access.

RECAP

- The network layer provides the network interface and a delivery mechanism to the transport layer, using such protocols as X.25, X.75, and X.21.
- The transport layer provides end system to end system connections using such protocols as ISO TP0 through TP4.
- The session layer provides session connections to presentation entities using protocols defined in ISO 8327 and CCITT X.225.
- The presentation layer provides syntax transformations on behalf of the application layer and employs ASN.1 to specify the syntax and required transformations.
- The application layer standards define services common to most applications as well as services that are relevant to specific groups of applications and include such protocols as X.400, FTAM, and VT.

OTHER PROTOCOL STANDARDS

ISO and CCITT are not the only organizations creating standards for the data communications industry.

IEEE 802 COMMITTEE

In 1980, Digital Equipment Corporation, Intel Corporation, and Xerox Corporation published a set of specifications for a local area network (LAN) called Ethernet, which they hoped would become the de facto standard for local area networking. While it met with some success, Ethernet did not attain the status of a de facto standard in its early years. Other vendors continued to introduce non-Ethernet LAN products to the market, and few of them bore any resemblance to Ethernet or to each other.

Seeing the profusion of local area network technologies and products, the *Institute of Electrical and Electronic Engineers* (*IEEE*) chartered the 802 committee in 1980 to create the definitive LAN standard, on the assumption that there could be one standard for all LAN environments. The reality, almost 10 years later, is that the 802 committee consists of at least seven subcommittees that have written an entire family of local area network standards because:

- The environments in which LANs are used are very diverse.
- There are a multitude of technologies available for LAN implementation.

- Manufacturers of competing technologies have promoted their interests in the standards committees.

Figure 9-1 contains a list of the current IEEE subcommittees with their areas of standardization. **Figure 9-2** shows the tree structure of the core portion of the IEEE standards, from the logical link control (LLC) sublayer, through the medium access control (MAC) sublayer, to the physical layer at the bottom (the LLC and MAC sublayers both reside in the OSI data link layer).

IEEE has submitted the recommendations from several of its subcommittees to ISO, which has adopted many of them as standards in the 8802 series. For example, ISO 8802/3 corresponds to IEEE 802.3, ISO 8802/4 corresponds to IEEE 802.4, and so forth.

802.1	Architecture and Overview
802.2	Logical Link Control
802.3	CSMA/CD
802.4	Token Passing Bus
802.5	Token Ring
802.6	Metropolitan Area Networks
802.7	Broadband Local Area Networks
802.9	Integrated Voice and Data LANs
802.10	Interoperable LAN Security

Figure 9-1   IEEE 802 subcommittees.

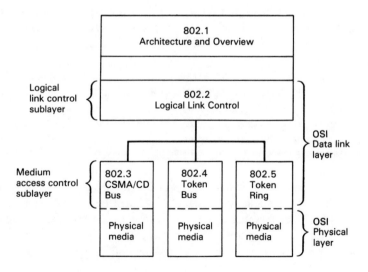

Figure 9-2   IEEE family of LAN standards for physical and data link layers.

MAP/TOP

For users of local area networks, the profusion of standards and products makes it difficult to buy a set of products from multiple vendors that will all work together. Two large companies, General Motors and Boeing Computer Services decided to do something about that problem.

MAP

General Motors (GM) was the organizing force behind the development of the *Manufacturing Automation Protocol* (*MAP*). The problem faced by GM and other manufacturers was the proliferation of factory-floor computers (for example, process control equipment, robots, and inventory systems) that needed to talk to each other over local area networks in the factories in order to drive the manufacturing process. These computers were built by a large number of different vendors using their own protocols, so the primary objective for MAP was to develop a single, standard stack of protocols to which all vendors could conform. By doing so, GM and the other companies hoped to reduce or eliminate the millions of dollars per year that they spent to make incompatible (or nearly compatible) products communicate. GM sought support from other large manufacturing concerns on the assumption that their combined purchasing power would speak to the vendor community with a stronger voice.

From the outset, the MAP Users Group did not want to create new standards for MAP, but chose to adopt existing or emerging international standards wherever possible. When appropriate standards did not exist, or when the standards were insufficient in a particular area, the MAP committee created extensions and submitted them to the international standards groups for consideration.

The MAP effort has been remarkably successful in enlisting support from both user companies and from computer and communications equipment vendors. The former group saw a unique opportunity to drive the vendors in the direction of compatibility through standards, and the vendors saw the MAP effort as an opportunity to tap into the vast LAN marketplace in the manufacturing industry. By the beginning of 1988, numerous vendors had introduced products conforming to the MAP 2.1 specification, and many others were planning to do so.

The newest version of the MAP specification, MAP 3.0, contains significant enhancements and extensions to version 2.1 and will be voted on during 1988 for approval by MAP members. The 3.0 version of the specification already appears to be well on its way toward general acceptance, despite some resistance by vendors who have invested heavily in building products that conform to MAP 2.1.

The problem for MAP 2.1 vendors is the significant changes that make much of 3.0 incompatible with 2.1 and with the short life span of MAP 2.1.

To prevent similar problems in the future, the MAP Users Group has taken the unusual step of stipulating that there will be no incompatible changes introduced to MAP 3.0 for a period of six years from its final publication in 1988.

TOP

The *Technical Office Protocol* (*TOP*) was an attempt by Boeing to perform a similar function for standards for the office environment instead of the factory floor. TOP shares many standards in common with MAP, but there are a few differences, primarily in the use of 802.3 instead of 802.4 for the lower layer specification. The TOP and MAP user groups were separate operations for several years, but the two groups consolidated to form the MAP/TOP Users Group because they share common purposes and methods.

While vendor acceptance has not been universal for MAP and TOP, caused in part by the difficulty of building products to standards that are evolving and maturing from year to year, both groups have had a significant impact on the standards process. They have demonstrated that it is possible for a group of nonvendor companies to band together to drive vendors in a common direction.

DEPARTMENT OF DEFENSE

The United States Department of Defense (DoD) has been active in the development of communications networks for many years. The most frequently cited example is the DoD-funded *ARPANET* project under the auspices of the DoD Advanced Research Projects Agency. ARPANET was an attempt to interconnect multiple computers at dozens of universities, government agencies, and defense contractors so that information and computing power could be shared from any location on the network.

ARPANET pioneered many of the advanced communications concepts that are currently in commercial use in the world, including the concept of packet switching that is discussed in Chapter 15. To drive the effort to allow vendor-independent network connections and communications, DoD has developed many communications standards in what [Stallings1] refers to as the *DoD protocol architecture* (*DPA*). For additional information about any DoD protocols, refer to [DDN].

TCP/IP

At OSI layers 4 and 3, respectively, DoD created the *Transmission Control Protocol* (*TCP*) and the *Internet Protocol* (*IP*), which are referred to collectively as *TCP/IP*. TCP employs a rather large PDU header, containing a minimum of 20 octets. The protocol is used to transmit streams of octets between nodes on the same network. When used in conjunction with IP, the communicating nodes may be located on any interconnected networks, or *internets*.

IP resides in the upper portion of the network layer and employs a connectionless-mode service to exchange data with the IP layer on another system. IP appends its own protocol header (minimum of 20 octets) to the TCP-created PDU and then passes the resultant PDU to the network layer. TCP and IP are independent of the underlaying protocol layers and are commonly used on top of either X.25 or 802.3 subnetworks, for example.

The flexibility of TCP/IP allows straightforward data exchange among computers from different manufacturers across multiple types of intermediate networks. **Figure 9-3** shows an example* in which system A is transferring a file to system B. System A is attached to a public data network with an X.25 interface, and system B is attached to an 802.3 local area network. (Both of these network types are described later in the book.)

The TCP layer on system A receives a PDU to transfer from the next higher layer, adds its header, and passes the PDU to IP. The IP software adds its header and passes the data to the X.25 packet layer, which adds its header and passes the PDU to the data link layer, where the HDLC encapsulation takes place. The frame from this layer travels across the PDN to a gateway node where the X.25 software strips away the X.25 data link and packet information and passes the resultant PDU to the IP layer, which examines the IP header.

When the IP layer discovers that the intended destination can be reached over the LAN, it passes the PDU to the LAN layer 3 and 2 software, which does its own encapsulation and puts the data onto the LAN. Finally, system B retrieves the frame from the network, where it works its way up through the link and network layers to the IP and TCP layers for delivery to the file transfer software on system B.

While TCP and IP were developed by the DoD for use on ARPANET, they are being adopted at an increasing rate for use in commercial networking products. They are not necessarily better than their ISO counterparts, but they have one considerable advantage for customers who are interested in internetworking — they are available today. Until ISO transport and internet-work protocol products become widely available, TCP/IP products are likely to garner a significant share of the market for multivendor network compatibility and internetworking.

TELNET

TELNET is a virtual terminal protocol that is widely implemented on ARPANET and is often used on top of TCP/IP in other networks, too. TELNET

---

*Internetworking example adapted with permission of Macmillan Publishing Company from *Data and Computer Communications* by William Stallings. Copyright© 1985 by Macmillan Publishing Company.

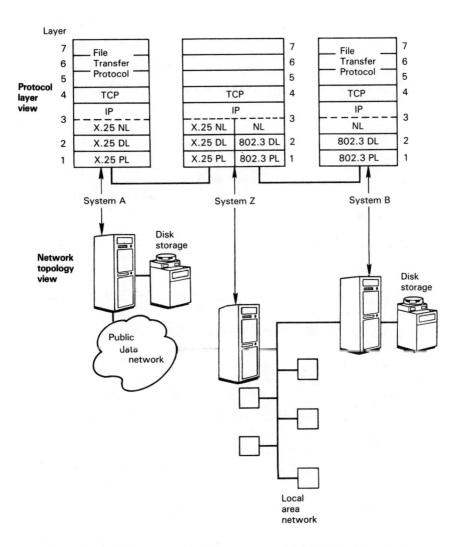

Figure 9-3 File transfer through TCP/IP internetwork. Using TCP/IP, system A is able to transfer a file to system B even though the two systems are physically attached to very different types of networks. See the text for a detailed explanation of the sequence of events that gets an application PDU from one system to the other.

was designed primarily for scroll-mode terminals and allows parameter negotiation in order to establish the bounds for the operation of a particular session.

FTP

FTP is the ARPANET File Transfer Protocol and has similar origins and current usage as TELNET. It is designed to allow various file types to be transferred between arbitrary host computers, providing format conversions as required.

SMTP

SMTP is the Simple Mail Transfer Protocol. It is a rudimentary electronic mail protocol allowing for transfer of mail items between users on multiple vendors' systems and relies on TCP/IP at the lower layers to allow delivery across multiple networks.

RECAP

- The IEEE 802 committee is working on a variety of standards related to local area networks.
- MAP and TOP have adopted IEEE and ISO standards where they are sufficient for their purpose and have made extensions to the standards where they are not.
- The Department of Defense created TCP/IP for the network and transport layers and TELNET, FTP, and SMTP for the upper layers.
- DoD protocols are widely used on ARPANET and are implemented on commercial networks when multivendor compatibility and internetworking are important.

Part III

CONVERSION DEVICES

Part III provides the details about the operation of the signal-conversion devices that were introduced in Chapter 3. The material in this section is divided into three chapters.

Chapter 10 describes the standards that have been defined for the interface between the signal-conversion device and the computer equipment.

Chapter 11 describes the techniques used by telephone line modems to achieve the transmission of data over the analog public telephone network.

Chapter 12 describes additional types of signal-conversion devices that were not discussed in Chapter 11, including null modems, short-haul modems, fiber-optic modems, and devices for connection of computers to digital transmission facilities.

10

INTERFACE STANDARDS

The development of the RS-232 recommendation for the interface between a computer and a modem was one of the earliest and most successful standardization efforts in the computer industry. RS-232 allowed computer vendors to develop their technology and their products independently from the development of modem technology and products. In addition, RS-232 ensured that a computer vendor could build a product that would function with a wide variety of modem vendor products, thus ensuring that the vendor would not become locked into the products of a specific modem vendor. This same independence was provided to the modem vendors, as well as to the users of the equipment at both ends of the RS-232 cable.

RS-232 is not the only computer-to-modem interface standard, but few others have gained its nearly universal acceptance. The other standards that do exist were developed because of the significant changes in the interface requirements of today compared to the 1960s era RS-232 specification.

For example, in the 1960s the maximum speed limitation of 20,000 bps for RS-232 was considered to be very reasonable (and perhaps, even beyond the realm of the possible). Today, speeds in the tens of thousands and even millions of bits per second are routine and require an interface that can operate in that range. In addition, microprocessor chips that could not have been imagined 25 years ago are now routinely used to build a variety of devices, including intelligent interfaces that have capabilities far exceeding those of RS-232.

It is an ironic testimony to the success of the RS-232 interface that the acceptance of newer, higher speed, and enhanced capability interfaces has been slowed by the widespread use of RS-232.

RS-232 AND V.24

The formal title of the newest version of *RS-232* is

Interface between Data Terminal Equipment and Data Circuit-terminating Equipment Employing Serial Binary Data Interchange.

RS-232 uses the terms *data terminal equipment (DTE)* and *data circuit-terminating equipment (DCE)* to describe the computer and the signal-conversion devices, respectively. RS-232 applies only to the DTE-DCE interface and has nothing to do with the operation of the communications line between the DCEs. Furthermore, the RS-232 interfaces at each end of a communications line are completely independent of each other. See **Figure 10-1**.

The RS-232 recommendation was drafted by the *Electronic Industries Association (EIA)* in cooperation with the Bell System, other modem manufacturers, and computer vendors in order to provide a common interface standard. The "RS" in the title stands for "recommended standard," and the single letter often used following RS-232 indicates the revision level of the recommendation. RS-232-C is the most commonly implemented version of the standard. RS-232-D was approved in late 1986 and published in January 1987.

In other parts of the world, the *V.24* recommendation from CCITT has been adopted and is very similar to RS-232. In this text, we will use RS-232 as our example, but virtually all the information about RS-232 applies to V.24. The interested reader should consult [McNamara] for a description of the specific differences between the two standards.

RS-232 specifies requirements for the mechanical, electrical, and functional aspects of the DTE-DCE interface. Each of these categories is described next.

Mechanical

The RS-232 connector contains 25 pins (or sockets depending on which connector you examine) arranged in the specific configuration shown in **Figure**

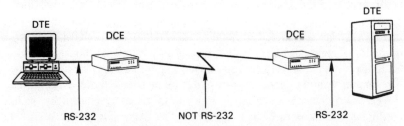

Figure 10-1 Location of RS-232 interface on communication line. The RS-232 interface is located between the DTE and DCE and does not apply to the communication over the telephone line between the DCEs.

10-2. Figure 10-2 also shows the physical dimensions of the *DB25 connector* that is used for RS-232. The 25-pin connector implies that there are 25 wires in every RS-232 cable and, in theory, this is correct. However, not all 25 wires have functions assigned to them, and even the wires that do have assigned functions are not used in all circumstances. Consequently, many RS-232 cables have fewer than 25 wires, even though the connector can accommodate 25.

Connecting two devices with an RS-232 cable requires caution to ensure that the cable has the correct wires for the particular application. Also, the DB25 connector is frequently used for other purposes than an RS-232 connection because it is widely available; while RS-232 always implies a DB25 connector, you should not assume that use of a DB25 connector always implies an RS-232 interface.

Electrical

RS-232 is a digital interface on which a positive voltage in the range from +3 to +25 volts represents a 0 or ON condition. A negative voltage in the range of -3 to -25 volts represents a 1 or OFF condition. A voltage in the range between -3 and +3 volts is considered to be in transition and does not represent a usable signal on the interface. See **Figure 10-3.**

The maximum speed recommended for RS-232 is 20,000 bps over a cable of 15 meters (approximately 50 feet). In practice, a longer cable is often used, especially when the transmission speed is less than the maximum or when the electrical characteristics of the cable in use are better than those listed in the recommendation. Similarly, it is possible to transmit more than 20,000 bps, but only when the cable is shorter than the maximum length or has electrical characteristics that are better than those in the recommendation.

Numerous suppliers offer cables that exceed the requirements of RS-232 by using shielding to reduce noise and interference or by using low-capacitance

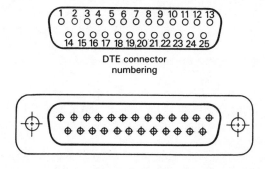

DTE connector
numbering

Figure 10-2   RS-232 mechanical characteristics. RS-232 specifies the use of the DB25 connector, which is pictured in this figure. [Adapted from *EIA Standard RS-232* (Washington, D.C.: Electronic Industries Association, 1987), Figures 3.1 and 3.2.]

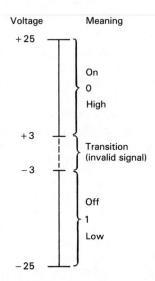

Figure 10-3   RS-232 electrical characteristics.

cable to reduce attentuation, or both. These cables allow transmission at considerably longer distances between the DTE and DCE. By whichever technique, RS-232 cables in the real world are often 50 to 200 feet or more in length. Strictly speaking, however, any usage over 20,000 bps or 15 meters is a violation of the RS-232 standard.

The speed and distance limitation of RS-232 results from the cable characteristics defined in the specification and from the use of an unbalanced electrical interface. On an *unbalanced interface*, a common ground wire is used for all the interchange circuits that will be discussed below. Another example of an unbalanced electrical system is an automobile electrical system: each light bulb or accessory has only one wire connected to it. The return path that completes the electrical circuit is provided by the common ground of the frame of the car. For RS-232, the common ground is provided by pin 7.

Functional

Figure 10-4 lists the functions of the most frequently used RS-232 interface wires, or *leads*. Note that each function is assigned a single wire and that each wire is used in only one direction. As noted above, the shared ground wire on pin 7 completes each electrical circuit.

For each of the most common pins on the interface, **Figure 10-4** also lists the pin number, the common name and abbreviation, and the EIA circuit designation, which consists of a two-letter name. The first two types of reference are more commonly used; that is, you are more likely to hear someone refer to pin 2 than to signal BA, or to talk about the state of "clear to send" or CTS than about the state of signal CB. The chart also shows whether each signal travels from the DTE to the DCE, or vice versa.

Data signals. The two most important signals on the RS-232 interface are the two that carry data: *transmit data (TD)* and *receive data (RD)*. All other signals on the interface exist to allow 0 and 1 bits to flow across these two wires. Note that TD and RD, like all other RS-232 signals, are named from the point of view of the DTE; that is, transmitted data are transmitted by the DTE, and received data are received by the DTE.

Control signals. Two of the signals in the control category, *data terminal ready (DTR)* and *data set ready (DSR)*, are used to indicate that the

Category	Pin No.	Common Name	Abbre-viation	EIA/CCITT Designation	Direction DTE DCE
GROUND	7	Signal ground	SG	AB/102	
DATA	2	Transmitted data	TD	BA/103	⟶
	3	Received data	RD	BB/104	⟵
CONTROL	4	Request to send	RTS	CA/105	⟶
	5	Clear to send	CTS	CB/106	⟵
	6	Data set ready (DCE ready)	DSR	CC/107	⟵
	8	Data carrier detect (received line signal detector)	DCD or CD	CF/109	⟵
	20	Data terminal ready (DTE ready)	DTR	CD/108.2	⟶
	22	Ring indicator	RI	CE/125	⟵
TIMING	15	Transmit clock (transmitter signal element timing, DCE)	TC	DB/114	⟵
	17	Receive clock (receiver signal element timing, DCE)	RC	DD/115	⟵
	24	External transmit clock (transmitter signal element timing, DTE)	ETC	DA/113	⟶

Figure 10-4   RS-232 functional characteristics. This figure shows some of the most common RS-232 signals. In cases where the common name is different from the name in the latest version of the EIA standard, the common name is given first, followed by the name from the standard. [Adapted from *EIA Standard RS-232* (Washington, D.C.: Electronic Industries Association, 1987), Figures 3.6 and 4.1.]

respective devices are powered on and functioning (*data set* is another name for a modem). There should never be data moving across an RS-232 interface unless both DTR and DSR are on.

Another pair of control signals, *request to send (RTS)* and *clear to send (CTS)*, are used to control the flow of data on TD and RD. The RTS/CTS exchange between the DTE and DCE is much like the children's game of "Mother, may I?". The DTE requests permission to transmit by applying the appropriate voltage to pin 4, thereby turning on RTS ("Mother, may I?"). When the modem detects the presence of RTS, it performs several functions, including turning on the outgoing carrier signal, and indicates permission for the DTE to transmit by raising CTS ("Yes, you may!"). At this point, the DTE begins to place bits on TD, which the modem receives and modulates onto the carrier signal. When it no longer has data to transmit, the DTE drops RTS, and the modem responds by lowering CTS.

Carrier detect (CD) is used by the DCE to notify its DTE that it is receiving a carrier signal on the telephone line and that the DTE, therefore, should be prepared to receive data on pin 3. On a half-duplex line where transmission can only take place in one direction at a time, the carrier must be turned on and off each time a modem transmits. Consequently, the CD signal will be turned on and off with each change in carrier. On a full-duplex line where the carrier can be left on constantly, CD will remain on as long as the carrier is present, which could be for as long as a connection exists.

These seven signals, TD, RD, DTR, DSR, RTS, CTS, and CD, along with pin 7, constitute the minimal RS-232 interface for an asynchronous, leased telephone circuit, as shown in **Figure 10-5a**. You will find RS-232 connections with fewer wires, but this means that some of the control signals are being ignored. One additional signal is often required for a dialup line. Ring indicator (RI) is used by the DCE to tell the DTE that there is an incoming phone call.

Timing signals. The signals listed previously are sufficient for most asynchronous lines because each DTE is responsible for providing its own timing signals so that it can place each bit onto TD or remove each bit from RD at the correct instant. For synchronous circuits, however, the DCE is responsible for providing the clock pulses, as shown in **Figure 10-6a**. The *transmit clock (TC)* and *receive clock (RC)*, pins 15 and 17, respectively, carry these timing signals from the DCE to the DTE. A synchronous DTE must only place bits onto TD when the "clock ticks" on pin 15 and must only remove the next bit from RD when the "clock ticks" on pin 17.

On some synchronous links, the DTE may provide its own clock instead of using the DCE clock. Pin 24, the *external transmit clock (ETC)* signal, can be used for this purpose. The modem then connects ETC to TC and RC as shown in **Figure 10-6b,** rather than generating its own clock pulses on these two leads. The DTE still takes its transmit and receive timing cues from pins 15 and 17, as if the DCE were the actual source of the original signal.

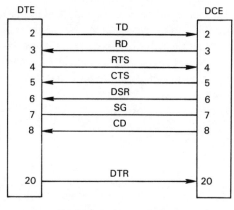

(a) Asynchronous interface

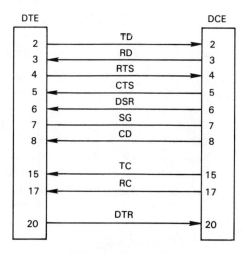

(b) Synchronous interface

Figure 10-5   Minimum RS-232 signals. These are the minimum required interface signals for asynchronous and synchronous operation over an RS-232 interface.

To summarize, the minimum pin configuration for a synchronous interface includes TD, RD, DTR, DSR, RTS, CTS, TC, RC, CD, and the signal ground on pin 7. Refer to **Figure 10-5b** for an illustration.

Miscellaneous signals. Signal quality detect (SQD) is also present on many RS-232 interfaces. This lead allows the DCE to tell the DTE that there is likely to be a problem with the received data, probably because the strength of the received carrier has dropped below an acceptable level.

Among the remaining RS-232 signals in **Figure 10-4** are a group of secondary signals. Their purpose is the same as the like-named primary counterparts, but they provide a second channel of communication between the DTE and DCE. The secondary signals are not widely used.

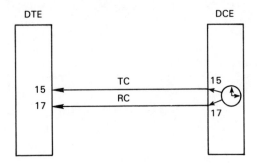

(a) DCE provides clock (normal case)

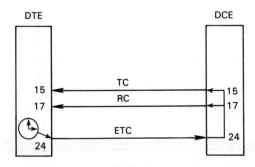

(b) DTE provides clock

Figure 10-6   RS-232 synchronous timing signals. Normally, the DCE is responsible for providing the clock signals on pins 15 and 17. The DTE may provide the clock signal by using pin 24, external transmit clock, if both DTE and DCE are configured this way.

RS-232 Example: An Asynchronous, Half-Duplex Line

To conclude this discussion of the RS-232 interface, we will examine an exchange of data on a half-duplex, asynchronous line on which the connection has already been established. This can be either a leased line or a dialup line on which the call has been placed and answered.

In **Figure 10-7**, the primary RS-232 leads are displayed from top to bottom, with system A on the top half and system B on the bottom half. Time is represented as moving from left to right, so an event to the left happened before an event to the right. This arrangement allows us to look at the events occurring at the same instant on the RS-232 interface at both systems A and B by looking vertically down the page.

For the purpose of this diagram, we assume that a telephone connection already exists between systems A and B and that both modems are powered on and ready. Consequently, DTR and DSR are on for both RS-232 interfaces.

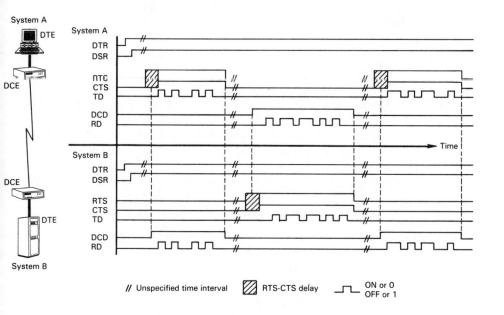

Figure 10-7   Example of half-duplex, asynchronous data flow.

In our example, system A is the next system to transmit a block of data. It raises RTS, and the modem begins to turn on carrier to the line after checking that there is no incoming carrier signal. After the outgoing carrier has stabilized, the modem raises CTS back to its DTE. The interval between RTS and CTS turning on is called the *RTS-CTS delay* or the *clear to send delay*. The value of the RTS-CTS delay for any modem is a design characteristic of the modem and is based on the modulation technique in use, among other factors. It should be apparent that in the half-duplex environment pictured here a shorter RTS-CTS delay will provide better overall throughput on the line.

When CTS comes on, the DTE begins to transmit data bits on pin 2. The modem receives the bits and modulates them onto the carrier. Meanwhile, the DCE at system B turns on carrier detect when it first notices the incoming carrier, thereby alerting its DTE to prepare to receive bits on pin 3. When the system B modem detects modulations in the carrier signal, it demodulates the signal and places the resultant bits onto pin 3 for reception by DTE B.

When its transmission is complete, DTE A turns off RTS, and the DCE drops carrier (to the line) and CTS (to the DTE). DCE B lowers carrier detect when it sees the carrier stop.

When system B is ready to send its reply, it signals its DCE by raising RTS and then waits for the DCE to start carrier to the line and return CTS. Now DTE B is free to send data on TD, which the modem receives and modulates out onto the line. On the receiving end of the telephone connection, DCE A had raised CD upon sensing the carrier signal and is now demodulating the data from the line and placing the bits onto RD.

When it has finished sending, DTE B drops RTS, which triggers the following events: DCE B stops sending carrier, DCE B drops CTS, and DCE A drops CD.

This cycle may be repeated hundreds or thousands of times during a typical interchange between two systems that are communicating over a half-duplex circuit.

Descriptions of other RS-232 environments can be found in [McNamara], [Stallings1], and [Seyer]. The RS-232 specification [EIA 232] contains a description in Section 5 of the signals that are required for a variety of common interface types.

RS-232 Compatibility

RS-232 is a recommendation that can be applied to many different communications environments, and many acceptable subsets of the full interface are in common use. In addition, there are many uses for parts of the RS-232 recommendation that, while they may not violate any aspect of the recommendation, do not fully conform to it either. The unfortunate result is that you must treat the phrase "RS-232 compatible" with extreme caution.

One vendor may advertise a modem that is "RS-232 compatible," and it may not function with a PC that is also advertised as "RS-232 compatible" because they have chosen different RS-232 subsets to implement. For example, the PC vendor may have tried to reduce hardware costs by not providing DTR or checking for the presence of DSR, while the modem may be expecting both signals to be used and checked.

In this case the PC will be able to transmit because it is not checking for DSR, while the modem will not be able to talk to the DTE because DTR is never presented. Minor violations of this type can cause endless hours of frustration to anyone troubleshooting an RS-232 interface. To further compound the problem, remember that many RS-232 cables do not have all 25 wires inside and that a cable that works correctly in one case may not do so in another.

Printer-to-PC interfaces can also cause potential problems. A printer is not a DCE, so there is really no DTE-DCE interface between a PC and a locally connected printer. However, many manufacturers have chosen to use RS-232 cables for this purpose because of their widespread availability and low cost. Furthermore, because this interface is not a DTE-DCE interface, there is considerable room for interpretation, and the ways in which PC and printer vendors use the interface vary widely.

[Seyer] contains dozens of charts of the pins used for personal computer and printer interfaces that could be useful if you are attempting to connect a printer to a PC. A number of vendors also sell "smart cables" that sense which pins are used and can simplify the task of connecting printers and PCs. The main point, however, is that printer interfaces for PCs are only slightly related to the original purpose of RS-232 and should not be confused with a true RS-232 interface.

RS-449

The EIA introduced *RS-449* in 1977:

> General Purpose 37-Position and 9-Position Interface for Data Terminal Equipment and Data Circuit-terminating Equipment Employing Serial Binary Data Interchange

RS-449 was intended to replace RS-232 by providing higher bit rates and longer cable lengths through the use of improved electrical specifications, while maintaining compatibility with RS-232. Industry acceptance of RS-449 has been hindered by the significant use of RS-232, as described earlier in this chapter. Indeed, many experienced data communications professionals have never seen or used an RS-449 interface.

Figure 10-8 shows the mechanical characteristics of the primary and secondary RS-449 connectors. The optional 9-pin secondary connector is used for the same type of secondary signals mentioned earlier for the RS-232 interface. **Figure 10-9** shows the relationship between the pins on the RS-232 and RS-449 connectors.

Aside from connectors and pin configurations, one primary difference between RS-232 and RS-449 is that RS-449 does not specify the electrical requirements for the interface. Instead, it allows the use of either EIA RS-422 or RS-423.

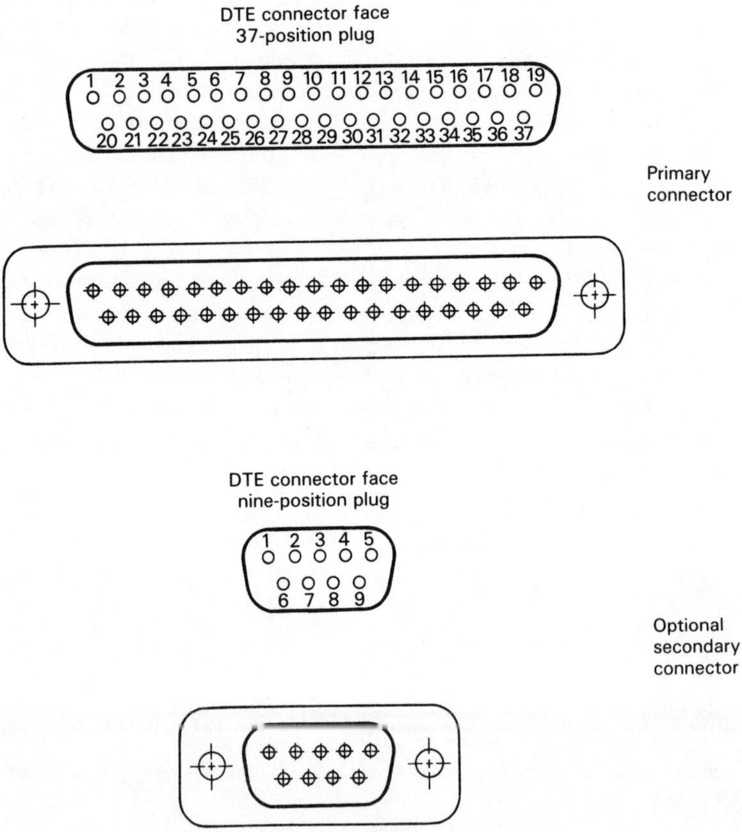

Figure 10-8   RS-449 mechanical characteristics. RS-449 specifies the use of a 37-pin primary connector and an optional 9-pin secondary connector. [Adapted from *EIA Standard RS-449* (Washington, D.C.: Electronic Industries Association, 1977), Figures 3.2-A and 3.2-B.]

RS-449		RS-232	
SG	Signal ground	SG	Signal ground
SC	Send common		
RC	Receive common		
IS	Terminal in service		
IC	Incoming call	RI	Ring indicator
TR	Terminal ready	DTR	Data terminal ready
DM	Data mode	DSR	Data set ready
SD	Send data	TD	Transmitted data
RD	Receive data	RD	Received data
TT	Terminal timing	ETC	Transmitter signal element timing (DTE source)
ST	Send timing	TC	Transmitter signal element timing (DCE source)
RT	Receive timing	RC	Receiver signal element timing
RS	Request to send	RTS	Request to send
CS	Clear to send	CTS	Clear to send
RR	Receiver ready	DCD	Received line signal detector
SQ	Signal quality	SQD	Signal quality detector
NS	New signal		
SF	Select frequency		
SR	Signaling rate selector		Data signal rate selector (DTE source)
SI	Signaling rate indicator		Data signal rate selector (DCE source)
SSD	Secondary send data		Secondary transmitted data
SRD	Secondary receive data		Secondary received data
SRS	Secondary request to send		Secondary request to send
SCS	Secondary clear to send		Secondary clear to send
SRR	Secondary receiver ready		Secondary received line signal detector
LL	Local loopback		
RL	Remote loopback		
TM	Test mode		
SS	Select standby		
SB	Standby indicator		

Figure 10-9   Comparison of RS-232 and RS-449 functional characteristics. [Adapted from *EIA Standard RS-449* (Washington, D.C.: Electronic Industries Association, 1977), Figure 4.2.]

RS-423 is an unbalanced electrical interface, similar to the electrical interface within RS-232, but it supports data interchange over longer cables and at speeds up to 100 Mbps. On the other hand, *RS-422* is a *balanced electrical interface* on which each signal uses its own pair of wires to form a complete electrical circuit. This technique, as opposed to the shared ground pin of the unbalanced interface, allows data transfers at rates up to 10 Mbps using cable lengths of up to 4000 feet. In **Figure 10-10**, note the definite relationship between cable length and maximum data transfer rate: it is not possible to transmit at the maximum data rate on a cable of maximum length.

X.21

The CCITT recommendation *X.21* is titled:

> Interface between Data Terminal Equipment (DTE) and Data Circuit-terminating Equipment (DCE) for Synchronous Operation on Public Data Networks

This recommendation provides a completely different style of interface than any of the others described in this chapter. Earlier interfaces assumed minimal intelligence in the interface hardware and, therefore, used simple techniques. Each interface wire has only one purpose and is either ON or OFF at any given moment. X.21, on the other hand, assumes the use of a micro-

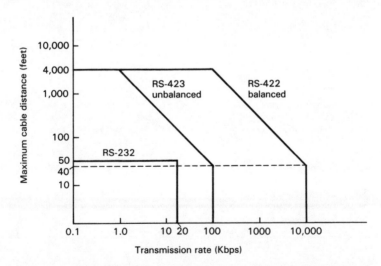

Figure 10-10   Interface cable length versus data rate. It is seldom possible to transmit data at the maximum data rate over a cable of maximum length for any given interface. This chart shows the distance/speed trade-off for several common DTE-DCE interfaces. [Adapted from Ken Sherman, *Data Communications: A User's Guide*, 2nd ed. (Englewood Cliffs, N.J.: Prentice-Hall, Inc., 1985), p. 78.]

processor-controlled interface and reduces the number of required wires on the interface by transmitting both user data and coded control information over the same lines. The rules of the interface allow the microprocessor to separate the data from the control information.

At the physical layer, shown in **Figure 10-11**, X.21 specifies a 15-pin connector. In normal use, there are only four active signals on the interface (remember that each consists of a pair of wires), exclusive of timing signals. X.21 uses 2 leads, called T and R, to transmit and receive data and also to pass control information. Two additional leads, called C and I, are used for control purposes and are always either ON or OFF. No data pass across the C and I leads.

The added sophistication of the X.21 interface gives it virtually unlimited future expansion possibilities. For example, additional control functions could be added by changing the programming for the interface. For RS-232 and RS-449, additional control functions could only be added by adding more wires to the interface.

If X.21 is so superior to the older interfaces, why do so few modems and computers have an X.21 connector? Because of the widespread use of RS-232, vendors are reluctant to introduce X.21 products until there is a sufficient

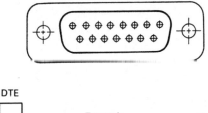

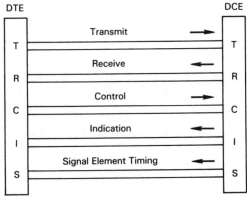

Figure 10-11 X.21 physical interface. The physical layer of the CCITT X.21 interface specifies a 15-position plug, uses a balanced electrical interface for improved speed and reliability, and assumes the use of intelligent interface hardware. On the interface, the T and R leads carry both data and control information, while the C and I leads are used for control purposes only and always have a meaning of either ON or OFF. The S leads provide timing information to the DTE.

base of other X.21 products on the market to which they can be connected. X.21 products are available in Europe but are less common in North America.

X.21 also includes recommendations for OSI layers 2 and 3 but only the physical layer is of interest in this chapter.

RECAP

- RS-232/V.24 is a DTE-DCE interface and is one of the earliest and most widespread standards in the data communications industry.
- RS-449 is a higher-speed, longer-distance replacement for RS-232/V.24, but is not widely used.
- X.21 is a DTE-DCE interface recommendation that provides greater capability and efficiency, but requires more intelligence in both the DTE and DCE.

TELEPHONE MODEM DETAILS

The function provided by a telephone line modem is to take a digital data signal and convert it into a form that will allow it to be transmitted across an analog network that was never designed to carry data. And since people tend to be impatient and want data to be moved more and more quickly, the added challenge for newer modems is to move data at ever faster speeds. Modem designers are constantly looking for more sophisticated techniques that will allow them to squeeze more data through a fixed-capacity telephone line.

Before we can describe some of the techniques for performing digital-to-analog conversion, we must first review the characteristics of the telephone line in greater detail.

THE VOICE-GRADE LINE

Ordinary copper wire, such as the type that probably runs from your telephone to the nearest telephone company *central office* (*CO*), has a reasonably large bandwidth and is capable of carrying all the frequencies of sound detectable by the human ear, from the lowest bass tones at a few cycles per second, to the highest treble sounds at approximately 20,000 hertz (Hz). In the early days of the telephone industry, however, telephone company engineers realized that the human voice does not generate frequencies over that broad a range and that the network did not actually need to transmit all 20,000 Hz in order for the words and the speaker to be recognizable at the other end of the line. Analyzing speech patterns led to the conclusion that only the tones of less than 4000 Hz were essential. The result is a network of 4000-Hz "pipes" called *voice-grade lines.*

Why were the telephone engineers concerned about using less bandwidth if the copper wire was capable of carrying all 20,000 Hz? The answer has relatively little to do with the wires that run from your telephone to the nearest CO, but instead lies in the way that calls are carried between telephone company central offices (see **Figure 11-1**). It would not be possible to have enough wires between every pair of central offices for every possible telephone call path.

Instead, network planners devised techniques to combine, or *multiplex*, several voice calls onto a single *trunk circuit* between two central offices. Reducing the amount of frequency spectrum (the bandwidth) occupied by any one call from 20,000 to 4000 Hz allowed a significantly greater number of calls to be multiplexed onto each trunk. In this way, network designers dramatically reduced the number of physical circuits that need to exist between any two COs.

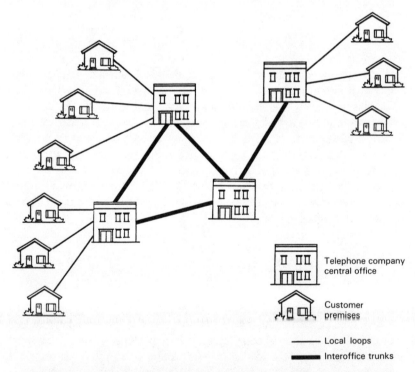

Figure 11-1   Local loops and trunk circuits. The local loop circuits from the customer premises to the nearest telephone company central office are usually copper twisted-pair wire. The bandwidth on each circuit is restricted to 4000 Hz by telephone company equipment so that calls from many local loops can be multiplexed onto each interoffice trunk.

The usable portion of the 4000-Hz bandwidth allocated for any one call is actually only about 3000 Hz wide, ranging from 300 to 3300 Hz. The frequencies below 300 and above 3300 are reserved as *guard bands* to prevent interference between telephone calls when they are "stacked" onto trunk circuits. See **Figure 11-2.**

Another important attribute of a typical voice telephone line is its maximum baud rate, which is approximately 2400 baud. This value becomes extremely

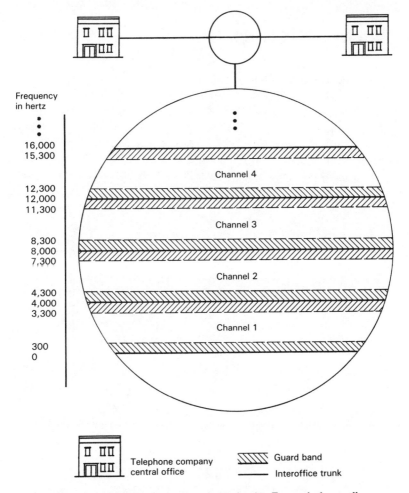

Figure 11-2 Call multiplexing on analog trunk circuits. Every telephone call crosses the local loop in the frequency range from 0 to 4000 Hz. At the nearest telephone company central office, each call is shifted upward in frequency to fit into the next available frequency slot on a trunk circuit. Each call must be shifted back down to the 0- to 4000-Hz band when it is placed onto the local loop at the distant end.

important as we examine modulation techniques that can only put 1 bit of data per baud, contrasted with other techniques that can pack multiple bits of information into each baud time.

The overall challenge for the modem designer is to place the converted digital data from a DTE into this 3000-Hz, 2400-baud pipe that was designed for voice traffic. Some common modulation techniques for doing so are described next.

MODULATION TECHNIQUES

Amplitude Modulation

A very simple technique for modulating a carrier signal with data is *amplitude modulation* (*AM*). The modem alters the amplitude, or strength, of the carrier signal to reflect the 0 or 1 value of the digital signal. **Figure 11-3a** shows a carrier signal that has been modulated to carry the bit stream 0101 0011 1000, using one amplitude to represent the 0 values and another to represent

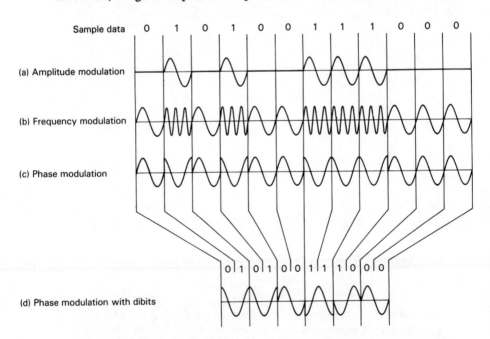

Figure 11-3   Analog modem modulation techniques. This figure shows the same bit pattern being modulated in four different ways. Using the first three techniques, the bit per second rate and the baud rate are the same since there is 1 bit per baud. In *part d*, however, there are 2 bits per baud, so the same data can be transmitted in half the time.

the 1's. As long as the receiving modem can detect the difference between the two amplitudes on the incoming signal, the original data can be extracted.

Recall from Chapter 4 that this may not be a simple task due to transmission impairments such as noise and attenuation. The received signal may look more like the weak, noisy signal in Figure 4-4, and, depending on the exact moment when the modem measures the amplitude of the received signal, it may or may not see the correct value.

The primary drawbacks of amplitude modulation are its susceptibility to noise and its low maximum baud rate within the bandwidth of a telephone circuit. It becomes difficult for the receiver to detect more than several hundred changes in amplitude per second, and the amplitude of the carrier signal can only be modulated once per baud, yielding a maximum possible data rate of several hundred bits per second. AM is not commonly used in telephone modems as a result.

Amplitude modulation is the same technique that is used for AM radio broadcasting. In the case of radio, the transmitter modulates a radio wave by the addition of music, and the radio receiver demodulates the carrier to extract the music.

Frequency Modulation

Frequency modulation (FM), one form of which is called *frequency shift keying (FSK)*, alters the frequency of the carrier signal to impress the 0 and 1 data values onto the carrier. The concept is identical to amplitude modulation except that the modem alters a different characteristic of the carrier wave. **Figure 11-3b** shows a frequency-modulated signal that represents the same data pattern, 0101 0011 1000, that was used in the AM example.

FM modems can change the frequency only once per baud time, so the bit-per-second rate of an FM modem will always equal the baud rate. However, FM modems can generate and detect more signal changes per second than AM modems, so the overall bit-per-second rate is higher than for AM modems. In addition, frequency modulation is more resistant to noise than AM. FM can support data rates up to about 1200 bps. FM radio broadcasts use the same principle and, as you may have noticed, the quality of FM radio transmission is generally better and less noisy than AM radio.

Phase Modulation

In a simple *phase-modulation (PM)* modem, a third property of the carrier waveform, its phase, is changed to indicate the transitions between 0's and 1's. Phase changes are not quite as simple to envision as amplitude or frequency changes, but **Figure 11-3c** shows the same data pattern used in the previous examples as it would be carried on a phase-modulated signal.

Phase modulation, one form of which is called *phase shift keying* (*PSK*), requires more sophisticated modem hardware to generate and detect shifts in the phase angle. It also has the capacity for carrying more information per unit of time than either AM or FM, because PM modems can be designed to generate and detect more than one phase shift per baud interval.

Whereas one of two different phase angles per baud can represent the binary value 0 or 1, if the receiving modem can detect four distinct phase angles in each baud interval, we now have the means to pack twice as much information per baud. For example, four phase angles of 0°, 90°, 180°, and 270° can represent the four possible combinations of 2 bits: 00, 01, 10, and 11.

These double-bit units, called *dibits*, double the data-carrying capacity of a line with a fixed baud rate. **Figure 11-3d** shows the same data pattern from previous modulation examples, but this time the encoding uses dibits and only takes 5 baud instead of 10 to transmit the same data. PM is the first modulation technique we have described where there is a difference between the baud rate and the bit per second rate.

We can extend this technique by using eight phase shift angles to represent all of the possible *tribits* shown in **Figure 11-4**, and, theoretically, by using 16 angles we can represent the 4-bit combinations (sometimes called *quadbits* or *quabits*) listed in **Figure 11-5**. If we plot these phase angles on an X-Y axis as shown in **Figure 11-6**, the resultant pattern is often called the modem *constellation*.

The more densely packed the points on the constellation become, the more difficult it is for the receiving modem to differentiate between adjacent signal values, especially when the incoming signal has been distorted by the types of transmission impairments described in Chapter 4 and later in this chapter. In practice, phase modulation generally reaches useful limitations at about 3 bits per baud. Consequently, other techniques or combinations of techniques prove to be useful for higher multiples of the baud rate.

Quadrature Amplitude Modulation

Quadrature amplitude modulation (*QAM*) is a technique that combines phase modulation and amplitude modulation to provide a data rate of four times the baud rate. In addition to looking for phase shifts, the receiving modem must detect amplitude variations as well, since the encoded signal represents 4 bits per baud. Modem vendors combine phase and amplitude shifts in a variety of ways to create the constellation for a particular modem model.

Naturally, each vendor claims superiority for their particular technique; however, each technique is more accurate with certain types of line distortion and less accurate with others. See **Figure 11-7** for examples of several common QAM constellations. **Figure 11-7** should make it apparent that QAM modems are not all compatible with each other.

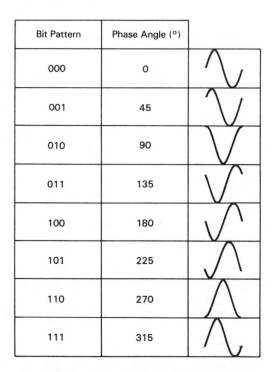

Bit Pattern	Phase Angle (°)
000	0
001	45
010	90
011	135
100	180
101	225
110	270
111	315

Figure 11-4 Phase angles for 8 tribits. Phase modulation allows 3 bits' worth of data to be packed into each baud interval. This figure illustrates one way in which each possible 3-bit data pattern could be represented by a change in the phase of the signal.

Many QAM modems that operate at higher speeds, such as 9600 bps, provide a speed fall-back capability if line quality is poor. For example, if the modem determines that it cannot transmit and receive at 9600 bps within the prescribed error limits, it will automatically fall back to 7200 or 4800 bps. Some will even test at 9600 bps periodically to determine whether it is possible to "upshift" back to the higher rate.

For many years, QAM modems that could carry 9600 bps over a leased line were the state of the art. However, newer techniques are proving that even 9600 bps is "slow" by comparison.

Trellis Coding Modulation

Trellis coding modulation (TCM) is a sophisticated technique that employs a microprocessor inside the modem. Similar to QAM, combinations of phase and amplitude are used to represent each bit grouping; however, there is an additional level of complexity in TCM. So many phase and amplitude values are used in TCM that they are arranged in conceptual "layers" or planes. As each signal arrives, the receiving microprocessor must first look at the value

Bit Pattern	Phase Angle (°)
0000	0
0001	22.5
0010	45
0011	67.5
0100	90
0101	112.5
0110	135
0111	157.5
1000	180
1001	202.5
1010	225
1011	247.5
1100	270
1101	292.5
1110	315
1111	337.5

Figure 11-5   Phase angles for 16 quabits. Phase modulation allows 4 bits' worth of data to be packed into each baud interval. This figure illustrates one way in which each possible 4-bit data pattern could be represented by a change in the phase of the signal.

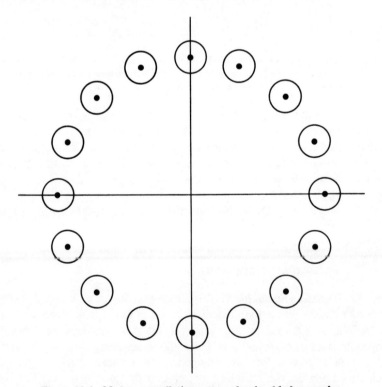

Figure 11-6   Modem constellation pattern showing 16 phase angles.

of the previous one or several signals to predict the plane upon which the new signal is likely to reside. Having made that determination, the processor can find the best match between the incoming signal and the reference values on that plane. The more memory that the modem contains, the larger the number of previous values it can use to predict the correct plane for the incoming signal and the more likely that the true value of a distorted incoming signal can be predicted correctly.

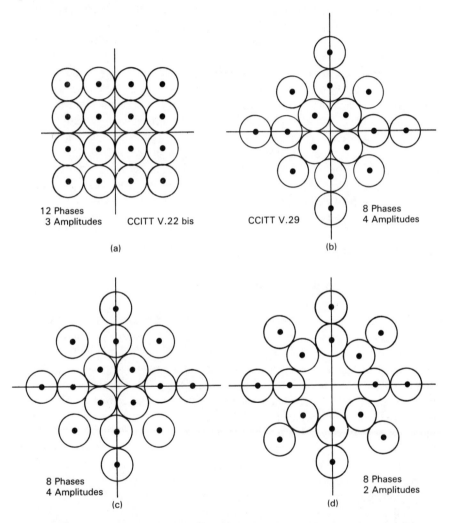

Figure 11-7   QAM modem constellation patterns. Modem vendors have adopted a variety of constellation patterns for QAM modems, each offering some advantage over the other. As you can tell from looking at these figures, not all QAM modems are compatible with each other. [Adapted from Ralph Glasgal, *Techniques in Data Communications* (Norwood, Mass.: Artech House, Inc., 1983), p. 83.]

While more complex than QAM, TCM actually provides significant performance improvements. See [Payton] and [von Taube] for specific technical details.

Multichannel Modulation

Microprocessors are also used in modems to implement other modulation techniques. Several companies build modems using a technique called *multichannel modulation* that divides the telephone circuit bandwidth into dozens, or even hundreds, of narrow-bandwidth subchannels and transmits a portion of the data on each subchannel. There are likely to be fewer errors overall because the data rate is slower and the modulation technique is simpler on each of the subchannels, and yet the aggregate data rate is exceptional. Several companies advertise data rates of 17,000 to 18,000 bps using multichannel technology.

Multichannel modems provide the added benefit of more gradual degradation if a particular circuit is noisy and cannot sustain the highest possible modem speed. For example, the modem may alter the number of subchannels in use to lower the bit rate in 100-bps increments until an acceptable transmission speed is found. Whereas a multichannel modem can drop from 14,400 to 14,300 bps, a conventional high-speed modem drops back in much larger increments, typically from 14,400 to 9600 bps, or from 9600 to either 7200 or 4800 bps. As line quality improves, the multichannel modem will shift back up to higher speeds to take advantage of the improved conditions.

Conditioning and Equalization

In the 1970s and earlier, most high-speed modems, which in those days meant modems operating at more than 4800 bps, required *conditioned lines*. To condition a line, the telephone company installed extra equipment, called *equalizers*, to counteract such transmission impairments as envelope delay distortion and attenuation distortion. (See [Glasgal], [FitzGerald], and [Held1] for technical details on these impairments.) There was an extra monthly charge for each of the several types of conditioning, but customers were willing to pay the extra fees in return for higher transmission speeds.

Advances in microprocessors and in signal-processing technology in the 1980s have reduced or eliminated the need for conditioned lines for all but the highest modem speeds (14,400 bps and above) by allowing the modem to perform the equalization on any phone line, whether leased or dialed. Many current modems compensate for the distortions of the line without any assistance from telephone company equipment. More advanced modems even provide *adaptive equalization* in which the microprocessor constantly monitors the incoming signal and matches the type and degree of equalization required to the line conditions at that moment.

Even with significant intelligence in the modem, the types of line conditioning available from telephone companies may not be sufficient for the highest-speed analog line modems, those operating at 19,200 bps, to operate at their highest speed all the time. Line conditions can fluctuate over time, forcing the modem to fall back to lower speeds such as 16,800 or 14,400 bps. In early 1988, AT&T announced plans to introduce a new type of line conditioning, called D6, that would be tailored to the requirements of available 19,200-bps modems.

In general, a modem with built-in equalization should not be used on a conditioned phone line. The modem will try to compensate for the same problems as the telephone company conditioning equipment, resulting in overcompensation or signaling confusion. You should rely on the modem manufacturer's instructions to determine whether conditioning is required.

FULL-DUPLEX TECHNIQUES

Bandsplitting

Full-duplex transmission is often achieved by *bandsplitting*, that is, splitting the bandwidth of a telephone line into two subchannels, one for communication in each direction. If the transmission path between two modems is a single pair of telephone wires, as is the case for a switched line, the total bandwidth available to be split between the two directions is 3000 Hz. If, however, there are the equivalent of two pair of telephone wires, as would normally be true for a leased line, the full 3000-Hz bandwidth is available for each transmission direction.

The size of the two channels may be equal or not, depending on whether there is likely to be an equal or unequal need for transmission in both directions. Some terminals, for example, may transmit data in one direction at 2400 bps, but only require intermittent and short acknowledgments in the other direction, which can be accommodated on a slower-speed *reverse channel*.

Time-Compression Multiplexing

Time-compression multiplexing (*TCM*) is a relatively new technique that is used in very limited applications, primarily on digital circuits. Rather than divide the bandwidth of the channel into halves as in bandsplitting, the channel is used at slightly more than double the nominal bit rate, first in one direction, then in the other. Nicknamed *"Ping-Pong multiplexing,"* this technique provides every appearance of a full-duplex circuit to the user, but in reality is an ultrahigh-speed, half-duplex link.

TCM is used to implement 56,000-bps, full-duplex transmission over switched digital circuits. Data are actually transmitted at 160,000 bps in each direction for extremely short bursts before reversing to transmit in the opposite direction. The user of this digital channel has 56,000 bps in each direction for a total of 112,000 bps. The remaining 48,000 bps are used for control information and to provide time for the line to turn around between bursts.

Echo Canceling

Another duplexing technique, enabled by microprocessors, is *echo canceling*. In echo canceling, the full bandwidth of the circuit is used to transmit in both directions simultaneously, with the implicit assumption that each modem will receive a combination of the signal from the other modem plus an echo of its own transmission. Each transmitter saves a digital image of its most recent transmissions and then subtracts that image from the incoming signal to cancel the echo, leaving only the desired signal to pass along to the attached DTE.

While difficult to envision, this is analogous to two people who face each other and talk simultaneously. The "collisions" between the two sets of sound waves do not interfere with each other, and if the human brain were capable of both talking and listening at the same time, the entire full-duplex conversation would be intelligible. While most of our brains are not capable of talking and listening simultaneously for any length of time, the microprocessor (or microprocessors) in a modem can be programmed to do exactly that.

Echo canceling modems usually operate at higher speeds and allow full-duplex operation over either leased or dialup lines.

INTELLIGENT MODEMS AND OTHER MODEM FEATURES

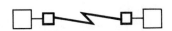

Modems are also getting smarter in ways that have little to do directly with modulating data onto a telephone line. Many modems have internal memory to store phone numbers, which helps to facilitate unattended operation, and automatic dialing by the attached computers or terminals.

Autodialing

In 1981, Hayes Microcomputer Products introduced the SmartModem® featuring a command set that the DTE could use to instruct the modem to automatically dial a telephone. This simple sounding feature eliminated the need for separate autocalling hardware connected with a second RS-232-like cable (using an interface called RS-366). The success of the Hayes SmartModem can be seen by the significant number of Hayes-compatible modems that are available on the market and by the singular lack of demand for the older RS-366 autodial equipment. For a description of *RS-366* and *autocalling units (ACU)*, see [Glasgal] or [McNamara].

Many dialup modems provide memory for the storage of telephone numbers, eliminating the need for the user to keep track of the numbers to be called. The phone numbers are usually provided to the modem from a PC or from a dumb terminal.

Dial Backup

Many leased-line modems offer automatic dial-backup facilities in the event of failure. The modem is preprogrammed with the telephone number of a port on the system to which its leased line is connected and is able to automatically dial that port if the primary line should fail. In this way, the user of the line suffers only minor inconvenience. For some modems the dialed connection is at a slower speed than the primary connection; other modems are capable of dialing a line at the same speed; still other modems can dial and use two separate lines for backup. As an example of the latter, a 19,200-bps modem could dial two 9600-bps lines and, by splitting the traffic over the two circuits, could still yield 19,200 bps to the user.

File Transfer

Other microprocessor-based modems provide batch file transfer protocols as a built-in feature. Popular choices include the Microcom Networking Protocol (MNP) developed and promoted by Microcom, Inc., along with several public-domain protocols such as Kermit and XModem. (Public-domain protocols are available to the public with no fees or royalties to a manufacturer. Public-domain protocols may be implemented directly into some vendors' modems; PC software implementations of public-domain protocols, for use with almost any modem, are available on many electronic bulletin boards.) CCITT is working on a modem standard called V.42 that includes specifications in this area.

Use of one of these protocols makes it relatively easy for a PC or other computer that does not have file transfer software to move files to other locations. Some of the modems in this category do everything; they may dial the correct numbers of other computers at a predetermined time of day, initiate the reading of data from the computer disk, and then transfer the data, error free, across the line. On the receiving end, these modems can answer the phone and store the received files on the computer's disk without operator intervention.

Other Features

Increased intelligence is also allowing modems to provide considerably greater self-maintenance and self-diagnostic features, as well as line diagnosis and troubleshooting assistance. Additional details of modem diagnostics are given in Chapter 19.

Modems have also benefited from the same size reduction as the rest of the electronics industry, and smaller modems and modems-on-a-chip are increasingly found built into everything from communications boards for PCs to credit card authorization terminals in gas stations and discount stores.

Modem vendors are adding data-compression techniques to their products as another way to increase the effective throughput on both dialup and leased lines. These products offer effective throughput in the range of 20,000 to 38,000 bps on either dialup or leased lines by combining advanced modulation techniques with sophisticated data-compression algorithms. Transmission at these speeds on analog lines offers communications solutions in a throughput range that was previously only possible with more expensive digital circuits. Chapter 14 describes data compression in more detail.

MODEM STANDARDS

As in most areas of data communications, there are standards for modem operation. For many years in the United States, the standards were the specifications published by Bell Laboratories. Outside of North America, modem standards have been published by CCITT in the V series of recommendations. The United States has begun to adopt the CCITT standards in the last few years. Among the more important current and emerging standards are the following:

V.22　　　　1200 bits per second duplex modem standardized for use in the general switched telephone network and on point-to-point 2-wire leased telephone-type circuits

V.22 bis　　2400 bits per second duplex modem using the frequency division technique standardized for use on the general switched telephone network and on point-to-point 2-wire leased telephone-type circuits

V.29　　　　9600 bits per second modem standardized for use on point-to-point 4-wire leased telephone-type circuits

V.32　　　　A family of 2-wire, duplex modems operating at data signalling rates of up to 9600 bit/s for use on the general telephone network and on leased telephone-type circuits

SUMMARY

Few areas of data communications technology have seen the magnitude of changes that have occurred in modems in the last five years. Sophisticated modulation techniques, echo canceling, and data compression are pushing against the theoretical upper limits of modem transmission speeds for a 3000-Hz channel, and all the while accomplishing this over lines of dubious quality that would not have carried data at considerably slower rates only a few years ago.

RECAP

- Modems use a variety of modulation techniques to convert digital signals to analog form for transmission over 3000-Hz telephone lines.
- Conditioning and equalization help to overcome transmission impairments; they may be supplied by the telephone company or by the modem.
- Full-duplex transmission is implemented using bandsplitting, echo cancellation, and time-compression multiplexing.
- Microprocessors and internal memory provide modems with a broad range of new features, including autodialing, improved diagnostics and maintenance, and file transfer.

OTHER SIGNAL-CONVERSION DEVICES

The modems discussed in Chapter 11 are used primarily for communication over telephone company-provided analog circuits, frequently over relatively long distances (tens, hundreds, or thousands of miles). Many users require data communications either over shorter distances or using specialized media. This chapter describes special purpose conversion devices, as well as the interface units required for the growing array of digital communications services.

NULL MODEMS

Null modems, also called *crossover cables* or *modem eliminators*, are used in situations where two DTEs are located within 50 to 100 feet of each other. In this case, there is very little point in using a telephone line to connect them because they are close enough to be cabled directly together. It would seem that the simplest solution would be to connect an RS-232 cable directly to the communication port on each system. Recall from Chapter 10, however, that the RS-232 interface is a DTE-DCE interface, and not a DTE-DTE interface.

Consequently, the function of a null modem is to appear to both DTEs as a DCE and to perform the equivalent function of the telephone network by delivering signals from one DTE to the other. While this may sound like a complex task, it is extremely simple in the case of asynchronous communications and only slightly more complicated for synchronous circuits.

Since all RS-232 DTEs use pin 2 to transmit data and pin 3 to receive data, one obvious requirement of a null modem is to connect pin 2 from the DTE on one side to pin 3 on the other side, and vice versa. Perhaps less obvious, the modem eliminator must also handle the RS-232 control signals, usually by:

- turning pin 4 back to pin 5, thereby providing CTS whenever the DTE raises RTS;
- using RTS to generate DCD for the opposite DTE;
- connecting DTR from one DTE to DSR for the other, and vice versa;
- connecting pin 7 across to provide a common signal ground.

Asynchronous Null Modems

Figure 12-1 illustrates these connections for an asynchronous null modem. Physically, the device pictured in **Figure 12-1** may be nothing more than an RS-232 cable that has had its pins wired as shown. It may also be a plastic housing with two RS-232 connectors and a small printed circuit board that does

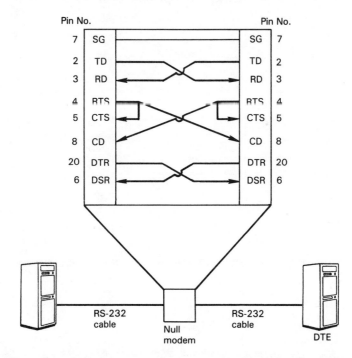

Figure 12-1 Asynchronous null modem. An asynchronous null modem allows two DTEs to communicate over a short distance by simulating the actions of two DCEs and the intervening network.

nothing more than connect the appropriate pins on the two connectors. Typical prices for an asynchronous null modem are $15 to $50.

Synchronous Null Modems

Recall from Chapter 3 that for synchronous transmission the modem is normally responsible for providing the clocking signals on pins 15 and 17. Clearly, the device in **Figure 12-1** cannot do that since it has neither a clock generator nor any wires connected to pins 15 and 17.

One solution to this timing dilemma is to let one of the DTEs provide the clock on the external clock lead, pin 24. **Figure 12-2** shows the additional wiring required for a synchronous null modem using external clocking. This style of modem eliminator is also very inexpensive because there are no electronics required, merely several additional wires in a cable or on a small circuit

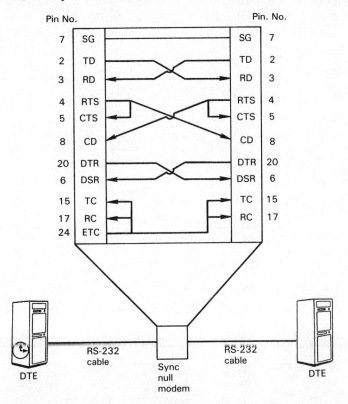

Figure 12-2   Synchronous null modem with external clock. A synchronous null modem allows two DTEs to communicate over a short distance by simulating the actions of two DCEs and the intervening network. Unlike an asynchronous null modem, a synchronous null modem must provide clock signals on pins 15 and 17. In this example, one of the DTEs is the actual source of the clock signal that the null modem places on pins 15 and 17.

board. This solution is only possible when one of the DTEs can provide the clock pulses.

A real *synchronous modem eliminator* (*SME*) must provide the TC and RC signals by itself, so it must include clock generator circuitry and will be wired like **Figure 12-3**. A typical SME would be sold for $50 to $300, depending on the design. Some SMEs require an external power source, usually standard household current; others make use of the small amounts of power on the RS-232 interface itself and do not need external power.

SHORT-HAUL MODEMS

When the transmission distance is longer than 50 to 100 feet, but less than a few miles, a *short-haul modem*, also called a *limited-distance modem* (*LDM*)

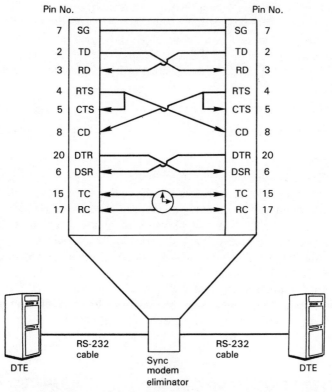

Figure 12-3 Synchronous modem eliminator (SME). A synchronous null modem allows two DTEs to communicate over a short distance by simulating the actions of two DCEs and the intervening network. Unlike an asynchronous null modem, a synchronous null modem must provide clock signals on pins 15 and 17. In this example, the SME is the source of the clock signal.

or a *line driver*, may provide the solution. These devices typically require dc voltage continuity; that is, they require continuous copper wire and will not operate over a conventional voice-grade line that passes through a telephone company switch. The continuous copper wire needed for LDMs may be installed by users within their own facility, or they may hire someone else to install the wires within or between buildings. Some local telephone companies can also supply continuous copper wires to two locations within the service area of a single central office by directly connecting the two sets of wires together at the CO. They provide the required dc continuity by not adding the loading coils normally used to improve circuit quality for voice traffic.

LDMs function by altering and boosting the digital signal from pin 2 of the RS-232 cable in such a way that it can be sent over longer distances than is allowed by RS-232. The LDM on the other end converts back to RS-232 levels to complete the circuit. Line drivers can operate at distances of up to about 5 miles and are relatively less expensive than conventional modems, but they do have the disadvantage of requiring continuous copper wire.

Note that an LDM is not a modem, in that it does not convert digital signals to analog form, but transmits a digital signal from end to end. Many short-haul modems make use of RS-422 (see Chapter 10) for the end-to-end transmission, since the balanced electrical signal of RS-422 can be transmitted over significant distances.

FIBER-OPTIC MODEMS

When the transmission medium is fiber-optic cable, a *fiber-optic modem* that uses the incoming data to modulate a light source is employed. Chapter 13 describes the applications, advantages, and disadvantages of transmission over fiber-optic cable. Just as with any other type of modem, a matching fiber-optic modem is required to recover the data from the carrier signal.

Several vendors sell fiber-optic line drivers as a substitute for copper-wire line drivers. Like conventional line drivers, the fiber versions are used to extend the range of communication beyond the RS-232 limit of 50 feet without using telephone lines and modems. Fiber line drivers allow transmission of several thousand feet between DTEs and are especially attractive in electrically noisy environments due to the high noise immunity of the fiber cable.

RADIO-FREQUENCY MODEMS

Radio-frequency modems (*RF modems*) are used in specialized applications in which data transmission is to take place over a facility such as a coaxial cable that carries RF signals. They operate in the same manner as telephone line modems by modulating a carrier with the value of the incoming data signals. Instead of modulating a carrier in the range of 300 to 3300 Hz, however, they modulate an RF carrier in the 10- to 400-MHz range. This type of modem is usually found in local area network applications, running over coaxial cable (coaxial cable is discussed further in Chapter 13).

DIGITAL SERVICE UNITS

A *digital service unit* (*DSU*) is the interface device used to connect a DTE to a digital transmission facility. Since both the source (the DTE) and the transmission path are digital, at first it would appear that no conversion device would be required at all. However, the DTE typically uses an RS-232 interface and expects to be connected to an RS-232 DCE, so the DSU must provide that interface. In addition, the digital signaling on the transmission link is somewhat different from that which is used on the DTE-DCE interface, so the format of the digital signal must be converted. The DSU is not a modem in that it does not modulate and demodulate an analog carrier signal, but it does provide the conversion from the RS-232 signaling scheme to the network signaling scheme.

R E C A P

- Null modems can be used to connect two DTEs that are 50 to 100 feet apart.
- Limited-distance modems operate over continuous copper wire to connect DTEs up to 5 miles apart.
- RF modems connect DTEs to high-bandwidth circuits such as coaxial-cable local area networks.
- Fiber-optic modems connect DTEs to fiber-optic transmission circuits.
- DSUs connect DTEs to digital communication lines.

Part IV

COMMUNICATION CHANNELS

Part IV describes the characteristics of the channels used to communicate data, both for long-haul and for local communications. We will discuss a wide variety of communication facilities, the majority of which have traditionally been provided by "the telephone company." Prior to the AT&T divestiture, which took effect on January 1, 1984, we all knew what the phrase "the telephone company" meant. In the years A.D. ("after divestiture"), however, there is no one telephone company, and most long-distance communication circuits involve a minimum of three telephone companies: two local service providers and one long-distance service company in between.

To simplify the discussion in the chapters that follow, we will refer to the telephone company or a telephone service supplier in the general sense. We will also use the term telco as a convenient shorthand reference to any telephone company.

Chapter 13 discusses the characteristics of copper wire, coax, fiber, and other communications media. It also introduces more detail about the public telephone network by describing switched lines, leased lines, digital circuits and T-1 trunks, and software-defined networks.

Chapter 14 describes equipment and techniques, such as multiplexers and data compression, that can be used to increase the effective throughput of communications lines.

Chapter 15 discusses the concepts of message and packet switching and describes the X.25 and X.75 recommendations.

Chapter 16 describes special considerations for communicating over the "last mile," that is, the distance from the subscriber to the nearest telephone company central office. This chapter includes such topics as the divestiture of AT&T, bypass technology, and ISDN.

Chapter 17 is devoted to a description of local area networks and covers their applications and technology. In addition, this chapter describes the international standards activity that affects the LAN community.

Chapter 18 describes the telephone private branch exchange (PBX), with particular emphasis on its data-handling characteristics. This chapter compares the use of a PBX and a LAN for local data movement and describes Centrex services.

Chapter 19 defines several views of network management and discusses the importance of managing a network today. The effects of divestiture on network management are discussed, along with the current activity in defining international network management standards. We also look at some of the tools and equipment that are available to manage a network.

TRANSMISSION FACILITIES:
LONG HAUL

Chapter 11 describes the basic characteristics of a voice-grade telephone line in order to explain the operations of telephone line modems. This chapter describes telephone lines in more detail, emphasizing the physical and transmission characteristics of the various media that are used by the telcos, especially as they relate to the long-distance portion of the telephone network.

MEDIA TYPES

Twisted Pair

The copper wire used in the telephone network is referred to as *twisted pair* because an individual circuit consists of one pair of copper wire that is twisted along its length in order to reduce the amount of electrical interference between adjacent pairs. Multiple pairs of wires are collected into cables with 25, 50, or even hundreds of pairs of wires.

Twisted pair wire forms the backbone for much of the local telephone network that is described in Chapter 16, but is almost never used for long-distance transmission. Media such as coax cable, fiber-optic cable, and microwave links are much more suitable for long-distance circuits. Twisted pair is mentioned in this chapter because it serves as a basis for comparison among the other media types described here.

Coaxial Cable

Coaxial cable (or *coax*) is so named because the two conductors over which signals travel share the same axis, that is, they are co-axial. As shown in **Figure 13-1**, the center copper conductor is surrounded by an insulating material, called a dielectric, which is usually some type of foam or plastic, but may even consist of air with occasional spacers of some other material. The second conductor forms a sheath around the dielectric and is, in turn, encased by a layer of insulating material such as plastic.

The design of coax cable gives it considerably better signal-carrying capabilities than twisted pair. Coax is capable of carrying signals in a frequency range of from 5 or 10 MHz up to about 400 MHz, yielding a useful bandwidth of almost 400 MHz. Coax requires fewer amplifiers for transmission over a given distance because there is considerably less attenuation for transmitted signals than is true for twisted pair. The most common use for coax in the telephone network is for the connections between telephone company central offices (COs).

Fiber-Optic Cable

A *fiber-optic cable* is a thin glass or plastic filament surrounded by a plastic jacket, or cladding, that can be used to transmit data by placing a controllable light source at one end and a light-sensitive receptor at the other. The light source is usually either a laser or a *light-emitting diode (LED)*, and the receptor is some type of *photodiode*. Just as a conventional modem modulates a carrier signal to transmit data over a wire, a fiber-optic modem controls the light source for fiber-optic transmission in order to transmit data over the fiber.

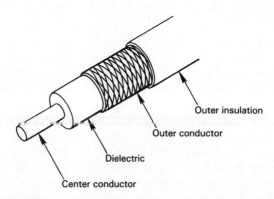

Outer insulation

Outer conductor

Dielectric

Center conductor

Figure 13-1   Cross section of coaxial cable. A center conductor is surrounded by a dielectric (insulating) material. This in turn is surrounded by the second conductor, which is a solid or braided wire sheath. The entire cable is encased in plastic or some other insulating and protective material.

The bandwidth of fiber-optic cable is measured in the hundreds of millions, or even billions, of bits per second. It is smaller and lighter than any metallic transmission medium, which, when coupled with its vast bandwidth, provides many times the transmission capacity per cross-sectional diameter of cable. While these qualities make fiber attractive in many situations, weight and space savings are especially important in applications such as crowded building conduits, under city streets, or on utility poles, where space is at a premium. Less common applications, such as on airplanes or ships, also take advantage of the space, weight, and bandwidth characteristics of fiber.

Fiber is virtually immune to electromagnetic interference, unlike its copper counterparts, so it suffers almost no noise-related signal degradation. Further-more, fiber is an extremely secure transmission medium since it does not radiate any electrical energy and is extremely difficult to tap. Unlike most metallic circuits that can be tapped merely by making contact with the metallic conductors, fiber can only be tapped if it is broken and reconnected. It is highly unlikely, therefore, that a fiber cable could be tapped without being noticed.

Occasional reports in the trade press suggest that the intelligence com-munity has developed ways to tap the signals on a fiber-optic cable, but that is certainly beyond the interests of this text. It is also beyond the realm of concern for most people in their business lives. Fiber is an exceedingly secure transmission medium for most users.

What are some of the disadvantages of fiber? The cost of fiber is still somewhat greater than that of high-capacity metallic circuits, and splicing fiber cables together to make repairs or to extend a cable requires a precision that is not necessary with metallic circuits. Nonetheless, costs for fiber have declined significantly and will continue to decline. In addition, *connectorized cable* (fiber cable lengths with preattached connectors that can be easily joined without special tools) and other techniques continue to reduce the handling problems of fiber-optic cables.

The current commercial benefit and the future promise of fiber are so strong that the long-distance carriers are spending billions of dollars each year to install fiber in their networks. They recognize the advantages of high bandwidth, low error rate, and low maintenance of fiber-optic cable. The carriers have even taken to extolling the virtues of fiber in their consumer advertising, attempting to attract customers based on the technical superiority of their fiber connections.

Microwave Transmission

Another staple of the telephone industry is *microwave transmission*. Micro-wave signals are transmitted through the air, between pairs of microwave antennas mounted on towers, with the only requirement being that the antennas must be in sight of each other. Microwaves do follow the earth's curvature to some degree, so the line of sight for a microwave link is slightly longer than the visual line of sight.

Figure 13-2 shows a typical microwave link that consists of a set of microwave repeaters, each of which is located on a tower in the highest possible location in order to extend the line of sight from any one antenna farther over the horizon. Spacing for microwave antennas is usually 30 to 50 miles.

Microwave transmission is subject to attenuation or distortion from atmospheric conditions. Heavy fog or rain can interfere with signal transmission, causing problems lasting either minutes or hours depending on the weather.

Perhaps the greatest advantage of microwave circuits over wire or fiber media is that microwave circuits do not require a physical right of way. They can be installed without the need to dig trenches and lay cable. Microwave circuits are used extensively where long, unpopulated distances need to be traversed, or when it is difficult for legal or topographic reasons to secure the right of way to lay cable.

Satellite Transmission

A *satellite link* is a microwave link with one of the repeaters in orbit around the earth. It uses some of the same frequencies as a microwave link and consists of two or more ground stations and a communications satellite. Satellite links, like terrestrial microwave links, do not require cable rights of way, and they provide a high-bandwidth alternative to cable media. Satellite earth stations for data transmission are similar to the dish antennas that have become common in recent years for reception of television signals from satellites.

Communications satellites are usually placed into a *geosynchronous* orbit, which is an orbit that is timed to the rotation of the earth. A geosynchronous orbit allows the position of the satellite to remain fixed with respect to a given antenna on the earth, eliminating the need for constant reaiming and readjustment of the earth stations. Most geosynchronous satellites are located approximately 22,300 miles above the earth. See **Figure 13-3a**.

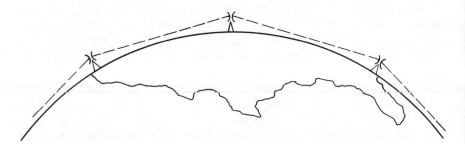

Figure 13-2   Microwave relay towers. Microwave antennas are usually mounted on towers on higher elevations to extend the line of sight between antennas. Tower spacing is 30 to 50 miles.

A satellite is composed of a number of *transponders* that receive signals on one channel, called the *uplink*, and amplify and then retransmit the signals on a second channel, known as the *downlink*. Each transponder on the satellite uses a slightly different pair of frequencies for the uplink and downlink, allowing multiple, simultaneous transmissions per satellite. A typical satellite may have 12 to 24 transponders for a total bandwidth of approximately 500 MHz.

Satellite links have several properties that make them unique among the transmission media we have discussed. First, satellite transmission is inherently a broadcast medium; that is, any signal transmitted by a satellite can be "heard" by any earth station that is both pointed in the correct direction and tuned to the right downlink frequency.

This property is both a tremendous advantage and a significant disadvantage. It is an advantage, since it allows a single transmission to be received at any number of earth stations within the footprint of the satellite (the *footprint* is the geographic area that is "illuminated" by the satellite beacon; see **Figure 13-3b**). Adding additional receiver locations requires no change in the hardware of the communication channel itself (that is, the satellite); it merely requires adding another earth station that is aimed at the satellite and tuned to the correct frequencies. This contrasts sharply with the need to add new telephone circuits or microwave links in order to add new locations to these transmission channels.

The broadcast nature of satellite transmission raises potential security questions also. For data that are confidential or restricted, some form of signal scrambling may be desirable. One example is in the television industry, where satellite transmissions are very common. The major networks and cable programming suppliers rely on satellites to broadcast their programs to hundreds of local TV stations and cable TV companies and, in some cases, to broadcast directly to thousands of individual subscribers who have installed satellite dishes. While most TV broadcasts are not scrambled, many programming suppliers scramble their satellite signals to prevent unauthorized receivers from capturing and utilizing the signal. For data communications users, the same security issues may arise if a satellite network is being used to move confidential or sensitive corporate data.

Transmission delay. The second potential disadvantage of satellite transmission is the relatively long propagation delay inherent in satellite usage. Because the typical satellite is 22,300 miles above the earth, the minimum trip from one earth station to another is about 45,000 miles. At the speed of light, the minimum delay for a 45,000-mile trip is approximately

$$\frac{45,000 \text{ miles}}{186,000 \text{ miles/second}} = 0.25 \text{ second (approx.)} = 250 \text{ milliseconds}$$

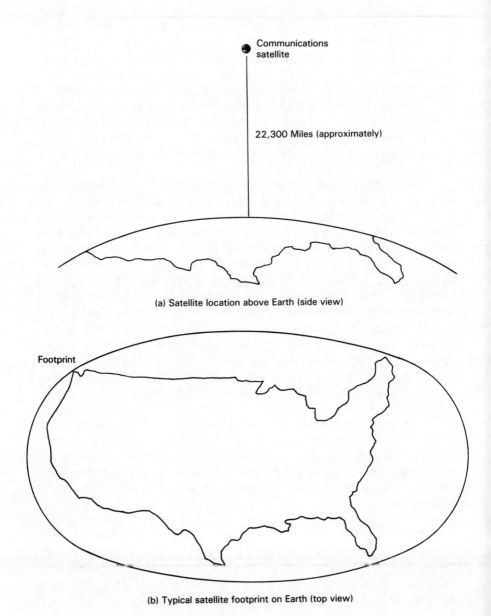

(a) Satellite location above Earth (side view)

(b) Typical satellite footprint on Earth (top view)

Figure 13-3   Geosynchronous satellite characteristics.

155

This delay will be unnoticed in a continuous one-way transmission, such as a television broadcast, but will be very noticeable for any type of two-way interchange, including a voice conversation. You may have noticed this delay on long-distance telephone conversations, especially on overseas calls. While you can compensate for satellite delay when you talk on the telephone, the effects of delay can be disastrous for data communications. As an example, refer to the discussion of the effects of satellite delay on a polling protocol in Chapter 6.

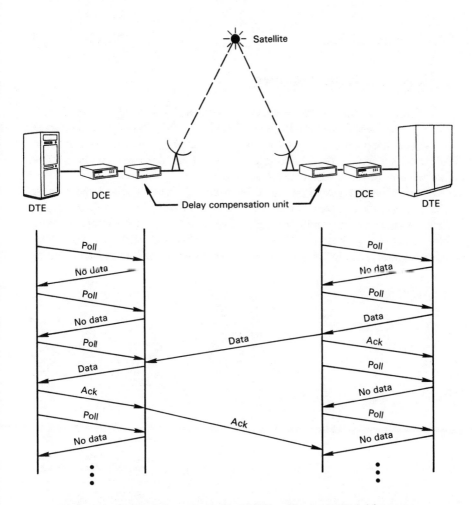

Figure 13-4 Satellite delay compensation unit for polling protocol. A delay compensation unit allows polling protocols to function more efficiently over satellite links with long delivery delays. The compensation unit on the host end of the link acts like a secondary device, responding to polls and selects locally. The unit on the slave end of the link generates polls and selects to satisfy the protocol requirements of the slave. The compensation units employ a full-duplex protocol, such as HDLC, on the satellite link.

To counteract the lengthy delay inherent in polling across a satellite link, several manufacturers offer satellite delay-compensation units. As shown in **Figure 13-4**, the compensation unit fools the master device into thinking that the poll has been answered immediately, while the corresponding compensation unit on the other side of the network is independently polling the slave device. The two delay-compensation units communicate with each other over the satellite link using a nonpolled protocol, probably HDLC or some variation.

SWITCHED LINES

Circuit-Switched Networks

Circuit switching is the technique for connecting a specific set of circuits into a path between users on demand. Circuit switching takes place whenever you dial a telephone, whether for voice or data transmission. The specific facilities that are used to build a circuit for your use may consist of any combination of the media types described above.

For a typical circuit, the link between the subscriber and the nearest telephone company central office will be twisted pair. The remainder of the circuit will be a combination of coax, fiber, satellite, or microwave between intermediate COs, leading ultimately to a final twisted pair connection from the last central office in the chain to the remote subscriber. **Figure 13-5** illustrates a typical set of connections.

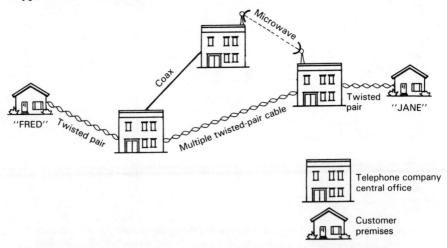

Figure 13-5 Composition of typical switched circuit. A dial-up circuit from "Fred" to "Jane" consists of the copper twisted pair that connects each to the nearest telephone company central office, plus one channel from each trunk between telephone company offices.

Circuit-switched connections are most common in the public telephone network where the circuits may be supplied by any number of service providers, including the local telephone company, MCI, AT&T, and many others. Some organizations have installed or leased a sufficiently large pool of private lines and switches that they can provide private, switched-line services for their communications users. Much more typically, however, companies rely on the pool of circuits and switches provided by the telephone carriers.

The primary advantage of switched data communications circuits is the flexibility to connect to any other telephone number in the world. Costs are based solely on usage, so you pay only as long as the communications facilities have been switched into place for your use.

Circuit-Switching Techniques

Earlier textbooks, such as [Black], describe the hierarchical approach that was used to switch calls in the former Bell system. With the advent of computerized telco switches, a newer and more efficient technique that relies on a private packet-switching network is used.

When a call request is received at a computerized telco switching office as a result of someone dialing a telephone, the calling and called telephone numbers, along with some additional accounting information, are sent through a private packet-switching network that is maintained for that purpose by AT&T (Chapter 15 contains a description of packet switching). The data message is routed to the central office nearest to the called party so that the switch there can determine whether the called telephone line is available to receive a call. If it is not, a message is sent back to the calling CO, which generates a busy signal in the handset of the caller. If the line is available, the routing information is passed back to the originating switch and the call setup is completed.

Using the previous hierarchical method, when the call request is received at the calling party's CO, that switch finds a circuit heading in the correct direction and allocates it to the call. The next switch along the way does the same thing, until a collection of links has been built all the way from the calling party to the CO nearest to the called party. If the last switch discovers that the line to the called party is busy, it signals that information back along the newly constructed circuit, resulting in a busy signal to the caller. During this entire time, a collection of telephone company circuits is tied up, only to be released when it is discovered that the call cannot be completed.

A significant advantage of the new, nonhierarchical switching method is that telephone company circuits and bandwidth are not committed to any one call unless the call can actually be completed. This may not sound significant in the context of a single phone call, but consider the advantage to the telephone company for the millions and millions of calls that cannot be completed each day because the called party is already on the phone.

Other Switched Network Services

AT&T and the local telephone companies use the packet data network and the databases within the network to provide other services than routine call setup to subscribers. For instance, some local phone companies take advantage of the calling and called telephone number information to provide "call-blocking" services. They maintain a database of numbers from which you do not want to receive calls and then automatically block all calls to you from one of those numbers. As a second example, if you predefine a list of numbers from which you will accept collect calls (perhaps your son or daughter who is in college), those calls can be completed without an operator having to ask for your permission each time.

AT&T also uses its data network to provide more advanced features as part of its toll-free 800 area code service. One such 800 service allows a company, which we will call the Apex Widget Company, to have a single toll-free 800 number for the entire country. Even though all of Apex's customers call the same 800 number, each incoming call is automatically routed to whichever of Apex's 27 offices is nearest the caller. AT&T matches the caller's phone number against a database containing the locations of the 27 sales offices and uses that information to complete the call. This database is maintained for Apex by AT&T as part of the long-distance network and is accessed via the AT&T packet-switching network mentioned earlier in the discussion of call setup procedures.

The Advanced 800 call routing is sufficiently flexible that routing can be varied based on the time of day or the day of the week. A call received from New York City after the New York Apex office has closed can automatically be routed to the office in Chicago or Los Angeles. If Apex maintains one 24-hour facility or uses an answering service when all its offices are closed, all calls received during that period can be routed to that location.

The same packet-switching network is used by AT&T to implement other advanced services, such as software-defined networks, which are described at the end of this chapter. Other network providers, such as MCI and US Sprint, offer services similar to the AT&T services used as examples in this chapter.

LEASED LINES

Analog Circuits

When communications requirements dictate a permanent, fixed connection between locations, companies often turn to *leased lines*, also called *dedicated* or *private* lines. Like a switched line, a leased line may consist of almost any combination of the media types described above. In this case, however, the user contracts with the communications service provider to have a line dedicated to its use for the terms of the lease.

The user of a leased line pays a fixed, monthly charge for the circuit whether it is being used or not. The decision to install a leased line may be justified based on a frequent need to communicate, the requirement for instantaneous access when communication is required (a switched connection takes from one to many seconds to establish), the need to connect multiple locations back to a central site, or a need for the higher transmission speeds that are usually possible on a leased line.

Higher data rates on analog leased lines are possible primarily because of the fixed routing for a leased line. A leased line minimizes the variability in routing and quality that are typical of a switched line and supplies a consistent-quality circuit (in practice, a leased line may be consistently good or consistently bad, but at least it is consistent).

The quality of a leased line can be improved, at an additional monthly cost, by requesting line conditioning. The telephone company agrees to provide a better-quality circuit, as measured by specifications that they publish, to compensate for one or more of the transmission impairments that can occur in normal usage. They accomplish this by the installation of additional electronic equipment along the circuit path.

Improvements in modem technology and transmission media have reduced the need for conditioned lines, although some high-speed modems may still require conditioning. Before ordering line conditioning, you should check the modem manufacturer's specifications because, as mentioned in Chapter 11, the equalization provided by many newer modems may actually counteract that which is provided by the phone company for a conditioned line.

Digital Circuits

Chapter 4 described the characteristics that make a digital communications line superior to an analog circuit. Both AT&T and other long-distance and local communications providers in the United States are delivering an increasing number of digital circuits to customer premises. AT&T's earliest digital offerings were in the *Dataphone* ®*Digital Service* (*DDS*) family. DDS service is available at speeds of 2400, 4800, 9600, and 56,000 bps. Pricing is based on speed, so the user pays more for 9600-bps service than for 2400-bps service.

The primary advantage of DDS-type circuits is the significantly reduced error rates that result from digital transmission. Some telcos have advertised, for example, that they will guarantee 99.5% error-free seconds on a digital line. It is safe to assume that if they are willing to guarantee performance that good the actual performance must be even better.

One problem with DDS-type services is that there is such a large gap between 9600- and 56,000-bps services. What do users do if they determine that they need approximately 20,000 bps of capacity, for example? One solution is to pay for a 56-Kbps line and use less than half the capacity. Another idea is to divide the load among several 9600-bps circuits, although careful attention must be paid to the cost of this approach, since the aggregate cost of multiple lower-speed circuits could exceed the cost of the higher-speed service, even if some of the capacity of the latter is unused.

Other than finding additional applications that could make use of the excess capacity of the 56-Kbps circuit, the user in this situation is left with little choice of digital alternatives. Reverting to analog transmission and using modems of the types described toward the end of Chapter 11 provides another possibility, as some of these newer-technology modems offer 14,400 bps, 19,200 bps, and even higher data transmission rates.

Switched Digital Circuits

Most digital circuits are leased lines because the telcos have not had sufficient CO equipment to switch digital circuits. This has begun to change as field trials and actual service offerings for 56-Kbps dialup, digital circuits have become available.

Switched 56-Kbps service offers an exciting range of applications for data communications. Several obvious choices include:

- Dial backup for 56-Kbps DDS leased-line service
- 56-Kbps service on an as needed basis for users who cannot justify the cost of a leased DDS-type circuit
- Occasional high-speed data transfer between mini- or microcomputers and mainframe computers
- Communications between high-speed digital facsimile machines

Nondata applications, such as video conferencing, are possible on switched 56-Kbps services, also. One reason for the relatively slow deployment of this service is the cost of the special equipment that is required at both the customer and telephone company offices. In addition, several incompatible techniques are being used to implement 56-Kbps switched digital service, and until one technique or a set of compatible techniques is agreed on, there cannot be universal service. One modulation technique for dialup digital service, called time-compression multiplexing, was described in Chapter 11.

T-1 CIRCUITS

One of the most explosive growth areas in digital data communications is the use of T-1 circuits by end users. High-capacity digital circuits have been the backbone of the AT&T long-distance network since the 1960s, but have only been offered to customers since the 1970s in the form of T-1 circuits.

The origin of T-1 service stems from AT&T's recognition of the value of digital techniques for improving the efficiency and quality of voice transmission on interoffice trunks. Then current voice digitization techniques required 8000 eight-bit samples per second, or 64,000 bps, to accurately represent a voice call in digital form (see **Figure 13-6**). By multiplexing 24 digitized calls, plus some additional bits for control purposes, AT&T created digital signaling rate 1, or *DS-1*. The DS-1 data rate is 1.544 Mbps, which is derived as follows:

24	channels
× 8	bits per channel
192	bits
+ 1	framing bit
193	bits per frame x 8000 frames per second=1,544,000 bps

DS-1 is the first step in a hierarchy of digital signaling in the network. The complete North American hierarchy, from DS-1 through DS-4 (274.176 Mbps) is listed in **Figure 13-7**. When DS-1 signaling is used on twisted pair wire, AT&T calls it *T-1*. The name T-1 and the term *T-carrier* have come to be commonly used in the industry (outside of the telephone companies themselves) for any 1.544-Mbps service, not just for service over twisted pair.

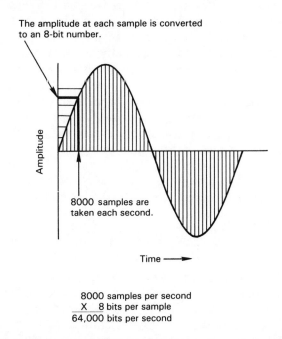

Figure 13-6   **Pulse code modulation (PCM) for voice digitization.** An 8-bit value is assigned to represent the amplitude of the analog signal at each of the 8000 samples per second. The result is 8000 8-bit samples, or 64,000 bps, to represent an analog signal in digital form using PCM.

North American			CCITT		
Carrier Name	M bps	Number of Voice Channels	Level No.	M bps	Number of Voice Channels
DS-1 (T-1)	1.544	24	1	2.048	30
DS-1C	3.152	48	2	8.448	120
DS-2	6.312	96	3	34.368	480
DS-3	44.736	672	4	139.264	1920
DS-4	274.176	4032	5	565.148	7680

Figure 13-7   North American and CCITT digital transmission hierarchy. T-1 carrier is commonly used on twisted pair and operates at the DS-1 rate in North America and the CCITT level 1 rate in other parts of the world. Higher digital signaling rates are used on other media, such as coax, microwave, and fiber.

The first customers for T-1 services were major voice network users who wanted to gain the economy of scale provided by having a single physical connection to the telephone company that provided 24 voice channels. The economics of a T-1 circuit are such that the cost of a single T-1 line may be equivalent to as few as 5 or as many as 20 conventional circuits, depending on the circuit length and local tariff structure. Especially at the lower end of that range, T-1 circuits can provide a significant number of channels for free, which can be utilized for additional voice traffic or for data traffic.

As you might expect, it did not take long for data network users to realize the significant value of T-1 circuits for data communications also. Each 64-Kbps channel can be used as a single high-speed communications link or, by using a multiplexer, can be shared among multiple, slower-speed channels.

The same cost justification that applies to consolidating multiple voice circuits onto a single T-1 line can be applied to multiple data circuits. Many companies have saved even more by combining voice and data onto a single T-1 link. In addition, applications that could not effectively be implemented with 56-Kbps digital lines because they required more bandwidth can now be considered.

For example, a T-1 sized pipe allows very high speed, bulk file transfers to be accomplished in minutes, which would have taken hours or even days at slower speeds. See **Figure 13-8** for a comparison of sample data transmissions at various data rates. Graphics terminals and other devices with large-bandwidth requirements that were previously restricted to locations relatively near the source of their data can now be located at any location serviced by T-1 facilities.

Before you conclude that T-1 services are the answer to all capacity problems and do not have any drawbacks, consider the implications when a T-1 circuit fails. Will you have adequate backup facilities for critical applications once you have combined all your circuits onto one link? Can you shift part of the traffic from the failed T-1 channel to another link? Can you use dial

Quantity of Data to Be Transmitted (in bits)	At a Data Rate of		
	9600 bps	56 Kbps	1.544 Mbps
1,000,000	104.2 sec	17.9 sec	0.65 sec
10,000,000	1042 sec	179 sec	6.5 sec
100,000,000	10,420 sec (2.9 hr)	1790 sec	65 sec

Figure 13-8   Transmission time versus data rate for various file sizes. Transmission times shown in this figure do not include protocol overhead; that is, they are the result of dividing the number of bits to be transferred by the bit per second rate. Therefore, these figures are not indicative of the actual throughput performance you can expect, but show the relative relationship between line speed and transmission time.

backup, probably at much slower speeds, until the T-1 link is available? You should not gloss over these issues merely because the economics of T-1 can be so attractive.

The immense popularity of T-1 circuits for both voice and data usage has resulted in two phenomena. First, the installation lead time for T-1 lines can be many months in some parts of the country. For some users, the lure of significant bandwidth is there, but the reality may be months into the future. Second, T-1 (DS-1) service is so successful that some carriers now provide DS-2 and DS-3 services to their largest customers in order to satisfy the seemingly insatiable demand for bandwidth.

T-1 Multiplexers

The need for effective utilization of T-1 bandwidth has created an entirely new segment of the industry for T-1 multiplexers. There are many established companies and numerous start-up companies building and selling T-1 multiplexers that are designed to handle an incredible range of input channel requirements for both voice and data links.

Some multiplexers feature flexibility in allocating bandwidth to any given channel on the basis of the time of day, or according to a predetermined schedule, or based on statistical analysis of traffic demand. Many T-1 multiplexers have sophisticated networking capabilities that allow a user to structure an entire network around a collection of T-1 lines and multiplexers.

T-1 Resale

An interesting sidelight to the increased use of T-1 facilities is the number of companies that have gotten into the communications resale business as an indirect result of their use of T-1 circuits. A company that has cost-justified installation of a T-1 line, but does not need the full 1.544 Mbps, may look at the extra capacity as a potential revenue source if they can find another company interested in subleasing the unused bandwidth.

This opportunity has led many T-1 users to seek other companies with offices in similar locations who could share a T-1 link. This is not risk-free revenue for the initial T-1 user, however, and they should not make the decision to resell service lightly. What happens when the T-1 circuit is down, for example? Is there legal liability for the company that sublet the channel capacity? Who is responsible for troubleshooting the problem? Who is responsible for providing alternate facilities if the outage is too long? Who decides what constitutes "too long"? A T-1 owner may also be required to register with federal or state regulatory agencies before they can resell capacity. Despite these and other questions, many corporations have entered the communications resale business as an indirect consequence of their T-1 circuit installations.

Other T-1 Services

Most T-1 service is available as leased lines. AT & T packages all its T-1 offerings into the Accunet® family of products, which includes:

- The DDS services mentioned earlier
- Accunet T1.5 and T45 offering 1.5- and 45-Mbps terrestrial lines
- Accunet Reserved, which can provide DS-1 and DS-3 capacity links on demand

Accunet Reserved service requires installation of special equipment at the customer premises and usually requires a minimum of 30-minute advance notice for the service to be enabled. Possible uses for Accunet Reserved include:

- Backup for Accunet T1.5 links
- Disaster planning so that T-1 communications can be rerouted on short notice to a backup computer site
- Periodic bulk file transfer between computer sites, for example, weekly backup of a database between two locations where data transmission is more convenient than physical delivery
- Nondata uses such as video teleconferences or other temporary television hookups

Vendors other than AT&T provide a similar complement of T-1 services in both the local and long-distance markets.

T-1 Outside North America

Outside North America and Japan, T-1 usage exists, but the CCITT has recommended a different multiplexing strategy that results in a T-1 circuit with a bandwidth of 2.048 Mbps instead of 1.544 Mbps. The CCITT T-1 concept is the same, but the implementation is different, so the two systems are incompatible. **Figure 13-7** shows both the North American and CCITT digital trunk hierarchies.

SOFTWARE-DEFINED NETWORKS

The *software-defined network* (*SDN*), also referred to as a virtual network or a virtual private network, is an interesting amalgam of leased line and switched line concepts that has evolved in the 1980s. The underlying idea is for large, switched-network vendors to provide the functional equivalent of leased line services to their customers without actually installing leased lines. This is accomplished by using sophisticated databases, computing power, and software within the telephone network to monitor SDN user requirements and network capacity and to provide bandwidth when and where it is needed.

Typical software-defined networks require leased line access from the customer site to the nearest central office, although MCI and AT&T have both announced switched SDN access (for example, via an 800 number for SDN users who are away from their office). The customer numbering plan, which need not bear any resemblance to the conventional area code and exchange numbering scheme, is stored in a database by the SDN provider so that each customer location in the SDN has a unique 7-digit telephone number. The locations served by the SDN may be either domestic or international locations, with the SDN database providing the translation from the customer's 7-digit SDN numbering plan to whatever digits are needed to reach the intended location. The same database that is used to complete calls within the SDN can also be used to provide additional services, such as call blocking and screening, access authorization, and management reports.

Software-defined networks can carry both voice and data traffic, offering either analog or digital circuit equivalents depending on customer need. SDN providers also allow varying degrees of customer access and control of their virtual network. A terminal on the customer site can be used to access and update the database that governs operation of the virtual network, and the customer may also be able to alter call routing, bandwidth allocation, and other parameters on an ad hoc basis.

AT&T believes that SDNs are likely to be most effective for customers with 20 or more sites when 40% of the calls are placed within the company and can be less expensive than leased lines for sites with calling times of less than 200 hours per month.

SDNs provide the network supplier with better utilization of their existing switched-network facilities by not locking circuits into fixed configurations for each customer. The user gains increased flexibility by not being tied to a rigid network of leased lines, while still taking advantage of the benefits of leased line services such as higher bandwidth, lower costs, and user control. While still a relatively new service from the primary switched-network vendors, software-defined networks are likely to become a significant force for both voice and data communications. SDNs use computing power and the inherent flexibility of the switched network to leverage the billions of dollars of existing investment in the telephone companies' networks.

RECAP

- Common media types for long-haul communications links are twisted pair, coaxial cable, fiber-optic cable, microwave, and satellite.
- Switched circuits offer considerable flexibility and economy when traffic is intermittent and of relatively short duration.
- Computerized switches and large databases in the telephone network make more efficient use of telco resources through nonhierarchical call routing; they also allow advanced services, such as call blocking.
- Leased lines offer fixed monthly costs and better quality than dialup lines and are appropriate when traffic is frequent and of long duration or requires instant access.
- Digital signaling, now available over switched lines as well as leased lines in some locations, offers considerably higher quality and data rates than analog lines.
- T-1 service use is growing extremely quickly and allows consolidation of multiple voice and data circuits onto a single physical link.
- Software-defined networks provide a telco customer the equivalent of a private network over the public, switched network through extensive database and software in the network.

INCREASING LINE UTILIZATION

Communication lines are a valuable and expensive corporate resource, and data communications managers want to use them as efficiently as possible. This chapter describes several techniques and devices that increase throughput or decrease costs for transmission facilities.

MULTIPLEXERS

A *multiplexer*, sometimes referred to as a *mux*, combines two or more independent data streams and allows them to be transmitted across a single communication line. Whenever a multiplexer is used on the transmit end of a link, a *demultiplexer* must be used on the receive end of the circuit in order to reverse the process and re-create the original, separate signals. The box containing the demultiplexing function typically is identical to the multiplexer; the manufacturer usually builds both functions into a single product.

Figure 14-1 shows a common multiplexer configuration with several communications lines consolidated onto one actual telephone line. In this example, the multiplexer is eliminating the need for three additional telephone lines by consolidating the traffic from four lines onto one. You might also use a multiplexer when you need additional communications capacity between two locations, but it cannot be installed, perhaps because of long installation lead times from the telephone company. The multiplexer would allow you to add the new traffic to your existing link.

167

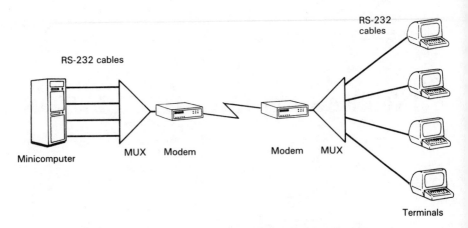

Figure 14-1 **Typical multiplexer configuration.** Multiplexers must be used in pairs so that multiplexed signals can be demultiplexed at the other end of the line. The modem in this illustration may be a separate piece of hardware, or it may be built into the multiplexer.

The primary techniques for multiplexing multiple signals onto a single line are frequency, time, and statistical multiplexing, which are described next.

Frequency-Division Multiplexing

Frequency-division multiplexing (FDM) combines multiple analog signals onto a single communication link and can be used whenever the total available bandwidth is greater than or equal to the sum of the input signal bandwidths. FDM works by creating multiple subchannels on the output medium and then shifting the frequency of the carrier and data from any one source up or down into one of the subchannels. For example, several lower-speed input devices can be frequency division multiplexed onto a single voice-grade line as shown in **Figure 14-2a**.

FDM makes efficient use of a circuit when all its sources are relatively busy, but it cannot make efficient use of the overall bandwidth when some or all of its sources are inactive. Consider **Figure 14-2a** if one or more of the transmitters are quiet 50% of the time, which is not an unusual situation for interactive terminal sessions. While overall costs have been reduced and line utilization has been improved somewhat by multiplexing the data, there will still be unused bandwidth whenever a source is not transmitting.

FDM is not as common on voice-grade telephone circuits as it once was because the average speed of computer terminals is significantly higher than in the past. When there were large numbers of teletype terminals communicating at 110 bps, as many as 12 to 24 of them could be multiplexed onto a single voice-grade circuit using FDM. However, a large number of terminals today operate at rates of 1200 to 4800 bps or higher; there is not sufficient bandwidth in a voice-grade circuit to use this multiplexing technique for more than a few devices.

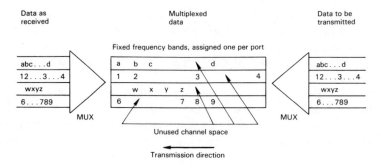

(a) Frequency — division multiplexing

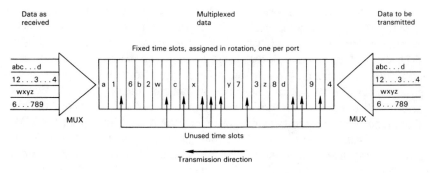

(b) Time-division multiplexing

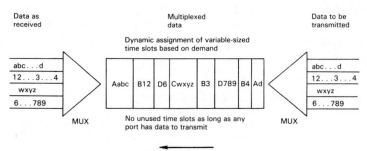

where uppercase A,B,C,D are unique identifiers assigned to the ports on the sending MUX (on the right) so that receiving MUX knows which output port to put the characters on.

(c) Statistical multiplexing

. . .Represents an indeterminate time interval between characters.

Figure 14-2   Multiplexing techniques. These figures show multiplexers that operate by interleaving characters of data. Other types of muxes operate by interleaving either larger or smaller amounts of data at a time.

However, FDM is a very useful technique on large-bandwidth analog circuits such as broadband coax cable links, since the large bandwidth allows the multiplexing of dozens or even hundreds of low- and high-speed data channels. FDM is mentioned again in Chapter 17 when we discuss broadband local area networks.

Fiber-optic circuits generally carry a single frequency band, but newer techniques in fiber optics suggest the future possibility of applying FDM to fiber-optic circuits. On fiber this is sometimes referred to as *color multiplexing*, since different frequencies of the visible light spectrum appear as different colors.

Time-Division Multiplexing

Time-division multiplexing (*TDM*) combines multiple input signals by assigning fixed time slots to each digital input according to a rotation pattern. Each device has the full circuit bandwidth available during its time slots. **Figure 14-2b** shows that the multiplexer places the data, which may be a single bit or a group of bits depending on the multiplexer type, from one computer device into its assigned time slot and then does the same for the next device. Because there is still a one-to-one ratio between input sources and time slots, the sum of the input transmission rates cannot exceed the output line speed for TDM.

TDM has the same general weakness as FDM if some of its sources are frequently inactive; that is, there is no way to use a time slot for other than its assigned source. Consequently, overall line utilization will be reduced, because some slots will not be filled.

Although TDM operates with digital input and produces a digital output, it is used with analog telephone lines by feeding the output of the multiplexer into a modem as shown in **Figure 14-2b**. TDM is widely used on digital communication lines and is the technique used for the T-1 multiplexing scheme described in Chapter 13.

Statistical Time-Division Multiplexing

Statistical time-division multiplexers (*STDM*), more commonly known as *statistical multiplexers* or simply *statmuxes*, apply statistical techniques to assign time slots on a demand basis. The objective is to make use of time slots that would otherwise go unused because a particular source is quiet. Since each time slot can carry data from any of the input sources, each slot must also carry an identifier of the data source so that the demultiplexer can pass each unit of data to the correct recipient. **Figure 14-2c** shows a typical statmux configuration.

The aggregate input bandwidth to a statmux may exceed the output bandwidth because we make the assumption that there will be idle time for each input line. It is not uncommon, for example, for a statmux using a 9600-bps output line to have inputs totaling almost twice that amount. Given that this is true, what happens if all the input lines are transmitting at once?

To accommodate this possibility, a statmux must be able to buffer and hold incoming data until they can be transmitted. This may induce additional delays in transmission for some channels; consequently, an extremely time-sensitive application or protocol may not operate well over a line containing a statmux. Some muxes do allow the user to establish priorities for each channel so that time-sensitive data streams can be expedited at the expense of less critical data.

Most statmuxes are built around a microprocessor that analyzes the incoming signal to determine which device has data to send. The same microprocessor is often used to provide additional features such as error correction, data compression, collection of performance statistics, speed conversion, and diagnostics.

Some statmuxes offer networking capabilities as shown in **Figure 14-3**. In this diagram, each mux has the capability to reroute traffic on alternate paths through other muxes in the event of a link failure, in addition to handling normal multiplexing chores.

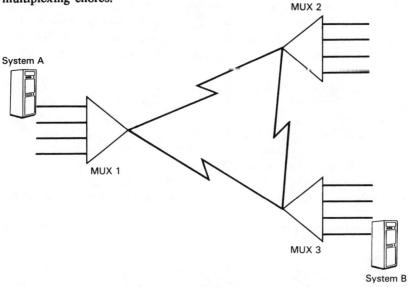

Figure 14-3 Switching multiplexers. If system A is talking to system B on a direct path from multiplexer 1 to multiplexer 3 and the link fails, mux 1 can reroute that, and any other, traffic via mux 2.

DATA COMPRESSION

Data compression increases the effective throughput rate on a data communication link by reducing the number of bits that need to be sent across the line for a given quantity of data. Most products offer a compression ratio of 2:1 for a typical data stream. Some data-compression units realize 3:1 or 4:1 reductions by combining several compression techniques or by adjusting the compression technique to fit the characteristics of the data.

Data compression may achieve either of two benefits for communications users. On one hand, it may be possible to transmit two or more times as much data through an existing circuit. On the other hand, it may be possible to use less expensive, lower-speed modems to send a given quantity of data in the same amount of time.

In the first case, compression may reduce expenditures when traffic volume increases. In the second example, compression may reduce initial implementation expenses, especially when there is a significant differential between prices for the higher- and the lower-speed modems.

An adjunct benefit of data compression is increased data security. If unauthorized personnel were to tap into a circuit carrying compressed data, they would be unable to interpret the information unless they had the identical compression technique available. Some compression product vendors even encrypt the compressed data stream to render it incomprehensible anywhere other than at a location that has the correct combination of decryption and decompression products.

Data compression is often implemented in add-on boxes, as shown in **Figure 14-4**. However, a growing number of modems and multiplexers incorporate compression technology in order to improve throughput. You may also find data compression implemented in software running in the DTE. Regardless of the implementation technique, there must be a corresponding decompression function at the other end of the link.

Two product examples illustrate the benefits of data compression. Symplex Communications Corporation (Ann Arbor, Michigan) offers a product that

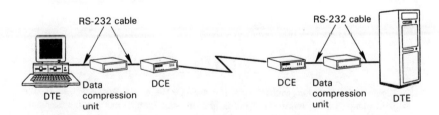

Figure 14-4   Typical data compression configuration. Data compression units are used in pairs and may be implemented as separate hardware devices as shown here. Alternatively, the compression unit may be built into the modems or multiplexers.

doubles the throughput of a 14,400-bps leased line modem. Telcor Systems Corporation (Natick, Massachusetts) sells a modem capable of transferring files at nearly 38,400 bps on a dialup line, with somewhat slower speeds for interactive applications. Telcor achieves this throughput by combining a modulation technique that transmits and receives at 9600 bps with a patented data-compression algorithm that achieves up to a 4:1 data compression ratio. The Telcor product also performs continual analysis of the data stream and dynamically adjusts the compression algorithm to suit its specific characteristics.

Compression Techniques

Run-length encoding replaces a repeated occurrence of a data pattern with one occurrence of the data pattern and a counter. This type of encoding is most commonly performed on repeating 8-bit characters, but it can be used for larger groups of bits. It is especially effective for data streams that are likely to have significant numbers of repeated characters, such as the following:

- Computer-generated report text or CRT screen images that consist predominantly of blank characters and may also have other repeated characters
- Program source code files that contain many blank characters and repeated words or word groups
- Financial data that contain repeating digits or number groups

Word-processing text files and program object code files are not likely to be compressed significantly by run-length encoding because they are not likely to contain repeated characters or digits. Examine this paragraph, for example. How many places can you find where the same character or word appears more than once or twice in a row?

Figure 14-5 contains the general format for the output of run-length encoding along with several examples.

Huffman Encoding

Computer character sets, such as EBCDIC and ASCII (see Chapter 2), use fixed-length bit patterns to represent each transmittable character. *Huffman encoding* replaces the conventional bit patterns for the most frequently transmitted characters with shorter bit patterns to reduce the number of bits sent on a communications line. Naturally, this means that some characters are encoded with a bit pattern that is longer than their original representation, but these characters are chosen because they are the ones that appear less frequently. The net effect is to transmit fewer bits overall for the complete data stream.

A simple Huffman encoding scheme uses fixed substitutions for each data character based on prior analysis of frequency of occurrence and can yield up

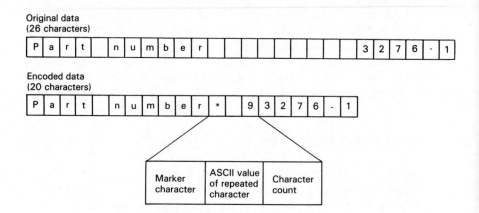

Figure 14-5   Run length encoding. Run length encoding replaces repeating characters or groups of characters with a three-character field: (1) a marker to indicate that replacement has occurred, (2) the ASCII value of the repeated character, and (3) a count of the number of characters that were in the original text.

to a 50% reduction in the number of bits required for a given amount of data to be transmitted. **Figure 14-6a** shows a hypothetical frequency distribution for a set of five characters: A, B, C, D, and E. Without Huffman encoding, the minimum number of bits required to represent each of these five characters is three. With Huffman encoding, the letter A only requires a single bit while the letter E requires four. The actual bit patterns for each of these five characters are derived by following the tree diagram in **Figure 14-6a** from left to right, yielding the bit patterns shown on the far right. At the other end of the line, the receiver of encoded characters examines them using the decision tree shown in **Figure 14-6b** to yield the appropriate data characters.

To prove to yourself that this encoding is worthwhile, look at the calculations in **Figure 14-6c**. Based on the probable number of occurrences of each character in a 100-character message, the total number of bits required without Huffman encoding is 300. With Huffman encoding, the total is only 210 bits, or a reduction of 30%.

A more sophisticated Huffman encoding technique takes on several forms, all based on the assumption that different types of data will have different characteristics. ASCII text will have a different character frequency distribution than program object code, or a financial database, or a facsimile image. In each case, a modified Huffman encoding that takes unique data characteristics into account will yield more efficient data compression than a standard method on the type of data for which it is designed.

Some devices offer a selection of encoding algorithms based on the dominant traffic type over a link. Even more sophisticated devices, such as the Telcor modem mentioned earlier, provide dynamic encoding that actually changes the encoding scheme in use "on the fly" as the characteristics of the data being transmitted change. Some devices also offer substitution for commonly

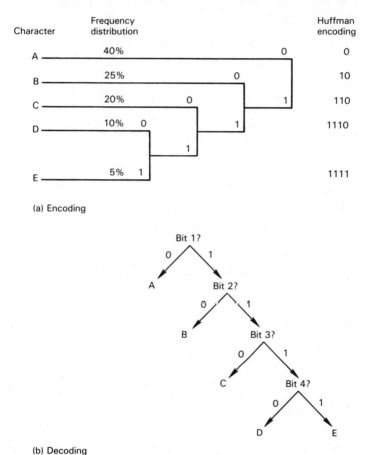

(a) Encoding

(b) Decoding

Figure 14-6 Huffman encoding. Huffman encoding replaces bit patterns of the most frequently occurring characters in a data stream with shorter bit patterns. The least frequently used characters will have longer bit patterns; but if the frequency distribution analysis is correct, the total number of bits transmitted will be less than the original, as shown in *part c*. The calculations in *part c* assume that the 5 characters shown (A, B, C, D, E) are the entire character set, so only 3 bits are needed to represent them if Huffman encoding is not used. [Adapted from Uyless D. Black, *Data Communications and Distributed Networks*, 2nd ed. (Englewood Cliffs, N.J.: Prentice-Hall, Inc., A Reston Book, 1987), p. 111.]

	A	B	C	D	E	Total bits for 100-character data message
Character count for 100-character data message	40	25	20	10	5	
Without Huffman encoding Bits per character	3	3	3	3	3	300
Bit count for this character for 100-character data message	120	75	60	30	15	
With Huffman encoding Bits per character	1	2	3	4	4	210
Bit count for this character for 100-character data message	40	50	60	40	20	
						Net reduction of 30%

(c) Transmission savings

Figure 14-6 Continued

occurring words and phrases, not just characters, allowing text with long, repeated character strings to be compressed to only a few bits. Consider the advantage of this latter approach when transmitting a COBOL source code file; commonly used verbs such as PERFORM and WRITE could be replaced by just a few bits, creating the potential for a dramatic reduction in the number of bits being transmitted.

RECAP

- Frequency division, time division, and statistical multiplexers provide more efficient use of communication circuits by combining multiple data streams into one.
- Data-compression techniques can provide better line utilization by transmitting fewer characters.

PACKET SWITCHING AND X.25

Chapter 13 described circuit switching as a technique for connecting two locations by switching a set of physical facilities into place on demand. For data communication, circuit switching is appropriate when very flexible connectivity is required, when communication takes place at irregular intervals, and when it is convenient to take advantage of the existing telephone company networks.

A circuit-switched network merely organizes a collection of "wires" into a circuit at the user's request, however. Once the connection has been made, there is no value added to the transmission by the network; that is, there is no error detection, no recovery in the event of failure, and no possibility for data on that circuit to be broadcast to all users or to be delivered anywhere other than to the two end points of the circuit.

STORE AND FORWARD SWITCHING

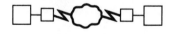

In contrast to circuit switching, store and forward switching relies on some intelligence in the network to accept, examine, store, and then forward a message toward its final destination. A computer using a store and forward network typically has either a permanent connection to the network or the ability to dial into the network on demand.

The network itself consists of switching computers that are permanently connected together, usually with large-bandwidth circuits, and that have the intelligence to move users' data from one location to another, to detect and retransmit corrupted data, and to work around communication link or processor failures. In short, there is value added to the transmission by the network. For a number of years, public data networks were called *VANs*, an acronym for *value-added network*; this acronym is not as widely used today.

A store and forward network may be owned and operated by a user or may be owned and operated as a service to one or more users. The former is called a *private data network*, the latter, a *public data network* (*PDN*).

Store and forward switching can be broken down into two subcategories, message switching and packet switching, both of which are examined in this chapter.

Message Switching

Message switching consists of the storing and forwarding of whole messages, which may range in size from several characters to hundreds or even thousands of characters. A typical message-switching network might look like the network in **Figure 15-1**. In this figure, assume that a message of 1000 characters is being sent from a user on computer A to a user on computer E. Computer A

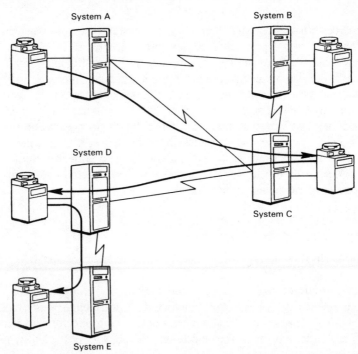

Figure 15-1 Message switching. As a message travels through a message-switching network, it is first stored on disk at each intermediate node and is then forwarded to the next node that takes it closer to its eventual destination.

packages the message and sends it to node C, which receives it, stores it on disk, and then forwards it to node D. Node D stores the message on disk and then determines that the message does not belong to any users directly connected to itself, so it forwards the message to node E, which is its final destination.

At each step along the way, the intermediate node holds the stored message so that it can retransmit it if needed, until it receives notification that the message has been successfully received at the next node along the path. In this way, the network ensures successful delivery of the message to the intended end system. Note, too, that each intermediate node was forced to store the entire 1000-character message before it could begin to transmit it to the next node. Contrast this with the description of packet switching, which follows.

Typical message-switching applications include electronic mail and messaging systems where the network user wants the flexibility to send messages to many different recipients and where the volume of traffic is too large for a dialup application. The primary disadvantage of message-switching systems is the lack of efficiency of the networking operations. The requirement to wait until an entire message has been received, to store it on disk, and then to forward it requires significant disk space and processing time on each intermediate switching node.

Packet Switching

Packet switching is another category of store and forward switching in which the emphasis is on forwarding and *not* on storing. In fact, the goal of packet switching is to ensure the timeliest delivery of data by not storing it other than for the shortest possible time in the main memory of the switching computers.

To achieve this goal, the size of each unit of data to be handled must be kept relatively small. Any message to be sent through a packet-switching network is first broken into pieces, called packets, that typically have a maximum length of 64 or 128 characters. After transmission, the packets are reassembled into the original message format for delivery to the destination system.

A *packet-switching network* (*PSN*) provides excellent support for almost any interactive application that does not require instantaneous response time and for low- to moderate-volume batch transfers, such as electronic mail and messaging. Depending on frequency and volume, packet networks may not be as appropriate for bulk data transfer. Neither are PSNs appropriate for applications that require guaranteed delivery times, since the delivery delay through a PSN will vary considerably depending on traffic volumes within the network.

Another important factor to consider when choosing between building a private, leased line network and using a PSN is how the network will be managed. A company that has no interest or skill in tracking down telephone line failures or equipment failures, in dealing with the telcos to arrange service, or in handling billing may be well advised to choose a packet network vendor who can do all these things. The company that wants to retain internal control and has the

Consideration	Packet Switching	Leased Telephone Lines
Bandwidth	Variable/on demand	Fixed
Billing	Usage sensitive	Distance/time sensitive
Reliability	Built in	By user
Delays	Can be significant	Minimal
Redundancy	Built in	By user
Speeds	To 56 Kbps	To 1.544 Mbps or greater
Coverage	Nearly universal	Universal

Figure 15-2   Comparison of packet switching and leased telephone lines. This figure shows some of the factors that you might consider in deciding whether to install leased telephone lines or to use a packet-switching network for any given application.

skills to do so could opt to build a private network of leased lines. See **Figure 15-2** for a comparison of factors to be evaluated in deciding between use of either leased lines or a packet-switching network.

Public and private packet-switching networks.   To build a private PSN, a company installs a number of switching computers that are interconnected by a set of high-speed trunks (typically 56 Kbps). When each of the company's computers has been connected to one of the PSNs by means of a single line, each computer has access to all the others in the network without requiring any

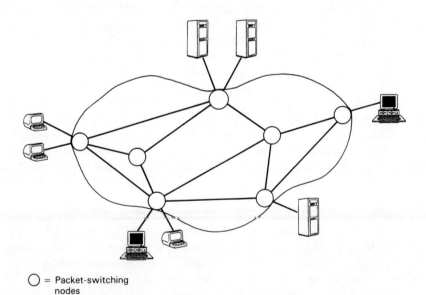

○ = Packet-switching
    nodes

Figure 15-3   Packet switching. In this typical representation of a packet-switching network, the computer equipment belonging to the user is outside the "cloud," while the packet switches and the mesh of communication lines connecting them reside inside the "cloud."

additional physical connections. As in **Figure 15-3**, the collection of PSNs and interconnecting trunks is often represented as a "cloud" in network illustrations.

Public packet-switching networks provide the same degree of connectivity as private networks but are built and maintained by a company that is in business to provide network services to many customers. Users of public packet-switching networks connect their systems to the public network and can then communicate with their own systems or with those of other subscribers to the network. The interior of the network cloud is the province of the network provider; outside the cloud is the user computing equipment. Typically, the user only needs to be concerned with connecting to the cloud since all internal connections are invisible to his or her computers.

Hybrid networks exist in cases where a company may find that traffic volumes, security considerations, geography, and costs combine to suggest a private packet network to reach some of their facilities (often the ones with the heaviest traffic volumes). Other facilities, however, can be serviced more economically by connecting them to a public packet network and then interconnecting the two networks. **Figure 15-4** shows a hybrid network.

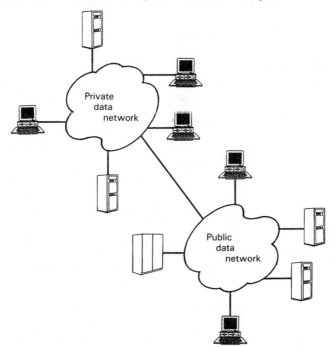

Figure 15-4   Hybrid private and public data networks. Private data networks are often connected to public data networks to allow access to computers that are not on the private network. In many private corporate networks, the private network is installed to connect high-volume traffic locations, and the public network is used to reach those low-volume locations that do not justify the cost of connection to the private net.

X.25

The title of the primary international standard related to packet switching, CCITT recommendation X.25, is:

Interface between Data Terminal Equipment (DTE) and Data Circuit-terminating Equipment (DCE) for Terminals Operating in the Packet Mode and Connected to Public Data Networks by Dedicated Circuit

X.25 was developed to provide a standard interface between computers and data networks, but, more specifically, to provide an interface between specially programmed computers (terminals operating in the packet mode) and public data networks. Development of the X.25 recommendation occurred at a time when public data networks were beginning to appear in many countries, especially in Europe, and was designed to standardize the emerging packet-switching technology. **Figure 15-5** shows several types of DTE connected to a network and highlights the location of the X.25 interface in each case. Note that the X.25 usage of the term DCE is not exactly the same as the more familiar RS-232 usage. An X.25 DCE is the point of connection to the network, which may or may not be accomplished by means of an RS-232 DCE, that is, a modem, as is illustrated on several of the X.25 links in the figure.

The first version of X.25 was published by the CCITT in 1976, and subsequent updates have been published on the CCITT schedule of every 4 years. Despite having many areas left for future study, the 1976 version was sufficiently complete that implementations began to appear in the late 1970s, with widespread implementations available in the early 1980s. The most recent versions of X.25, published in 1984 and 1988, added several new features and significantly reduced the areas left open to interpretation.

Having described what X.25 is, it is equally important to point out what X.25 is not. X.25 is *not* a recommendation for internal network operation. It has absolutely nothing to do with the way in which data are formatted or moved inside of the network cloud in **Figure 15-5**. Public data networks are very likely to have strikingly different internal network protocols. In the United States, for example, Telenet and Tymnet use unique and incompatible means to package and transport data from one side of the network to the other, even though both use X.25 as their external interface. Consequently, the commonly used phrase "X.25 network" does not describe the internal operation of the network, but indicates that the network supports the X.25 interface.

X.25 deals with the lower three layers of the OSI model, each of which is discussed on the following pages.

X.25 Physical Layer

CCITT selected the physical layer of the X.21 specification (see Chapter 10) for X.25. X.21 actually specifies all three lower layers of the OSI reference

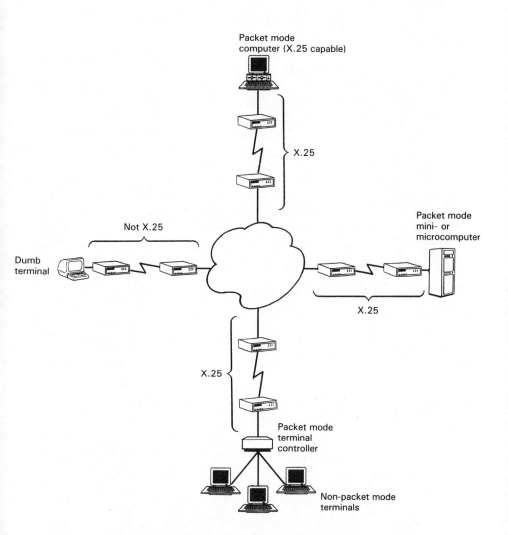

Figure 15-5 Location of X.25 interface. X.25 specifies an interface between terminals operating in packet mode and a public data network. It has nothing to do with the internal operation of the packet-switching network.

model; however, CCITT chose only the physical layer of X.21 for inclusion in X.25.

Because there were so few products on the market in the middle 1970s that had implemented the X.21 interface (there are still relatively few), CCITT allowed for an interim set of interface standards for the X.25 physical layer called *X.21 bis*. These interim standards included RS-232 and V.24 for slower-speed interfaces and RS-449 for high-speed interfaces. Most implementations of X.25

that are in use today are implemented using RS-232/V.24 because of the widespread availability of computer and communications hardware built to those specifications.

X.25 Data Link Layer

Single-link procedure. Once again, at the data link layer CCITT chose to use an existing standard as the basis for X.25. Layer 2 of X.25 employs a subset of HDLC called *Link Access Procedure Balanced (LAPB)*. Under LAPB, all stations are *peers*; they are all equal and can either initiate commands or issue responses.

LAPB allows for the establishment of a logical link connection across a physical medium, for information transfer using information frames, and for link disconnect. It also provides link reset procedures for recovery from certain types of errors. **Figure 15-6** contains a list of the LAPB commands and responses that comprise the HDLC subset that is used for the X.25 data link layer. **Figure 15-7** shows a typical link establishment, data transfer, and disconnect sequence.

Frame Type		Command		Response
Information	I	Information	I	Information
Supervisory	RR	Receive ready	RR	Receive ready
	RNR	Receive not ready	RNR	Receive not ready
	REJ	Reject	REJ	Reject
Unnumbered	SABM	Set asynchronous balanced mode		
	DISC	Disconnect		
			DM	Disconnect mode
			UA	Unnumbered acknowledgment
			FRMR	Frame reject

Figure 15-6   LAPB subset of HDLC used for X.25 data link layer. This figure shows the asynchronous balanced mode subset of HDLC commands and responses that are used for the X.25 LAPB data link layer. In this usage, asynchronous does not refer to async transmission but to events that can occur independently of each other, as is the case with a full-duplex protocol like HDLC. [Adapted from *CCITT Red Book* (Geneva: CCITT, 1985), Fascicle VIII.3, Table 5/X.25, p. 120, by authorization of the International Telecommunications Union.]

Multilink procedure. The 1984 version of X.25 added a new feature to the data link layer that allows for multiple, physical connections between the X.25 DTE and DCE. Only one physical link had been supported in previous

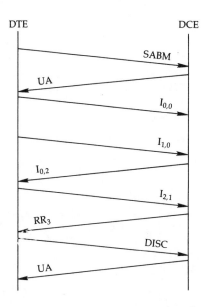

Figure 15-7   Typical X.25 data exchange. This figure illustrates a typical exchange of commands and responses that serve to establish the link, transfer data, and disconnect the link. Refer to Chapter 7 for the meaning of each of the commands and responses.

versions of the recommendation. The multilink sublayer of X.25 distributes each packet that it receives from layer 3 to one of the single-link procedures, each of which is responsible for a specific physical connection.

One attractive aspect of this implementation approach is that existing data link software can be used unmodified, because each single-link procedure still receives a packet from above and the operation of the LAPB procedure associated with each physical link is unaffected. **Figure 15-8** illustrates the addition of the multilink procedure to the X.25 layers and demonstrates that the preexisting data link layer software is completely unaware of the additional actions of the multilink procedure.

The multilink procedure adds an additional control field to each layer 3 packet before passing the PDU to the single-link procedure. The receiving multilink procedure uses the multilink control field to identify and resequence the incoming packets. The multilink procedure does not perform any error checking as it assumes that all error-handling functions have been performed by the single-link sublayers. See **Figure 15-9** for the format of the multilink control field.

The major advantages of supporting multiple, physical links for the X.25 interface are to provide redundancy in the event of link failure and to increase the overall DTE-DCE bandwidth without exceeding the bandwidth of the physical

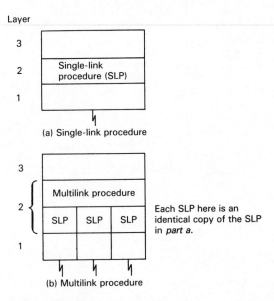

(a) Single-link procedure

(b) Multilink procedure

Figure 15-8　X.25 data link layer. The single-link procedure is the original data link layer for X.25 and allows for one physical connection from an X.25 host to the network. The 1984 version of X.25 added the multilink procedure to allow more than one physical layer connection. Addition of the multilink layer is completely transparent to the single-link procedure; it still receives a PDU from the layer above, which it packages in an HDLC frame for transmission.

layer interface (for example, the RS-232 maximum of 20,000 bps). The multilink procedures also allow new links to be added or service to be performed on an existing link without taking the entire X.25 interface out of service.

X.25 Packet Layer

The packet layer of X.25 corresponds approximately to the network layer of the OSI reference model; however, it does not include a specification for how the network layer will interface with the transport layer. It does provide for the establishment of virtual circuits from a DTE on one side of the public data network to a DTE on the other side of the network. A *virtual circuit* (*VC*) consists of the combination of a logical channel between one DTE-DCE pair, a path through the network, and a logical channel between a second DTE-DCE pair. See **Figure 15-10**.

One of the most valuable functions of X.25 is to multiplex multiple data exchanges over a single X.25 interface. This has always been true of X.25 and has no relationship with the 1984 feature that provides for multiple physical links. Multiple data exchanges are handled by means of *logical channel numbers* (*LCN*). X.25 allows for a maximum of 4095 logical channel numbers between

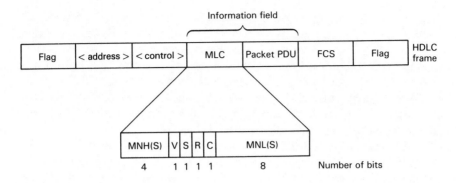

Where
MLC is multilink control field
MNL(S) is bits 1 to 8 of multilink send sequence number
MNH(S) is bits 9 to 12 of multilink send sequence number

V is the void sequencing bit ⎱ Used in combination to control whether and
S is the sequence check option bit ⎰ how multilink sequence numbers are used

R is the reset request bit
C is the reset confirmation bit

Figure 15-9 Format of the X.25 multilink control field. The multilink control field is added to the front of the packet-layer PDU, and the resultant PDU is passed to one of the single-link procedures below. The information in the multilink control field allows the receiving multilink procedure to resequence the incoming packets. Operation of the multilink procedure is completely transparent to the single-link procedures. [Adapted from *CCITT Red Book* (Geneva: CCITT, 1985), Fascicle VIII.3, Tables 9/X.25 and 10/X.25, pp. 135-7, by authorization of the International Telecommunications Union.]

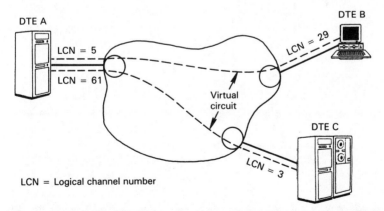

Figure 15-10 X.25 virtual circuits between DTEs attached to the same public data network. Whether there is a single physical connection or multiple connections between an X.25 host and the network, X.25 supports multiple virtual circuits across the link. This allows the X.25 host to have more than one logical connection to other terminals or computers.

each DTE-DCE pair. In most X.25 implementations, however, the actual limit is much lower due to capacity limitations of either the DTE, DCE, or both.

LCN 0 is reserved for use by the packet layer when interface operations have become so confused that a complete restart is necessary. The lowest-numbered LCNs above 0 are reserved for permanent virtual circuits (PVC). PVCs are preconfigured virtual circuits that are activated whenever a DTE is powered on and active. A given X.25 interface may or may not have any PVCs assigned, depending on the communication needs of that DTE.

All other LCNs are assigned in ranges as shown in **Figure 15-11**. The DTE assigns an LCN whenever it wishes to initiate a call to some other DTE, and the DCE assigns an LCN whenever it receives an incoming call request

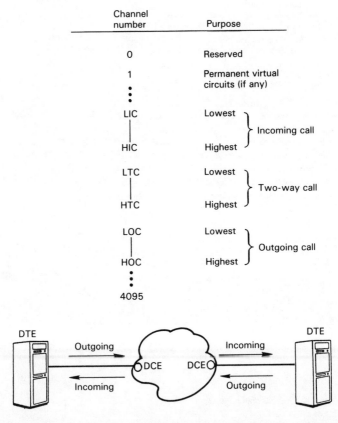

Figure 15-11   Logical channel number assignments. The lowest LCNs are assigned to permanent virtual circuits. The DTE assigns the highest available LCN for each outgoing call, and the DCE assigns the lowest available LCN for incoming calls. The numbers in the middle can be designated for use by either DTE, DCE, or both, to provide more flexible LCN assignment. LCN 0 is reserved for packet layer restart and diagnostic messages.

from the network. Note in **Figure 15-11** that "incoming" and "outgoing" are always from the point of view of the DTE.

Typically, a block of numbers is reserved for incoming calls, a block for outgoing calls, and a two-way zone for either call type. By having the DTE and DCE assign numbers from opposite ends of the available list of numbers, the chance of both devices assigning the same number is greatly reduced, although the packet procedures of X.25 have rules to sort out that type of collision in favor of the DTE. (The DTE and DCE are like the characters in George Orwell's *Animal Farm*; the DTE and DCE are equals, but the DTE is a little more equal.)

The number assigned to the logical channel on one end of a virtual circuit has absolutely no relationship to the LCN on the other end of the same VC. LCNs are only relevant to one specific X.25 interface, as shown in **Figure 15-10**, where one VC consists of LCN 5 and 29 plus the network path connecting them, and the other consists of LCN 61 and 3 plus the connecting path.

Every X.25 packet has a header with the format shown in **Figure 15-12**. The first three octets of the header are mandatory, and the remaining octets may be present or not depending on the specific packet type. **Figure 15-13** lists some of the most commonly used packet types. Note that, just as there are control frames and information frames at the data link layer, there are control packets and data packets at the packet layer, many of which have names and functions similar to their link layer counterparts.

Data packets and selected control packets contain send and receive sequence numbers, just as the link layer uses frame send and receive sequence numbers. Do not confuse the two, however; although they serve the same function, that

Octet
Number

1	General format identifier	Logical channel group number
2	Logical channel number	
3	Packet type identifier	
• • •	Optional octets based on packet type	

General format identifier contains bits that are used to select certain packet layer options.

Logical channel group number is combined with the *logical channel number* to form a 12-bit logical channel number.

Packet type identifier contains bit patterns to distinguish among the packet types listed in Figure 15-13.

Figure 15-12   X.25 packet header format.

From DTE to DCE	From DCE to DTE	Purpose
Call request	Incoming call	Call setup
Call accepted	Call connected	Call setup
Data	Data	Data transfer
RR	RR	Receive ready
RNR	RNR	Receive not ready
Clear request	Clear indication	Call clearing
Clear confirmation	Clear confirmation	Call clearing
Reset request	Reset indication	Reset one virtual circuit
Reset confirmation	Reset confirmation	Reset one virtual circuit
Restart request	Restart indication	Restart entire packet layer (that is, all virtual circuits)

Figure 15-13   A representative sample of the packet types used by X.25. [Adapted from *CCITT Red Book* (Geneva: CCITT, 1985), Fascicle VIII.3, Table 17/X.25, p. 170, by authorization of the International Telecommunications Union.]

is, to number units of data to prevent missing or duplicate data, the link layer and packet layer sequence numbers are completely independent of each other. If you have any doubts about this, think about the fact that a given X.25 interface may have several active virtual circuits, each with its own packet sequencing, all being carried in consecutively numbered I-frames at the data link layer.

Figure 15-14 illustrates the packet flow that would normally occur when DTE A, on the left in the illustration, establishes a connection to DTE B and transfers several data packets. **Figure 15-15** carries this example one step further by showing two independent packet level connections on the same X.25 interface. Note that there is no confusion about which packet belongs to which conversation because the LCN is always present in the packet header.

To further illustrate the point made about packets being carried on the physical link inside the information field in an I-frame, examine **Figure 15-16**. This figure corresponds exactly to **Figure 15-15**, but it shows the events occurring at the link layer.

PACKET ASSEMBLER/ DISASSEMBLER

The title of the X.25 recommendation specifies that X.25 applies to terminals operating in the packet mode. What happens to the hundreds of thousands of terminals that are not smart enough to know how to operate in packet mode? Are they excluded from use on public data networks? Definitely not.

A nonpacket mode terminal is connected to a public data network through a *packet assembler/disassembler (PAD)*. A PAD is a device that speaks to a terminal using the native protocol of the terminal, which might be async, bisync, or any other protocol, and converts the data stream into X.25 protocol for

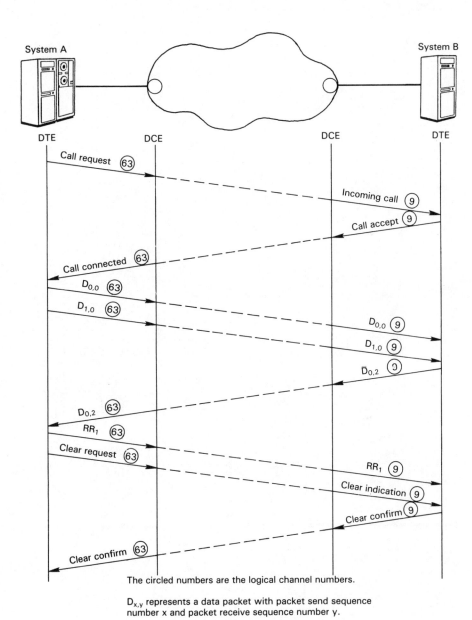

The circled numbers are the logical channel numbers.

$D_{x,y}$ represents a data packet with packet send sequence number x and packet receive sequence number y.

Figure 15-14 X.25 packet layer call establishment and data transfer.

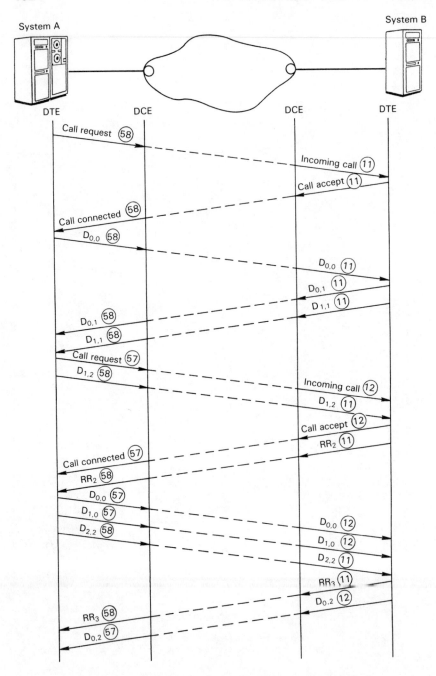

Figure 15-15   X.25 packet layer example. The LCNs used for each packet layer connection prevent confusion when there are multiple logical channels in use on any DTE, as shown in this example. Be sure to compare the packet layer traffic in this figure with the corresponding data link layer traffic between the same DTEs that is shown in Figure 15-16.

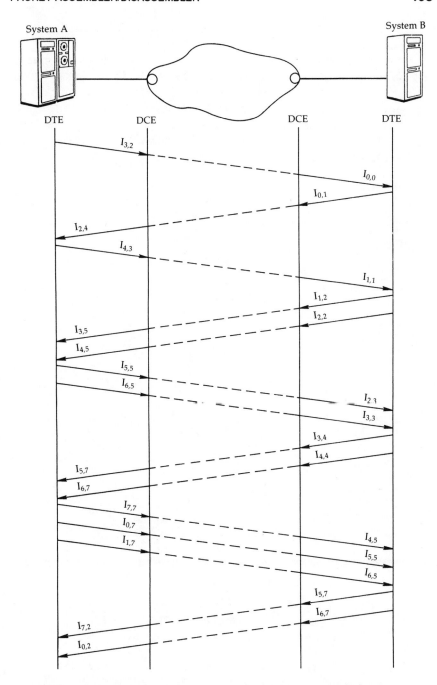

Figure 15-16   X.25 data link layer example. This figure shows the data link layer activity that corresponds to the packet layer traffic in Figure 15-15. Note that there is no relationship between packet sequence numbers and frame sequence numbers, although each provides the same function at its own layer.

communication with the network DCE. In essence, the PAD is an X.25 protocol converter.

The PAD function may be provided at several different locations and may be supplied by the DTE user or the PDN. **Figure 15-17** illustrates several nonpacket mode terminals connected to PADs and shows a variety of PAD locations. Note that the PAD for system F is part of the software in the network-switching node, and, strictly speaking, there is no X.25 interface in this case. Regardless of how it is implemented, the PAD function allows nonpacket mode terminals to have access to public data networks.

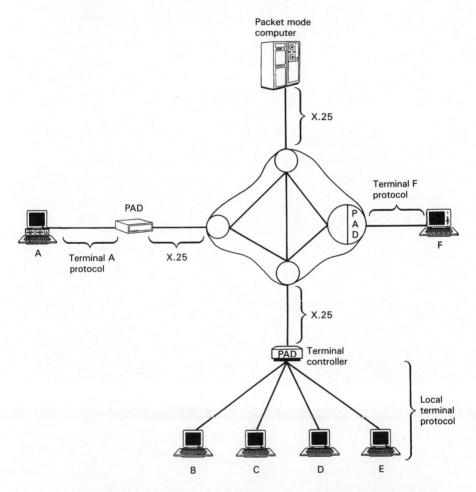

Figure 15-17   Use of PADs. A packet assembler/disassembler (PAD) allows connection of a nonpacket mode device to a public data network by converting from local terminal protocol into X.25 protocol. Note that the PAD function may be in the computer equipment, in the network vendor's equipment, or in hardware provided by a third vendor.

In many cases, the network provider may supply the PAD, as would certainly be the case for system F in **Figure 15-17**. The network vendor may also supply a separate PAD as shown for system A, or the user may buy this type of PAD from a third-party source. The PAD for terminals B through E might be obtained from either the network supplier, the supplier of the DTE, or a third party.

A wide variety of PADs exists to satisfy the needs of PDN customers to connect a broad array of nonpacket mode terminals to their networks. PADs for dumb terminals were developed first and are described next. PADs for bisync devices were a logical outgrowth of the economies of packet networks and the existence of millions of bisync terminals. PADs for SNA terminals, facsimile machines, and other special-purpose devices also exist.

Standards Related to PADs

Because of the significant numbers of asynchronous, dumb terminals, also called *start-stop* (*SS*)-mode terminals after the characteristics of asynchronous transmission, CCITT created three recommendations to describe the interaction between the user, a SS mode terminal, and a PAD. The titles of these recommendations are as follows:

X.3   Packet assembly/disassembly facility (PAD) in a public data network

X.28 DTE/DCE interface for a start-stop mode data terminal equipment accessing the packet assembly/disassembly facility (PAD) in a public data network situated in the same country

X.29 Procedures for the exchange of control information and user data between a packet assembly/disassembly (PAD) facility and a packet mode DTE or another PAD

In essence, X.3 defines a set of parameters to control the operation of a PAD; X.28 provides a means for a user at a SS-mode terminal to query and change PAD parameters; and X.29 provides a means for a packet mode DTE or another PAD to query or change PAD parameters. **Figure 15-18** illustrates the relationship between these recommendations and the various network devices in the network.

X.3. *X.3* parameters control the operation of a PAD by telling it the characteristics of the start-stop mode terminal to which it is connected. X.3 parameters exist to tell the PAD:

- What parity scheme is to be used between the SS mode terminal and the PAD

- Whether the PAD should insert a line feed after each carriage return it sends to the terminal

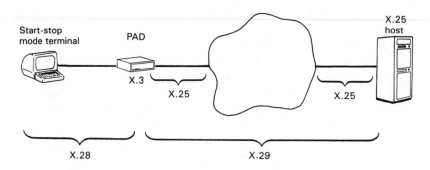

Figure 15-18   Relative location of X.3, X.28, and X.29 in the network.

• Whether the PAD is to echo characters back to the terminal or wait for characters to be echoed from the remote DTE
• What bit per second rate to use for the terminal

There are twenty-two X.3 PAD parameters in the 1984 version of the standard.

X.28. *X.28* provides a very simple list of commands that can be typed by a user to query and change PAD parameters. This may be necessary because different applications that the user wishes to run may have different requirements of the SS mode terminal. Also, the user may wish to access different computers at different times, and the characteristics of the computers may vary, necessitating changes in the operation of the terminal.

Many PADs provide a means to predefine lists of parameters so that an entire set of parameters may be changed at one time, thereby eliminating the somewhat tedious task of typing numerous X.28 commands. This parameter list function is not part of the X.28 recommendation, however; it is a service provided by the PAD vendor or the network vendor.

X.29. *X.29* allows a host DTE to affect PAD operation in the same way that a person can by typing X.28 commands. At first you may ask why the computer would want to change parameters in the PAD for a user connected to that computer through the network. The reason is actually quite logical if you consider that the computer application developer may want to eliminate the need for the user to know anything about PAD parameters. A computer application can use X.29 to send a set of X.3 parameters to the user's PAD on the other side of the network without the user even being aware that this is happening. X.29 can also be used for PAD to PAD communications.

Bisync Pads

PADs for polling protocols, such as bisync, must compensate for transmission delays that will be longer through a packet network than on a leased line. Polling protocols require a response from the polled devices within a specified period of time in order to know that the device is alive and well and to determine whether the remote device has any data to transmit to the host.

The additional delays of a packet network over a leased line can mean either or both of two problems for the polling device. First, if the delay in both directions is sufficiently long, the poll response may not arrive back across the network before the controller times out and gives up on getting a response. Second, even if the poll response does arrive in time, the round-trip time will be considerably longer through the PDN than it would be on a leased line, which may adversely affect each user's response time.

Figure 15-19 depicts the location and operation of a bisync PAD for use with a packet network. In addition to translating from bisync to X.25 protocol, the PAD compensates for the delay by "stealing" the poll on the host end and by generating polls on the remote end. The bisync requirements of both host and remote are satisfied, and we can still use the more efficient X.25 protocol to access the packet-switching network. You should note a strong resemblance between this description of a bisync PAD and the satellite delay compensation unit described in Chapter 13. In both cases, the added device is an attempt to make a polling protocol function over transmission links with relatively long delays.

The overall performance of polled terminals attached to a packet network will seldom be as good as when they are attached to a leased line; however, the use of the packet network may still make sense for other reasons, including the following:

- Flexibility for connection to multiple hosts through a single network connection
- Availability of a public data network when leased lines cannot be installed
- Availability of a corporate private data network on which incremental costs for new bisync connections are minimal compared to the costs of new leased lines

X.75

CCITT recommendation X.75 is titled:

Terminal and Transit Call Control Procedures and Data Transfer System on International Circuits between Packet-switched Data Networks

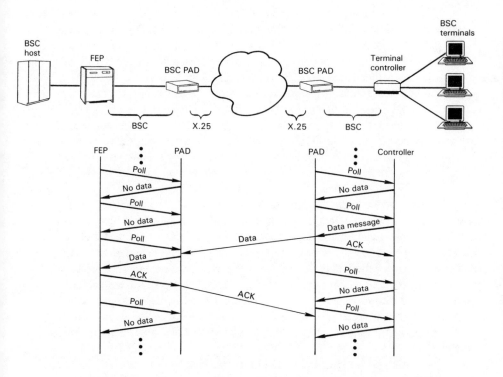

Figure 15-19   Use of bisync PAD to connect 3270-type terminals to mainframe. The host-end bisync PAD "steals" polls and selects from the front-end processor (FEP), while the terminal-end PAD generates polls and selects as though it were the FEP. This process eliminates the potentially lengthy delays that would result if every poll had to travel through the network and be answered through the network before the next poll could be issued. Compare with Figure 13-4.

X.75 is used to provide an interface between two X.25 interface networks. X.25 itself is not suitable for several reasons. First, it is a DTE-DCE interface, and the internetworking problem is really a DCE-DCE problem, as can be seen in **Figure 15-20** (refer also to Figure 8-2).

Second, the volume of traffic between networks may be such that X.25 does not provide enough virtual circuits or enough bandwidth. X.75 provides the additional capacity by supporting multiple physical links between networks.

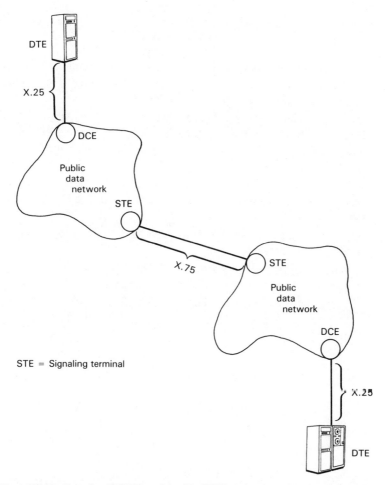

Figure 15-20   Location of X.75 interface. The X.75 interface is used to connect multiple X.25 packet-switching networks.

The success of multiple links in X.75 and the requirement for greater bandwidth in X.25 led to the adoption of multilink procedures in the 1984 version of X.25.

Third, X.25 call request procedures have no provision for handling parameter passing across intermediate networks, for accommodating multiple network billing information, or for handling a multitude of other complications that arise when an intermediate network is introduced.

RECAP

- Message switching is a type of store and forward switching in which whole messages are received by a node, written to disk, and forwarded; delays may be seconds, minutes, or longer.

- Packet switching is a type of store and forward switching in which messages are broken into small packets that are received by a node and immediately forwarded; delays may be tenths of seconds or seconds long.

- X.25 specifies the packet mode DTE to DCE interface for a public data network and covers the lower three layers of the OSI reference model.

- X.3, X.28, and X.29 specify how nonpacket mode devices can use a public data network.

- Bisync PADs must compensate for potentially long delays through the network by intercepting and generating polls and selects locally.

- X.75 specifies the interface between two X.25 networks.

16

TRANSMISSION FACILITIES:
THE LAST MILE

Most of the improvements in transmission technology described in the previous chapters, such as digital signaling and higher-bandwidth media, have occurred in the long-distance portion of the telephone network. It is the connection from the nearest central office to the end user, usually called the *last mile* or the *local loop*, that is the least economic for the telephone service providers to upgrade.

THE LAST MILE ENVIRONMENT

The costs for upgrading central office equipment or major interoffice trunks can be spread among many thousands of subscribers, but the cost to upgrade the last mile to a given location can only be applied to one customer. As a result, most subscribers are still connected to the public telephone network by copper twisted-pair wire. The largest corporate customers may be connected to the CO by higher-bandwidth media such as coaxial cable, fiber-optic cable, or microwave links. However, even some of the largest telephone customers are still connected to the telco CO via twisted-pair, albeit by thousands of twisted-pair lines.

The two primary motivations for a telco customer to consider alternatives to the copper wire local loop are economics and bandwidth, which are often two sides of the same issue. Those companies in which bandwidth demand stays relatively constant may still be able to reduce their expenses for communications facilities by using alternate local-loop technology. Those companies in which demand for additional bandwidth continues to climb may turn to alternative local-loop connections to satisfy their bandwidth requirements, rather than paying for additional twisted-pair lines each month.

The local-loop problem is not restricted solely to communication between the customer and the telco central office with the intent of communicating over long distance. Similar restrictions exist if a customer would like to communicate between two facilities that are connected to the same central office. In this case, the last mile may be the only mile, but similar constraints bound what the user can accomplish using voice-grade, twisted-pair lines.

DIVESTITURE

Before January 1, 1984, the cost of providing local telephone service throughout the United States had been subsidized by the revenues generated from the significantly more profitable long-distance services. This was possible because of long-standing arrangements between AT&T and the local telephone companies, most of which were AT&T subsidiaries.

MFJ and CI II

Two events in early 1980s changed all that. The first was the Federal Communication Commission's Computer Inquiry II (CI II), which was an investigation into the use of computers and the provision of computer services in the telephone network. It resulted in specific regulations that governed what telephone companies could and could not do with computer services.

The second was the *Modfied Final Judgment* (*MFJ*) that took effect on January 1, 1984. The MFJ, which settled an antitrust suit against AT&T, required AT&T to divest itself of the local operating companies. *Divestiture* strictly prohibited the subsidization of local service from long-distance revenues, which forced the local operating companies to shoulder the full cost of providing local service.

Divestiture broke the former Bell System into seven *regional Bell operating companies*, or *RBOC*s. Each RBOC has one or more of the local *Bell operating companies (BOC)* under its jurisdiction. The long-distance portion of the former Bell system is run by AT&T, and the other parts of AT&T are split into various divisions and subsidiaries.

LATAs and POPs

The *local access transport area* (*LATA*) delineates the service area for a local telephone company and is another creation of divestiture. Although there is some coincidence of boundaries, LATAs are not derived from telephone area codes.

The long-distance carriers, also called *interexchange carriers*, are prohibited from providing intra-LATA services, and the local telcos are prohibited from providing inter-LATA services. Each interexchange carrier that wants to provide service into or out of a LATA maintains a *point of presence* (*POP*) within the LATA.

BYPASS

Bypass is the application of alternative technology to circumvent the limitations inherent in the copper wire of the last mile. A customer may implement bypass by installing direct links between two or more of their own offices or by connecting their premises directly to the switch of a long-distance carrier. In either case, the result is that the customer bypasses the local telephone company altogether.

Even though bypass had existed before divestiture, the local operating companies saw it as a significant threat to their already diminished revenues. Consequently, bypass quickly became one of the hot buzzwords, and even one of the dirty words, of the postdivestiture period.

Compounding the problem for the local telcos were the economics of installing bypass equipment in the first place. Usually, only the largest customers within a given operating company's service area can justify the cost of bypass technology. And it is these same largest customers who make up the greatest percentage of the revenue, and most likely of the profit, for the local telephone company. Consequently, the threat of bypass strikes very directly at the bottom line for a local telephone company.

The state regulatory commissions that control the rates that local telephone companies are allowed to charge were worried about bypass for the reasons cited in the previous paragraph, also. For them the potential revenue loss to the local telephone companies was most likely to result in considerably higher rates for those subscribers who remained with the local carrier, especially for the small business and residential customers.

Justification

In spite of the misgivings of public utility commissions and local telephone companies, bypass is continuing to happen because it makes considerable sense for many companies and institutions. The motivation for bypass falls into four areas:

1. *Cost savings*: A large manufacturing firm that spends thousands of dollars per month on long-distance calls may save a percentage of that money by "eliminating the middle man," the local telephone company. They may install a microwave link directly to the long-distance carrier's offices to reduce local calling expenses.

2. *Increased bandwidth*: A company with offices in several buildings in the local calling area may choose to connect them with microwave, fiber, or coax links to facilitate very high speed data transfer among the offices.

3. *New technology*: Alternate service providers may offer services or technology that is not yet available from the local telco. For example, switched digital services or fiber-optic trunks may not be available from the local carrier, but may be available from another source.

4. *Installation lead time*: A corporate headquarters location that needs several additional T-1 circuits to connect to its computer network may not be willing to wait the six months quoted by the telephone company for installation. They may turn instead to an outside firm that can install the circuits much more quickly.

Bypass Providers

Who are the companies providing bypass services? First, there are small companies or divisions of larger companies that see bypass as a major business opportunity. They will install private microwave, coax, or fiber links between two customer locations or between the customer and a long-distance carrier.

Second, the interexchange carriers may install or allow a customer to install bypass circuits between the customer's office and the carrier's switch, thereby eliminating the local telephone company. Often however, the long-distance carrier arranges for the local telco to provide T-1 links between the customer's site and their POP. Strictly speaking, this arrangement does not constitute bypass because the local telephone company is providing the local links.

Third, it is important to note that the local telephone companies are not sitting idly by while all this is happening. Many have formed subsidiaries to install bypass services and facilities for their own customers, thereby ensuring that the lost local calling revenue does not disappear from their books entirely.

LOCAL-LOOP ALTERNATIVES

Regardless of whether a large volume user needs better access to a telephone company CO or whether a customer wishes to bypass the local operating company, several dominant technologies are involved in providing alternative local-loop connections. Any of these alternatives may be used to connect a user to the nearest CO, to connect multiple user sites together directly, or to connect a customer premises to a long-distance carrier's POP.

Figure 16-1 shows a variety of local-loop and bypass connections; these are described in the following paragraphs.

Twisted Pair

When analog twisted-pair circuits are insufficient for the local loop, you can order DDS-type digital circuits or T-1 circuits for local use, just as you could for long-distance use (see Chapter 13). DDS and T-1 services can be implemented over the same copper twisted pair as analog circuits are, with two major changes. First, the telco removes the *loading coils* that improve analog transmission over twisted pair because they interfere with digital transmission. Second, they install different equipment at the CO and the customer premises to terminate the circuit.

In **Figure 16-1**, the ABC Company office on the left has a T-1 link to the nearest CO due to its traffic volume. ABC multiplexes both voice and data traffic onto its T-1 circuit. This example is not bypass since the connection is to the local telco CO, but it does demonstrate a twisted-pair alternative in the local loop.

Microwave

Microwave facilities are one of the most common forms of private communication links, partly because they do not require the acquisition of land or land-use rights in order to string cable. As we discussed in Chapter 13, microwave communication only requires that small dish antennas be located within line of sight of each other.

A company with two offices in a metropolitan area, for example, could install a private microwave link between them and have multiple T-1 channels available for voice and data use. The costs to the company are for one-time installation and regular maintenance fees, but there are no monthly charges from the local phone company.

Do not assume that microwave installation is always simple or even that it is always possible, however. In urban areas such as Manhattan, a line of site may not exist between two buildings. In other cases, a proposed microwave link may cause radio-frequency interference with existing microwave links and would be disallowed by the *Federal Communications Commission (FCC)*.

All the major long-distance carriers have the capability to terminate private microwave links at the POP in many locations. As an example, in **Figure 16-1**, the corporate headquarters of XYZ, Inc., is located 30 miles outside a major city. XYZ has installed a microwave connection to their long-distance carrier's

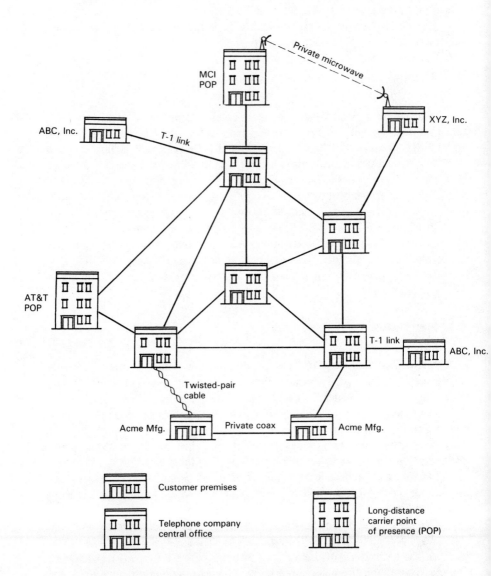

Figure 16-1 The local loop. This figure shows a portion of the local telephone network with several telephone company central offices and several types of interoffice trunks and local loop connections. It also illustrates coax and microwave circuits being used to bypass local telephone company circuits.

POP in the city. This link provides multiple voice and data circuits and eliminates any fees to the local phone company for traffic on the 30-mile loop to the city. As shown, XYZ, Inc. still maintains a connection to the local telco to allow assignment of local telephone numbers, to enable calling within the local area, and, perhaps, to allow access to a second long-distance carrier.

Coax Cable

Coax cable is another option for private communication links. Toward the bottom of **Figure 16-1**, Acme Manufacturing has several facilities within a relatively small geographic area and has installed several miles of coax to connect them directly together. The telephone switchboards, or PBXs, in each location are interconnected by T-1 links running over the cable so that local calls among company offices can be handled on the private facility instead of on the public network. Other channels on the cable can be used for video applications or for data communication at speeds from several hundred bits per second to T-1 rates.

Cable television companies are also a source of coax-based alternative communication channels. In many locations, especially in urban areas, there is an extensive network of coax cable installed for delivery of cable TV services. Frequently, there is unused bandwidth available on the cable that the cable companies will sell for private use. Even if there is no capacity available on their primary cable(s), some cable TV companies have installed or will install additional cable for private use.

Fiber-Optic Cable

Private fiber-optic cable provides an excellent communications link in situations where the high capacity and quality offset the somewhat greater expense of installation. As with microwave or coax, a private fiber link may connect multiple company locations, or it may connect the company to either the local CO or the long-distance carrier's POP.

Satellite

Some companies have chosen to install satellite dishes on their premises, giving them direct access to their other locations around the country and solving both their local and long-haul communication needs. The first available satellite systems transmitted on *C band* frequencies, on which the transmission to the satellite (the uplink) occurs at approximately 6 GHz, and the downlink transmissions take place near 4 GHz. C band transmission has the disadvantage of requiring large, 10-meter-diameter satellite dishes to overcome interference from terrestrial microwave sources. A 10-meter dish cannot be installed on top of or immediately adjacent to many buildings, often because of zoning restrictions or potential structural damage from wind.

Very small aperture terminals. In the 1980s, *very small aperture terminal (VSAT)* systems have made direct satellite communications feasible for more companies than ever. VSAT uses either C band or the *Ku band* (the uplink is at 14 GHz and the downlink at 12 GHz), which does not suffer from microwave interference and can use relatively small, 1- to 2-meter dishes. The smaller Ku band dishes can be placed more easily on rooftops, although the political and financial dealings required to get approval in some cases can cause severe difficulty [CommWeek].

VSAT networks generally consist of one large, central station with any number of remote VSATs and are particularly suited to one-to-many or many-to-one communication requirements. They are not suitable for peer-to-peer needs since most VSAT stations do not have sufficient power to transmit and receive to another VSAT station directly. Merrill Lynch and K-Mart have installed widely publicized VSAT networks to take advantage of this capability. In the case of Merrill Lynch, their network is used to connect their brokerage offices to a central site to allow transmission of updated financial information from the central site to all remote locations. K-Mart's network will eventually link several thousand retail stores with its corporate data center. Several hundred stores were already on line by the end of 1987 primarily to provide credit authorization services.

Cellular Telephone

The primary purpose of cellular telephone service is to provide mobility and flexibility in the local-loop connection. As such, use of cellular service is seldom justified based on the four reasons for bypass listed earlier in this chapter. The justification for cellular telephones is almost always based on mobility. Nonetheless, a description of cellular service is appropriate for this section because it represents a legitimate last mile replacement.

The principle behind cellular telephone systems is to use a network of low-power transmitter/receivers organized into small areas called cells, such as the network shown in **Figure 16-2**. A mobile user who places a call is handled by the antenna at the center of the cell in which he or she is located. The strength of the signal to and from the mobile user is constantly monitored as he or she drives through one cell and approaches another. As the signal weakens in the current cell and strengthens in a neighboring cell, a central computer will "hand off" the call from the old cell to the new one with no discernible interruption to the user. This process may repeat dozens of times as the caller moves within the network.

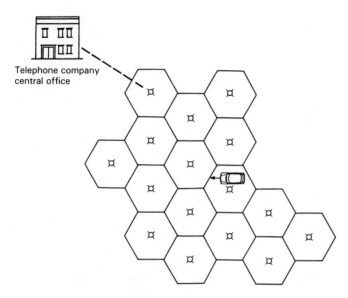

Telephone company
central office

¤   Low-power transmitter/receiver

— — —   Connection between cellular network and telephone company central office

Figure 16-2   Cellular telephone network. The service area for cellular telephone service is broken into small cells, each of which contains a low-power transmitter and receiver. As a vehicle moves within the service area, a computer constantly monitors the strength of its signal at nearby receivers and passes control of the call to the receiver with the strongest signal. Therefore, as the car in the figure moves from right to left, its signal is handed from one cell to the next, allowing the call to continue uninterrupted.

A cellular telephone user can place calls to any other telephone in the world just as you can from your office or residence phone. The cellular telephone company maintains connections to the local telephone company to allow access to the outside world. Most telephone markets have two cellular phone companies because the FCC granted two licenses for each market, one to a *wireline carrier* and one to a *nonwireline carrier*. The former is the local telephone operating company and the latter can be anybody else. Most cellular phone companies have agreements with cellular carriers in other areas to simplify accounting and billing if you use your cellular phone outside the local area and to allow calls to continue uninterrupted if the caller leaves one company's service area and enters another in the middle of a call.

Cellular telephones are a dramatic improvement over older radio telephones in the number of users that can be accommodated on the system at any one time. The older technology used fewer high-powered transmitters and receivers that covered large geographic areas. There was a fixed number of radio frequencies allocated by the FCC for mobile telephone use, so there was a fixed number of calls that could be handled at any one time within the entire large geographic area.

In most metropolitan areas, there were long waiting lists, of as much as several years, for people wanting to obtain radiophone licenses. And because the airwaves were crowded with people who already had licenses, it often took many minutes to be able to place a call. By dividing the service area into a larger number of cells with lower-powered transmitters, the same limited frequencies can be reused in any two nonadjacent cells, multiplying the number of active calls at any given moment dramatically. Except in the busiest cellular markets where demand has outstripped cell construction (for example, Los Angeles), cellular telephone users typically receive dial tone on demand, without waiting.

Data traffic. Voice traffic dominates cellular telephone usage today. Data communication over cellular telephone could be handled by conventional modems if the user stayed within one cell for the duration of the call. The real problem for a mobile data communication user occurs during cell handoff. If the handoff takes 1/10 second, which would be largely unnoticeable for a voice caller, some number of data bits will be obliterated. Consequently, several manufacturers of cellular modems have designed products that use additional buffering or other techniques to compensate for the potential data loss during cell handoff.

Cellular telephone service does have a small place in nonmobile applications. Emergency call boxes on the side of a highway or even on a city street may use cellular service when the cost of linking the boxes via either telephone wire or a private radio network is too high. In rural areas where houses are miles apart, it may be cheaper for the local telco to use cellular techniques rather than to string wire to each remote location.

FM Subcarrier Transmission

FM subcarrier transmission fills a niche in the local-loop market for simplex communication to subscribers. As the name suggests, *FM subcarrier* transmission makes use of a part of the frequency spectrum of existing FM radio signals to broadcast data to special receivers. The data are modulated onto a noninterfering subcarrier signal and broadcast along with the usual FM radio programming. The primary advantage of this technique is that the data provider does not need to build a transmission network; it merely needs to make arrangements with one or more FM radio stations and then provide the modulated signals that are added to the regular FM signal for transmission. Subscribers can either be stationary or mobile just as for FM radios.

Another advantage of FM subcarrier broadcasting is that adding new subscribers requires no new equipment or wiring. The service provider only needs to equip the new subscriber with the proper radio receiver. One disadvantage of this technology is that reception can be spotty within a given region. As you have noticed many times on your car radio, not every FM station can be received equally well in all areas. Buildings and interference from other nearby radio stations can also affect FM subcarrier reception.

One of the most common applications for FM subcarrier services is providing the electronic equivalent of the stock market ticker tape. The stock data supplier provides a special receiver to each customer. Whenever the radio receiver is on, all the stock data are received. Most devices of this type are programmable since most customers are interested in only a few or perhaps a few dozen individual stocks. The subscriber selects the issues of interest and the receiver records only these data, ignoring the thousands of other transactions that are broadcast. Many receivers can be programmed to alert the user if special events occur, for example, if the price of a stock is above or below a preselected threshold.

Other applications for FM subcarrier transmission include broadcast news services and pocket pagers. Improvements in the underlying technology that allow higher data rates to be transmitted over this medium will undoubtedly spur additional applications in the future. [LiCalzi] identifies several companies that provide FM subcarrier services.

ISDN

The *integrated services digital network*, or *ISDN*, is one of the most talked about communications subjects of the middle and late 1980s. The purpose behind ISDN is to provide every customer with a single, digital link that allows for fully integrated, simultaneous transmission of voice, data, video, or any other electronic signals, up to the maximum bandwidth of the provided link.

Current CCITT standards for ISDN define two channel types for the interface between the customer and the network. A *bearer channel*, or *B channel*, supplies 64 Kbps of bandwidth to the user and may be used for any combination of voice and data traffic that the customer desires. The *D channel* that is part of each interface carries network signaling information, such as dialing information when the ISDN user initiates a call. A portion of the D channel is also available to the subscriber to carry packet-switched data.

Basic Rate Interface

The ISDN *basic rate interface* (*BRI*) contains two B channels and one D channel (at 16 Kbps) in a configuration known as 2B+D, for a total capacity of 144 Kbps. A retail store served by a BRI, for example, might use one B channel for voice and the other to communicate between their PC and the computer at the headquarters location. They could also use the D channel to carry credit card authorization transactions in much the same way that stores dial into Telenet or Tymnet for that purpose today. All three of these functions occur simultaneously because the three channels are completely independent.

As a residential customer with a BRI, you could use the D channel to receive identification of the calling party so that you know who is calling (or at least where they are calling from) before you answer the phone. You might also use one of the B channels to have your PC order merchandise from a catalog, and then transfer money from your bank to your stock broker, while you use the other B channel to talk to your son at college. Meanwhile, on the D channel, the electric company could be reading your electric meter from their main office.

Primary Rate Interface

The *primary rate interface* (*PRI*) provides 24 digital channels in a 23B+D format, in which the D channel operates at 64 Kbps. Using the retail store example from the previous section, the chain's headquarters might be connected to the network using a PRI. They might allocate several B channels for voice traffic and use most of the remainder for 64 Kbps connections to each of their stores.

Because the bandwidth of an ISDN channel is under the control of the subscriber, the headquarters location may change the use of the B channels dynamically. At various times during the day, it may combine the capacity of several B channels to transfer orders directly to the computer of one of their suppliers at several hundred thousand bits per second, returning those channels to voice or other data applications when the transfer is complete. At night, it might use the consolidated bandwidth of all the B channels to accomplish bulk file transfer, at almost 1.5 Mbps, to another company location.

Benefits and Prospects

Part of the potential of ISDN results from having both B and D channels in simultaneous operation. Consider a customer service operation that uses their BRI interface to take the calling party information from the D channel, uses one B channel to read that person's account data from a database, and uses the second B channel to talk to the customer. At the instant that the telephone rings, the customer service agent already has the client's account information displayed on a terminal and can talk to the customer, all using a single network interface.

As of early 1988, field trials of ISDN are taking place in the United States and other parts of the world. One of the most widely publicized trials involves the headquarters of McDonald's Corporation and their local telephone company, Illinois Bell. Many communications and computer equipment vendors are testing their ISDN products as part of this and other field trials, and although the standards are not yet finalized, it appears that ISDN installations will become more prevalent from 1988 on.

For years, much of the communications industry has felt that ISDN was a solution in search of a problem, resulting in such tongue-in-cheek definitions of the acronym ISDN as "integration subscribers don't need" or "I sure don't know." The lure of ISDN is a single, integrated network accessible from a universally adopted interface on every communicating device. The hope is to eliminate multiple networks, the profusion of analog and digital circuits, and the proliferation of incompatible modems and interface devices that are required today for network connections.

Will ISDN deliver on that promise? The coming years will certainly tell. It is quite likely that ISDN will make significant inroads in reducing the clutter and variety described in the previous paragraph. The greatest impact will probably be in simplifying the local loop.

It seems unlikely that there will ever be one universal network, however. Many of the reasons that multiple public and private networks exist today will not go away with ISDN; competition, politics, economics, security, territorial imperatives — all these reasons suggest that there will always be multiple networks. Even if ISDN is successful at meeting customers' requirements for a simple, universal network interface, the result is still likely to be multiple, interconnected ISDN networks (both public and private), rather than one universal network.

R E C A P

- The local loop still consists largely of copper twisted pair, which offers limited bandwidth.

- Divestiture radically changed the structure of the telephone industry by separating AT&T from the local service providers.

- Reduced cost and/or increased bandwidth requirements usually drive customers to seek local-loop alternatives.

- Bypass may be used by a corporation to connect directly to its other facilities or to a long-distance carrier without going through the local telco.

- Bypass alternatives include such media as coax, fiber, microwave, satellite, and FM subcarrier.

- Cellular telephone service is a significant improvement over older radio telephones, and while the dominant use of cellular phones is for voice traffic, special modems allow use for data transmission.

- ISDN holds the promise for a single, all-digital network with a universal interface for all subscriber equipment; while the ISDN interface will become standard, it is more likely that there will continue to be multiple, interconnected networks.

LOCAL AREA NETWORKS

As this book is being completed in 1988, it looks as though the "Year of the LAN" may have finally arrived. The trade press has carried predictions of the "Year of the LAN" since the early 1980s, but the promise has failed to materialize until now.

For many of those years, the *local area network* (*LAN*) market was dominated by technologists who endlessly debated the merits of baseband versus broadband, CSMA/CD versus token ring access, and bus versus star or ring topology. Finally, however, the focus has shifted from the technology to the application for LANs.

The current application focus has not caused a significant increase in the number of LAN installations by itself. It has taken the maturing of LAN standards (albeit several standards not just one), the proliferation of PCs, and the availability of LAN software to finally make LANs a widespread phenomenon in the business world.

LAN APPLICATIONS

The primary functions of a LAN are to allow the sharing of resources and to facilitate communication within a work group. It makes more sense to share relatively expensive facilities such as laser printers, application programs, communication lines to other computers, and large-capacity disk drives among multiple users rather than to provide one to each user for his or her dedicated use. A LAN also enhances communication by allowing electronic mail, document and spreadsheet transfer, and other intragroup exchanges. Local area networks are especially effective in fulfilling these functions because they offer significant bandwidth and total connectivity; that is, every device on the network can access every other device directly.

The selection of products to provide shared resources and facilitate work group communications should not require detailed investigation of the underlying technologies. Instead, you should be able to apply a collection of products from multiple vendors to fit your particular needs. While it is more possible today than it was even two or three years ago to take that approach, the LAN market is not yet at that point. Consequently, a brief description of LAN technologies is presented next.

LAN CHARACTERISTICS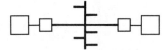

Baseband or Broadband

Local area networks are usually classified as either baseband or broadband. *Baseband* networks place a digital signal directly onto the transmission medium, using the entire bandwidth of the medium, which suggests that there can be only one data signal on the network at any given instant. To compensate for using the entire bandwidth for each transmission, data are usually sent in very short bursts. In this manner, multiple devices may share the network, but no two devices can use the network at exactly the same instant. Baseband networks can support hundreds or even thousands of devices with an aggregate data transmission rate in the millions of bits per second.

The maximum length of a baseband network is usually limited by the distance that a signal can travel before it becomes unusably weak. Additional devices can usually be added to a baseband network by tapping into the cable very simply and inexpensively. Baseband nets do not usually contain digital repeaters, but individual LAN segments can be joined together with repeaters. **Figure 17-1** contains a typical baseband configuration that is much like an Ethernet LAN.

Broadband networks employ radio-frequency modems and frequency-division multiplexing to split the overall network bandwidth into multiple channels. Each channel is entirely independent of all other channels, and all channels may be in use at any given moment without interference. Broadband networks have tremendous flexibility to allow multiple, simultaneous services. A typical broadband net may be carrying several dozen 9600-bps data channels, multiple 64-Kbps circuits, several T-1 links, several video channels, and numerous low-speed data links. Other multiplexing techniques may be combined with FDM to further subdivide the capacity of a broadband network. For example,

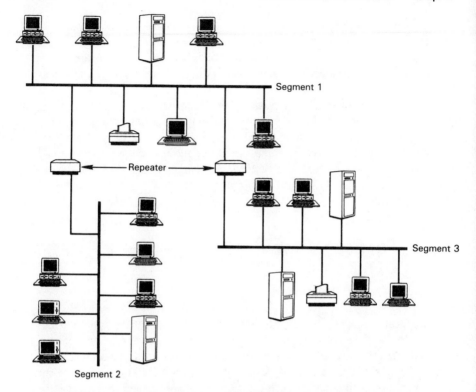

Figure 17-1 Typical baseband network configuration. This network has several base-band segments that are connected with repeaters to form one larger network.

one or more of the FDM channels may use TDM to allow multiple, lower-speed devices to share one channel. Refer to Chapter 14 for a description of multiplexing techniques.

Broadband networks use amplifiers to boost signal strength as necessary, and there is really no limit on the maximum size or number of users for a broadband network. The location of each amplifier, tap (the point at which the user connects a device to the network), and other hardware components is fairly critical, so broadband networks require that a specific network design be performed to ensure that all signals will be propagated correctly. Vendors of broadband LANs can usually perform site-specific network designs, but they may also offer predesigned kits from which users can assemble their own networks.

Adding new devices to a broadband network is very simple if taps are available near the desired location. However, some redesign of the network to compensate for the additional signal loss through the new taps may be necessary if no taps are available. Consequently, advance planning is extremely important

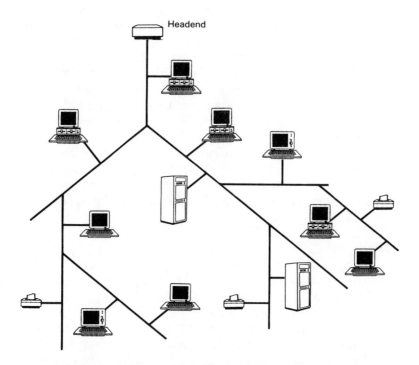

Figure 17-2 **Typical broadband network configuration.** Broadband networks contain a headend that loops all incoming signals back out to the network devices. Dual-cable broadband networks use one cable for all communications toward the headend and a separate cable for communications in the opposite direction. Single-cable systems use one portion of the bandwidth for signals moving to the headend and the remainder of the bandwidth for signals flowing outward.

for users of broadband LANs. Refer to **Figure 17-2** for an example of a broadband network.

A cable TV network is a broadband network. Multiple television channels are "stacked" onto the cable using FDM. Each cable subscriber uses his or her television set or VCR to select one channel at any given time, but all channels are available simultaneously.

Transmission Media

Coax cable is commonly used for LANs due to its low cost and large bandwidth. Coax can be used for either baseband or broadband transmission (although each typically uses a different type of coax) and is easy to install and maintain. Many of the components needed for coax cable installations are available off the shelf from cable television component suppliers.

Fiber-optic cable is used for LAN installations, especially where its extremely high bandwidth and excellent security properties are important. It is not appropriate for a highly changeable environment in which device movements are frequent because it cannot be spliced or tapped easily.

Twisted pair has always been a very desirable medium because it is so plentiful in office environments, because it is so easy to string and splice, and because it is the least expensive of all potential LAN media. It has the drawback of being very susceptible to crosstalk and interference problems and therefore has been better suited to relatively low speed applications. It has gained more prominence in the last few years as vendors have improved the ability of their products to deal with these problems. Twisted pair is likely to play an increasingly dominant role as data rates increase; several vendors have announced support for 10-Mbps transmission on twisted pair, providing exceptional speeds on a very low cost medium.

Topology

The *topology* of a network is the view of the network that you would have if you looked down on it from above.

Bus topology networks are configured with a central cable, or bus, to which each device is attached individually. **Figure 17-3a** shows a typical bus topology. Depending on the particular network, a failure at any one point in the network may not disrupt the entire network; it may be possible for one or both halves of the network to continue to operate until the problem is repaired. Traffic on the bus is bidirectional so that any device may talk to any other device.

A *branching tree topology* is a variation of the bus topology in which there is a *headend* from which some number of branches radiate out as shown in **Figure 17-3b**. Any two devices may communicate, regardless of where they are located, but all traffic proceeds from the transmitting device to the headend on one path and travels from the headend to the receiving device on another path. The two paths may be formed by using two separate but parallel cables on each branch, creating a *dual-cable network*. Alternatively, the two paths may be implemented on a *single-cable network* by using a frequency-shifting device at the headend. For this second implementation, all traffic moving toward the headend uses one range of frequencies; then the headend shifts all incoming traffic to another range of frequencies for the outbound trip.

Single- and dual-cable networks are functionally equivalent; however, the dual-cable approach provides the entire bandwidth of the cable in each direction, whereas the single-cable method can provide only a portion of the bandwidth in each direction.

Failure of the headend in a branching tree network is usually fatal to the network unless a spare headend can be switched into place. Most other failures may isolate one portion of the network but should not necessarily affect the network as a whole.

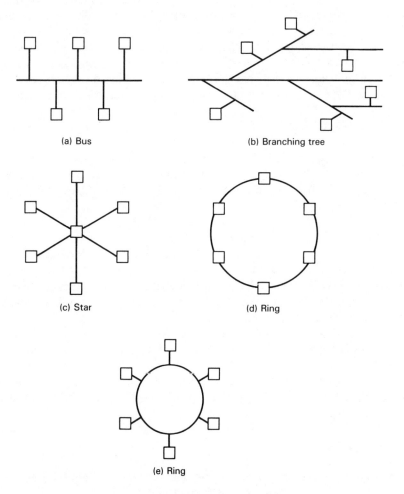

(a) Bus

(b) Branching tree

(c) Star

(d) Ring

(e) Ring

Figure 17-3   Common LAN topologies.

A *star topology* uses a central controller device as the hub of the network; all devices are wired directly back to the hub, and all communication between devices passes through the hub. While it can be used with any transmission medium, this design is particularly well suited to twisted-pair wiring because most building wiring runs from desktops back to central wiring closets. Implementation of a star topology could be as simple as installing the controller in a wiring closet and connecting the appropriate twisted pairs to the hub and to the user devices. **Figure 17-3c** shows a star topology network.

Failure of any one device or link in a star network usually only disrupts service to that end device. The one obvious exception is the controller at the hub of the network; failure there means that the entire network is down.

A *ring topology* connects all computer devices to each other in a circular fashion, and communication around the ring usually flows in only one direction. The ring may look like either **Figure 17-3d** or **17-3e**. Both designs provide the same communication functions, but **Figure 17-3e** isolates each device so that the network as a whole can still function if one device should die. Failure of one of the computers in **Figure 17-3d** would be fatal to the network since each device must actively pass the received signals on around the ring.

Access Methods

When all computer devices share a common medium, as is the case with a local area network, there must be a means to arbitrate and control access to the network. The two most common access methods are CSMA/CD and token passing.

CSMA/CD. *Carrier sense multiple access with collision detection (CSMA/CD)* is the formal name for an access method that can be described as "listen before talking, listen while talking." Essentially, each device on the cable is allowed to transmit whenever it has data to send after checking to see that the channel is not already in use ("carrier sense") by another of the other devices on the network ("multiple access").

The sending device must listen to its own transmissions on the channel in order to know whether there has been a conflict with another transmitter ("collision detection"). If a collision is detected, each transmitter stops immediately, waits a random amount of time, and checks for carrier again before starting over. The random time interval prevents the two devices from waiting the same amount of time, only to collide again.

Figure 17-4 illustrates the actions leading up to and following a collision between the signals from two devices.

At time (a)	System A begins to transmit because it does not sense a carrier at its location on the channel.
At time (b)	System B begins to transmit because it does not sense a carrier at its location on the channel.
At time (c)	System B, which is monitoring the channel (as required), senses a collision of its transmission with something else so it stops transmitting; meanwhile system A continues to transmit because it has not detected a problem, since system B's signal has not yet arrived.
At time (d)	System A detects a collision and stops transmitting.
At time (e)	Both systems are quiet and are waiting a random number of milliseconds before trying to transmit again.

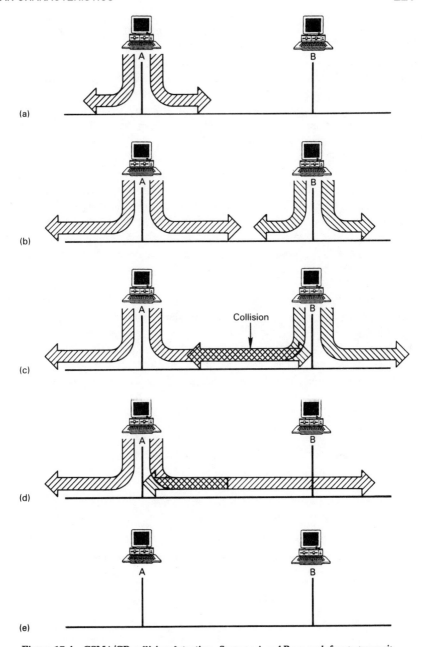

(a)

(b)

Collision

(c)

(d)

(e)

Figure 17-4   CSMA/CD collision detection. Systems A and B are each free to transmit whenever they have data to send and there is no carrier present at their location on the network.   Upon detecting a collision, as shown in *parts c* and *d,* each system stops transmitting, waits a random amount of time, and then attempts to retransmit.

Do not draw the conclusion from this diagram that collisions are a frequent occurrence on CSMA/CD LANs. They are usually quite rare because of the combination of three factors: the propagation speed of electrical signals is so fast, most LAN cables are very short, and traffic is very bursty and most devices are not transmitting a considerable percentage of the time. As a result, the time interval between when one device begins to transmit on an idle channel and the point when that signal has reached every other device is short, probably only microseconds or a few milliseconds.

CSMA/CD is well suited for traffic that occurs in bursts, such as interactive terminal sessions and small-quantity data transfers such as electronic mail delivery. Bulk file transfers could cause some performance degradation, since one station could easily dominate the network by always having additional data queued to send and therefore always seizing the network when carrier is not present. CSMA/CD is not as well suited to time-critical applications, such as a process control network in factory, where each device must have frequent and predictable access to the network.

Token passing. *Token passing* controls multiple device access to the shared LAN medium by means of a special bit pattern called a *token*. The token is circulated among the network devices, and a device may only transmit if it currently "owns" the token. Although it can be implemented on any network topology, token passing is most frequently implemented on a ring topology, hence the term *token ring*. **Figure 17-5** shows the motion of the token around a ring network.

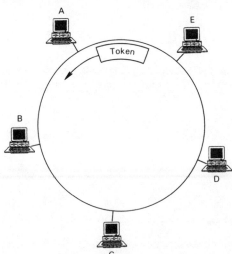

Figure 17-5   **Token passing on a ring network topology.** A special bit pattern, called the token, is passed around the ring. A device on the network may only transmit if it has possession of the token, thereby eliminating data collisions on the network.

When computer A receives the token, it has the option to pass it along immediately if it has no data to transmit, or it may mark the token as "in use" and then transmit its data. When the transmitted data are received back at the sending station (after making one round trip of the network), the token owner marks the token as "available" and sends it to the next station on the ring.

Because of the necessity to keep the token moving, special care must be taken to ensure that the token does not get damaged or lost. If, for example, station C receives the token but suffers a systems failure before it can retransmit it, the token will be lost. Generally, this type of problem is handled by having one or more control stations on the network whose job it is to constantly monitor the passing of the token. If the token does not arrive within a predefined maximum time period, the control station generates a new one.

One advantage of the token passing access method is the predictability of the arrival of the token. The maximum possible round-trip time before a station will next get the token is the sum of times that it would take for each station to accept the token, transmit one maximum-length message, and then forward the token to the next station. And unless every station has a message to transmit each time it receives the token, the actual round-trip time will be less than this maximum. When most stations are idle, the round-trip time will be extremely small.

The predictability of token passing makes it valuable in a network environment where predictability is important and where it is undesirable for one very busy station to dominate the network. By contrast, token passing is less desirable in a network in which several stations are generating bursts of traffic, but where there are many others that are quiet most of the time. In this situation, the overhead of passing the token to dozens of quiet stations before giving the busy stations another opportunity to transmit may result in reduced efficiency for the busy devices.

Another potential problem for token passing is the failure of any one station on the network. In a CSMA/CD network, a single station dropping off the net would not affect the operation of the network. However, a dropped station in a token ring environment would prevent it from receiving and passing the token. The usual solution is to build in some sort of bypass mechanism so that a missing station is ignored.

BRIDGES, ROUTERS, AND GATEWAYS

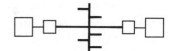

Bridges

Bridges are used to interconnect homogeneous networks at the data link layer. A bridge has very little protocol knowledge and does little more than shunt traffic from network A to network B when the link level destination address in a frame is not for a local device. Note that this implies that the bridge maintains a list of systems on its network or that the bridge is smart enough to construct its own list.

One procedure for building a dynamic list makes use of an extra flag in the data link frame header that has the meaning of "off network." This flag is set to FALSE by any sending station on a LAN, thereby indicating to receivers on the same network, including the bridge, that this is local traffic. The bridge begins building its list of local systems by storing the sending address of each frame it receives that has the off-network bit set to FALSE.

Whenever the bridge forwards a frame to another network, it sets the off-network flag to TRUE. The bridge determines whether to forward a frame to another network by using the following rules:

1. For frames received with off network set to FALSE (that is, locally generated traffic):
   a. If destination address is on the list for local network, do nothing.
   b. If destination address is not on the list for local network, forward the frame to the other network and set the off-network flag to TRUE.
2. For frames received with off network set to TRUE (that is, they were forwarded from another network):
   a. Do nothing. If the addressed station is alive and on this net, it will receive the frame; otherwise, the frame will be ignored.

Note that some frames will be forwarded through the bridge in error. In particular, if a frame has a destination address of a station that has not yet transmitted and whose address, therefore, is not on the local bridge list, the frame will be sent to the adjacent network. As you can see from case 2, this will cause no harm on the adjacent network as the frame will be ignored, because there is no receiver with a matching address.

Routers

A *router* connects dissimilar networks at the network layer by performing appropriate protocol conversions and routing of packets. An 802.3 to Token Ring router, for example, would be programmed to understand the format and protocol rules for both network types and would perform all necessary conversions before forwarding data from one network to another.

Gateways

A *gateway* connects two dissimilar networks at the application layer. It performs conversions between two different applications and uses the underlying protocol stacks for delivery. For example, a Wang OFFICE® to DEC All-in-One®gateway would take messages created by a user of the Wang system and convert them to the correct format for the Digital product. After converting the addressing information, the gateway software would pass the message to the DEC software.

LOCAL AREA NETWORK STANDARDS

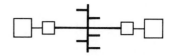

Most of the standards activity for local areas networks has centered around the IEEE 802 committee, which was described in Chapter 9. As an increasing number of standards-compatible products are delivered to the market, customers can buy with greater assurance that products from multiple vendors will interoperate. Eliminating or decreasing fears of buying incompatible products has prompted much of the surge in market demand for LAN products.

To date, the standard that has had the most significant impact on the market is the IEEE 802.3 recommendation, which is based on Ethernet but is not a 100% copy of the Ethernet specification. A significant number of products available today conform to this recommendation and offer a high degree of vendor independence and interoperability at the lower layers covered by the 802.3 specification. The next most significant market impact comes from the 802.5 recommendation, which was heavily influenced by IBM's Token Ring Network protocols and design. There are a large and increasing number of 802.5 products on the market.

RECAP

- LANs should be evaluated based on the application solutions they provide, and not necessarily on their underlying technology.
- LAN characteristics include baseband/broadband, topology, access method, and media type.
- Bridges interconnect homogeneous LANs at the link layer.
- Routers interconnect heterogeneous LANs at the network layer.
- Gateways interconnect heterogeneous networks at the application layer.
- LAN standards are having a significant, positive impact on the LAN market as more and more standards-compliant products are produced.

PRIVATE BRANCH EXCHANGES

A *private branch exchange* (*PBX*) provides some of the functions of the telephone network on a smaller scale and is usually used for communications within a single company. A PBX allows the user to dial the extension of someone else within the company or to select an outside line to dial an external phone number. PBXs also provide a variety of additional features, such as call forwarding, speed dialing, conference calling, and least-cost routing for outgoing calls.

Many PBXs are used within a single location, for example, within a single building or for just one company's communications within one building. Many PBXs can also be networked together to provide communications among multiple facilities over a wide geographic area.

The vast majority of the traffic handled by most PBXs consists of voice telephone calls. Many PBXs are capable of carrying data traffic also, and, for this book, we are more interested in the movement of data through a PBX within a local area. This chapter includes a comparison of a PBX and a local area network for local area data transportation.

PBX TYPES

Analog PBXs

Early PBXs were designed for analog voice traffic and cannot handle digital communications directly. Connecting a computer or terminal to an analog PBX

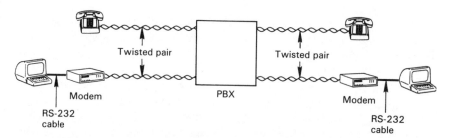

Figure 18-1   Analog PBX used for local data traffic. An analog PBX can transmit data after the digital signals have been converted to analog format.

requires a modem and a separate telephone port on the PBX, resulting in the configuration shown in **Figure 18-1**.

Data over voice (*DOV*) devices, available from PBX vendors and from third parties, make it possible for a telephone set and a computer device to share a pair of wires. The DOV converter modulates the digital signal onto a carrier that is at a frequency above the 4000-Hz voice channel (hence the term data *over* voice). Since the switch itself is only designed to handle signals in the range of 0 to 4000 Hz, the higher-frequency data signal must be stripped off before the signal actually enters the switch, leading to a configuration like the one shown in **Figure 18-2**. Data over voice arrangements do allow a pair of wires to be shared for both voice and data, but they do not really allow the data caller to take advantage of any of the features of the PBX.

Digital PBXs

Newer generation PBXs use digital rather than analog switching. Digital switching offers many advantages over the older analog technology, including the ability for virtually all switch operations to be controlled by software,

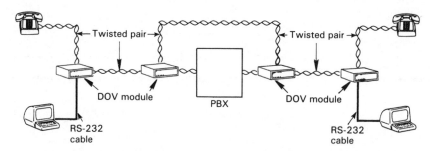

Figure 18-2   Data over voice. The data over voice (DOV) module places the data signal onto the same twisted pair as the voice signal by modulating it onto a carrier frequency that is above the 4000-Hz channel used for the voice traffic. Because the PBX in this example cannot handle the additional frequencies used for the data signal, the data must be stripped off and passed around the PBX before being placed back onto another twisted pair for delivery to the other computer device.

providing considerable flexibility over hardware-controlled designs. The use of digital switching also makes it easier for a PBX to handle data traffic, because all bit streams are essentially the same regardless of whether they originated as voice traffic or data traffic.

Analog phone signals must be converted into digital form in order to be processed by a digital switch. This is accomplished with a *coder-decoder* (*codec*), which is either located in an interface card in the PBX, which means that analog signals still travel along the twisted pair between the telephone instrument and the PBX, or in the telephone set itself. Newer digital switches tend to use digital telephone sets, in part due to increased availability and lower costs of codecs, so that all communication between the PBX and any device to which it is connected is in digital form.

All-digital communication is good news for data communicators because it offers considerably more flexibility in connecting devices to the PBX; there is no question about whether a particular port on the PBX is analog or digital since they are all digital. It also allows devices to share a pair of wires and a port more easily, since time-division multiplexing of bit streams is very simple to implement in telephone set hardware. Many of the digital telephone sets on the market have a built-in RS-232 connnector to facilitate connection of computer devices to the PBX, as shown in **Figure 18-3**.

Data Switches

In addition to PBXs, there is another similar category of device that is usually called a *data switch*. Data switches are not designed to handle voice traffic but are intended to provide extremely flexible connections between any computer devices to which they are attached. A data switch may be used to

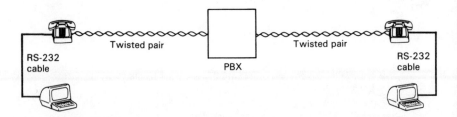

Figure 18-3   Data and voice carried by digital PBX. The RS-232 cable from the computer either plugs into an RS-232 port on the telephone handset or into a small data module that typically sits under the handset. No special equipment is needed at the PBX since it is designed to carry both digitized voice and data signals over the same twisted pair.

connect terminals to ports on a host computer, to connect microcomputers to each other or to host computers, to connect minicomputers to laser printers; the idea is to allow complete flexibility. Data switches typically have maximum speed limitations per port of 56 to 64 Kbps.

The decision to use a dedicated data switch or a digital PBX may have some technical components, such as the maximum number of ports, the maximum data rates, or protocol restrictions, but the decision criteria may very well be nontechnical. For example, if the data center manager in a large company needs device switching capability but there is little cooperation between her department and the internal telecommunications department, the decision to use a data switch instead of the corporate PBX may be a simple one.

If, on the other hand, the chief information officer for a company looks at both sets of requirements and controls the budgets for both MIS and corporate telecommunications, a digital PBX with the proper features may be the best answer.

PBX versus LAN for Local Data Transmission

Another great debate for many companies is whether to use a digital PBX with data capability or a local area network to handle data transmission within the office. Obviously, there is no absolute answer to this question, but the summary in **Figure 18-4** of the characteristics of both devices may provide some assistance in evaluating any given situation.

As capabilities of digital PBXs and LANs continue to converge, the decision will probably come down to wiring costs and data rates. The former generally favors a PBX, and the latter favors a LAN. Even this distinction will blur, however, as LAN products provide megabit data rates over existing twisted pair (and therefore at low cost) and as PBXs offer megabit per second data rates for data communication.

Consideration	LAN	PBX
Connectivity	Any to any	Any to any
Bandwidth/data rate	Up to many Mbps	Up to 56 or 64 Kbps
Asynchronous devices	Yes	Yes
Synchronous devices	Yes	Yes
Gateway functions	Maybe	Maybe
Use of existing wiring	Probably not	Probably

Figure 18-4   Comparison of PBX versus LAN for local data distribution. This figure lists some of the considerations when deciding between a LAN and a PBX for local data distribution.

CENTREX

As telephone users began to install PBXs instead of individual telephone lines for each telephone instrument, the telcos saw the potential loss of revenue as a significant threat. Studies have shown that as much as 70% of all business telephone calls are to another person at the same company location. Consequently, each PBX means that a significant portion of the calls originated during the business day never make it outside the PBX. In addition, the PBX reduces the number of outside lines required, because it can allocate calls to a pool of available lines rather than needing an outside line to every desk.

Local telephone companies have competed with PBXs for years with central office based services generically called centrex. For companies that do not want the responsibility of having a PBX on site or for companies that cannot cost-justify a PBX, centrex is a way to have the equivalent of an off-site PBX that is administered by someone else for a monthly service fee.

As digital PBXs have become increasingly sophisticated, some industry analysts have predicted the demise of centrex services. Divestiture added more weight to that argument as many observers predicted that the former Bell operating companies would not be able to compete effectively in the PBX market.

The years since divestiture have shown the operating companies to be capable of competing after all, with new features and services leading the push to retain existing customers and attract new ones. Many centrex offerings now supply the same range of advanced voice and data features offered by PBX vendors, including fully digital operation in some locations. Several centrex offerings even include central office LAN, or COLAN, services, whereby users can have the functional equivalent of a local area network over the telco twisted-pair wiring in their building.

R E C A P

- PBXs switch calls between devices connected to the PBX and provide access to outside communication lines.
- PBXs were initially designed to handle voice calls, but most modern PBXs can handle data calls also.
- Data switches are designed to make connections between data communication devices.
- For local data traffic, the twisted-pair wire used by a PBX may be cheaper than installing special LAN cable, but most LANs can support much higher data rates than PBXs.
- Centrex services provide the capabilities of a PBX from a telco central office.

19

NETWORK MANAGEMENT

The traditional view of network management focused on managing the links in the network. The most important activities included diagnosis, isolation, and restoral of service on those links, using a collection of tools that will be described later in this chapter.

The contemporary view of network management focuses on the entire network, including both the links and the systems, and tends to look at the network as a major corporate asset. Network management has become a key topic in the communications industry and is a critical issue to senior corporate managers for the following reasons:

- Networks are more important than ever to daily business operations; most network outages are nearly intolerable when the business of the corporation depends on the information flowing through the network.
- Networks are larger and more complex, making the task of management more complex.
- The divestiture of AT&T eliminated "the telephone company" as a source of assistance; no single provider can be responsible for an entire long-distance circuit, let alone for an entire network, leaving a greater percentage of the management responsibility on the shoulders of the user.
- Multivendor networks are the rule not the exception, and there are dozens of vendors of computer and communications equipment.
- Most network equipment vendors offer their own version of a network management solution, and few of the management systems are compatible with each other.

INTEGRATED NETWORK MANAGEMENT SYSTEMS

The last point above highlights the most significant problem and opportunity in the last few years: the integration of separate network management products into a unified system. The reality is that no vendor offers all the software and hardware required to completely manage a communication network in today's world. As a result, most network users are left with little choice but to maintain multiple management systems side by side.

Is there any hope for the people who are forced to run networks with multiple, incompatible management systems? The solution is similar to the emerging solutions discussed in Chapter 5 regarding incompatible vendor network architectures; there will be international standards and there will be vendor-provided de facto standards.

International Standards

Addendum 4 to the OSI reference model, called the OSI Management Framework [ISO 7498/4], is a broad outline for management in an OSI environment. It defines five sets of management facilities, called *Specific Management Functional Areas* (*SMFAs*), that are needed.

1. *Configuration and name management* includes setting and storing system parameters, collecting and storing status information, initializing and closing down managed objects, and associating names with network addresses.

2. *Fault management* includes facilities to detect, isolate, and resolve failures in the network.

3. *Accounting management* provides for the collection of data that can be used to allocate costs and control the use of network resources based on preset limits.

4. *Performance management* gives the network manager both real-time and historical data on various elements in the network.

5. *Security management* provides authentication and access control for network resources and management facilities.

OSI management standards, when they are completed in the early 1990s, will provide a means for vendors to build network management products that can share information and improve the possibility of an overall, integrated network management system.

For all the good they will do, however, OSI management standards are not the total solution to the daily needs of network managers. The OSI Management

Framework only addresses those portions of an open system that are involved in communications with another open system. It does not address issues of local system management, such as software distribution, disk space management, or control and allocation of buffer space in memory, and yet management of these items and others is essential to the overall management of the network. In addition, OSI management standards do not deal with the management of non-OSI resources and protocols. Consequently, those portions of a network that employ SNA or another vendor's network architecture will be outside the scope of OSI management.

Nonetheless, OSI management will provide the basis for a significant percentage of the vendor network management products that are brought to the market in the 1990s. The standards will also evolve to include a greater percentage of the real-world requirements of network managers, further increasing their usefulness.

Vendor Solutions

The dominant vendor offering is the family of NetView® products from IBM. Introduced in May 1986, the first release of NetView was IBM's attempt to organize its then current network management products into a coherent framework, with a common user interface and consistent use of color and graphics among the products. Subsequent announcements in 1986 and 1987 broadened the scope of NetView, most significantly by the inclusion of support for management of non-SNA devices, including processors on the IBM Token Ring, PBXs, T-1 multiplexers, and network equipment from other vendors.

Network management integration is enabled by a product called NetView/PC®in which a PC acts as a gateway between the non-SNA device (or a network of non-SNA devices) and NetView on the mainframe. IBM has published the specifications for the NetView/PC interface so that other vendors may transmit alert messages and status information in a format acceptable to NetView on the host. See **Figure 19-1** for a sample NetView and NetView/PC configuration.

NetView/PC centralizes the presentation of alert messages and status information from multiple vendors' products onto the mainframe. Depending upon the software provided by the other vendors or by IBM, it may also be possible to send commands to the remote, non-IBM equipment from the NetView console on the mainframe. In many cases, however, the flow of information will be primarily one way; that is, alarms and status will flow to the mainframe, but the other vendor's management console will still be needed to issue commands to its own equipment.

NetView has achieved widespread, though not universal, acceptance among network equipment vendors because of IBM's dominant position in the computer and communications market. Several dozen equipment vendors have announced

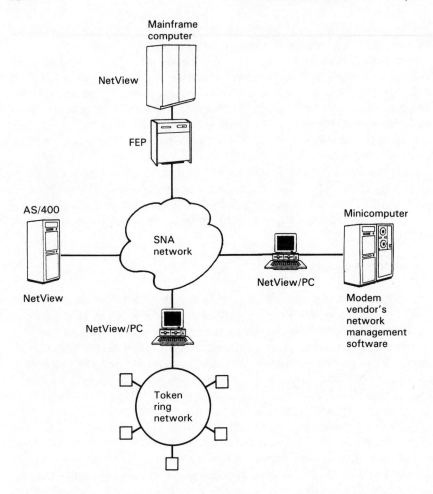

Figure 19-1 Network management using NetView. This figure illustrates a possible network configuration using NetView software to manage a network.

NetView-compatible products or plans for such; many others are thinking seriously about including NetView compatibility in their network management strategy.

NetView and OSI Management

Will NetView become the dominant vendor-sponsored management architecture? Most likely. Will it predominate over international network management standards? Not likely. The strongest possibility seems to be that

NetView and OSI management standards will follow much the same course as the SNA and OSI communications protocols.

The two protocol sets have taken parallel yet somewhat convergent paths in the last 10 years. They are more similar today than yesterday, and will be more similar tomorrow, but both will continue to exist for a long time. The same will be true of NetView and OSI management. They will become more similar in the coming years, but will remain distinct.

NETWORK MANAGEMENT TOOLS

The traditional tools of network management include breakout boxes, line monitors, patch panels, matrix switches, modem vendor network management systems, and DTE software. Each of these tools is described briefly next.

Breakout Boxes

A *breakout box* is a small device that can be inserted between the DTE and DCE on an RS-232 link to monitor the status of some or all of the 25 leads on the interface. The box consists of two DB25 connectors, an array of LEDs, a row of small switches, two metal contact points for each RS-232 lead (one on the DTE side and one on the DCE side of the box), and a supply of short wires that fit over the metal contact points. **Figure 19-2** shows a typical breakout box and its location on a circuit.

The LEDs show the on or off state of each lead. To reduce the cost of the box, there is usually not an LED for each RS-232 wire, but merely one for each of the major pins on the interface. A typical breakout box has an LED for each of the signals listed in Figure 10-5a or 10-5b.

The row of switches on the breakout box allows you to interrupt any of the signals on the interface for troubleshooting purposes. Similarly, the rows of test points and the jumper wires allow you to change the condition of any of the interface leads. As an example, if your terminal is not transmitting and you connect a breakout box and notice that the modem never turns DSR on, you could put a jumper wire from DTR (assuming that it is on) across to DSR, forcing that signal on. If the link then works correctly, you have isolated the problem to an incorrectly configured or faulty modem and can rectify the problem.

You might also use a breakout box if you are connecting a PC to a printer and you do not know which signals are used by the PC and which are used

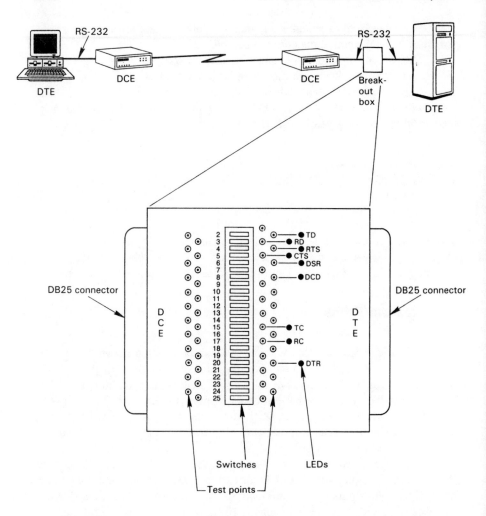

Figure 19-2   Breakout box. A breakout box is used to examine and possibly modify the state of the control signals on an RS-232 interface.

by the printer. A breakout box can show you which pins are active on each device, so you can use the switches and jumper wires to complete the correct circuits.

Keep in mind that a breakout box shows you the status of each lead and not the actual data. You will see the LED flash on and off rapidly as the zeros and ones representing the data move across TD and RD, but the box does not provide any interpretation or translation of those flashes. To see the actual data, you must use a line monitor.

[Held2] describes breakout boxes in detail and discusses their application in troubleshooting network problems.

Line Monitors

A *line monitor*, or *datascope*, allows you to view the data moving across the TD and RD wires between a DTE and a DCE. You place a datascope on the RS-232 interface in the same manner as a breakout box, but the datascope has appropriate hardware and software to display the actual data bits on the line.

Most line monitors can display the TD and RD data in uninterpreted form, that is, they show you the actual ones and zeros directly; or the monitor can convert the bits into ASCII, EBCDIC, or other character sets. Most datascopes also provide protocol interpretation. On an HDLC link, for instance, you can instruct the scope to show you the frame types and contents so that you are not required to interpret the data manually. On an X.25 link, you can see the frames at the data link layer or the packets at the network layer, much like Figures 15-15 and 15-16 in this book.

A datascope consists of a processing unit, a display screen, a keyboard, and some amount of memory (see **Figure 19-3**). A few datascopes feature only internal memory, but most also contain external storage such as a cassette or diskette drive. A few years ago all datascopes were specialized pieces of hardware, but the widespread availability of the PC has changed that. You can buy add-in boards and software that enable a PC to serve as a line monitor, eliminating the need to purchase specialized test equipment.

The cassette or diskette in a monitor allows you to record line activity when data transmission rates are too fast for real-time analysis. Any data rate above a few hundred bits per second cannot be viewed in real time. External storage also allows you to send the recorded data stream somewhere else for analysis. For example, when a communication problem occurs at a remote location, you could instruct the remote site personnel to install and activate a line monitor to capture the problem. They can then forward the tape or disk to you for analysis.

Datascopes contain numerous other features, such as the following:

- Traps and filters that display or capture only the portions of the data stream that meet criteria that you define
- Counters to record statistics such as the number of frames, packets, or errors on a link
- The ability to simulate the operation of either the DTE or DCE for testing an RS-232 interface

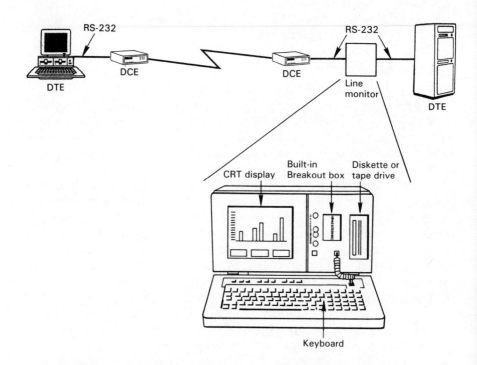

Figure 19-3 Line monitor. A line monitor is used to examine the data and protocol information on the transmit data and receive data leads of the RS-232 interface.

- A built-in breakout box
- Color graphics to show the state of the RS-232 leads or to display statistics in graphic form

This is by no means an exhaustive list of line monitor features, since active competition brings new products and features to the market regularly.

The main application for a datascope is analyzing protocol failures on a line. If a polled terminal appears to be out of service, for example, a datascope lets you examine the traffic on the line to ensure that poll messages are being sent out from the master device. A computer vendor would use a line monitor to test a new X.25 protocol implementation, for example, before actually connecting to a network.

Line monitors also exist for LANs, T-1 links, and other non-RS-232 connections. Although these devices contain features specific to the interface and protocol used on non-RS-232 connections, their basic purpose and feature set are the same as described above.

Patch Panels

Patch panels are a simple means of changing the connections between DTEs and DCEs without connecting and disconnecting RS-232 cables. A typical patch panel may have dozens or hundreds of on-line devices connected to it, along with a bank of spare modems. In this way, if a modem or port should fail, a spare can be connected to the DTE in seconds.

A *patch panel* consists of one or more rows of connectors similar to the ones depicted in **Figure 19-4**. Each vertical column is connected to a DTE and a DCE on the back; the front contains sockets for patch cords that can connect to either the DTE or the DCE. There is also a third socket on the bottom of the column for connection of a line monitor between the DTE and DCE. Many patch panels also contain LEDs at the top of each column to provide a visual indication of the state of the key RS-232 leads.

When no patch cord is connected, as in **Figure 19-4a**, the DTE and DCE in each column are connected to each other. When a patch cord is inserted, it breaks the default connection and allows any DTE on the panel to be connected

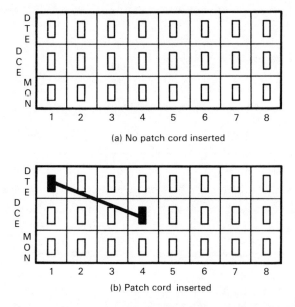

(a) No patch cord inserted

(b) Patch cord inserted

Figure 19-4   **Patch panel.** The patch cord in *part b* is used to connect DTE 1 to DCE 4. When a patch cord is not present, as in *part a*, the DTE and DCE in any given column are connected to each other. The third row on the patch panel, labeled MON, can be used to insert a line monitor between the DTE and DCE without physically breaking the RS-232 connection.

to any DCE, as shown in **Figure 19-4b**, where DTE 1 is now connected to DCE 4. The other devices in those columns, DCE 1 and DTE 4, are not connected to anything unless another patch cord is used to link them to some other device.

Matrix Switches

In simplest terms, a *matrix switch* is a computerized patch panel. The interface cables from the various computer ports, modems, and line monitors are connected to the switch as in the case of a patch panel, but there is no front panel. All interconnections are made electronically using a terminal to issue commands to the switch.

One major advantage of a matrix switch over a patch panel is that multiple connections can be made at one time. If, for example, a front-end processor on a mainframe should fail, one command to the matrix switch could cause several dozen communications lines to be switched to a backup FEP. With a patch panel, this same operation would require an operator to insert dozens of patch cords to yield the same result.

Some switch vendors use the computer in the switch to provide additional, nonswitching features, such as inventory control programs or other administrative support services.

Modem Management Systems

Modems and multiplexers are involved with network management in several ways. Many vendors offer modems with some or all of the following:

- Loopback features that assist in isolating line problems
- Status monitoring and statistics collection with reporting back to a computer at a central site
- Reconfiguration of remote modem parameters from a central site
- Administrative support software for such activities as problem management, change management, and inventory management

Modem loopback. *Loopback testing* is an important technique for successively testing portions of two DCEs and the phone line between them in order to prove the success or failure of each component on the path. **Figure 19-5** illustrates four types of modem-generated loopback tests. Loop 1 tests only the digital circuitry in the near-end modem by looping the incoming digital signal from the DTE back through the digital circuitry on the receive side of the modem for comparison. An exact match constitutes a successful test.

Loop 2 tests both the digital and analog circuitry in the near-end modem. It performs the digital-to-analog conversion on the transmit side of the modem and then loops the analog signal back to the receiver in the modem. After converting back to digital form, the original and resultant signals are compared. Loop 3 adds both the phone line and the analog circuitry in the remote modem to the test loop. Loop 4 includes the remote modem digital circuitry in the test.

As you can see in **Figure 19-5**, remote loopback testing requires the cooperation of the remote modem to perform the loopback function. Older modems required an operator at the remote location to manually switch the modem into loopback mode and then back out upon completion. Most current modems are able to respond to commands from a central site to enter and leave loopback mode, which greatly simplifies testing. Central control of testing means that tests can be run at off hours when no one is at the remote location and, with some modems, that tests can be preprogrammed to run at preset times when no one is at either location.

Status and statistics.   Central network control is enhanced by modems that collect and report their own status and statistics to a central site. The computer at a central site can analyze incoming statistics and generate alarm messages for critical conditions. In addition, the central system can record the data for subsequent analysis and planning.

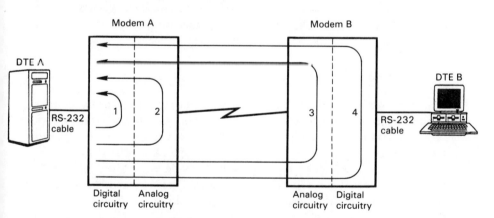

Figure 19-5   Modem loopback testing. Modem loopback facilities test successively larger portions of the connection from a local modem to a remote modem to help isolate problems. When a loopback test is initiated from DTE A or modem A, the loops shown test the following parts of the communications link:

1:   Digital circuitry in local modem
2:   Digital and analog circuitry in local modem
3:   Digital and analog circuitry in local modem, plus the telephone line and the analog circuitry in remote modem
4:   Digital and analog circuitry in local modem, the telephone line, and both analog and digital circuitry in remote modem

Reconfiguration. Older modems or multiplexers required that operating parameters be set with jumper wires inside the modem, with switches inside the modem, or with switches on the modem front panel. Many modems can now be configured from a central site, which simplifies both the initial installation and subsequent reconfiguration process.

Administrative support. Data communications equipment vendors have used their central site modem control computer to provide additional competitive advantage by offering administrative support systems. In addition to statistical analysis, for example, the central system can store network inventory information and print inventory management reports.

Vendors also offer problem management systems that allow customers to record each reported problem and track it until it has been resolved. The problem database stores historical data, providing reports on the failure history of each device in the inventory or on the performance of a vendor's products over a period of time.

Change management is an application for scheduling and tracking changes to the network, whether they involve adding new modems and lines or moving a group of terminals from one location to another. Networks are constantly changing, and it is critical to be able to make additions and changes without adversely affecting the existing operations. The change database also provides a historical record of the alterations that have been made to the network, which can be extremely helpful when troubleshooting problems.

Bit Error Rate Testers

Bit error rate testers (BERT) are devices that generate a known bit pattern for transmission across a telephone line. The bit pattern can either be tested on the far end of the line or can be looped back and checked at the originating end when used in conjunction with modem loopback capabilities.

BERTs can be stand-alone boxes built for this purpose or the BERT function can be incorporated into a line monitor. Several brands of modems incorporate BERT functions in the modem, allowing the line to be tested without the need for additional equipment.

DTE Software

The DTE may be an active part of the traditional network management operation. Both computer vendors and third-party software vendors offer packages that run the gamut from simple line monitors to sophisticated statistical analysis and modeling tools for network planning and design. DTE software packages may be designed to supplement or to replace some of the other tools listed above.

SUMMARY

If you ask ten people for a definition of network management, you will probably get at least eleven answers. Nevertheless, the size, complexity, and importance of networks to business operations, combined with continuing changes to networking technology and communications regulation, will ensure that network management remains one of the most significant data communications topics of the next decade.

RECAP

- The traditional view of network management focused on managing the links in the network.
- The contemporary view of network management focuses on managing the entire network, both the links and the systems, as a corporate resource.
- Integrating network management systems is the greatest challenge for users and vendors of network equipment.
- NetView is the dominant vendor-sponsored attempt at network management integration.
- The OSI Management Framework from ISO is the standards approach to integrated network management, but only applies to those elements of the network that are involved with communications between open systems.
- Network management tools include breakout boxes, line monitors, bit error rate testers, patch panels and matrix switches, modem management systems, and DTE software.

GLOSSARY

Most glossary entries are followed by a page number and in some cases a figure number. The page number refers the reader to the place in the book where the term is explained and used, providing an example of usage in context. The figure number refers to a picture or an example in the text. Words in boldface within a definition refer to other glossary entries that provide additional information.

Accounting management   The process of collecting data about network operations such that billing and other accounting functions can be performed. Accounting management is one of the Specific Management Functional Areas highlighted in the OSI Management Framework. (p. 232)

ACK   See **Acknowledgment**.

ACK0, ACK1   Acknowledgments used in bisync protocol. (p. 69/Fig. 7-2)

Acknowledgment (ACK)   An indication of successfully received data that is sent by the receiver to the transmitter. (p. 56)

Acoustic coupler   A signal conversion device that connects a DTE to a telephone line via a sound (acoustic) connection rather than an electrical connection; used where an electrical connection via modem is not possible.

ACU   See **Automatic calling unit**.

Adaptive equalization   An electronic technique that allows a modem to continuously analyze and compensate for variations in the quality of a telephone line. (p. 134)

ADCCP   Advanced Data Communication Control Procedure. A bit-oriented data link protocol created by the American National Standards Institute as a derivative of IBM's SDLC. Not widely implemented. (p. 74)

Address field   That portion of a protocol message format containing a unique identifier of either the sender (more frequently) or the receiver (less frequently). (p. 75/Fig. 6-6)

AM   See **Amplitude modulation.**

American National Standards Institute (ANSI)   A U.S. organization involved in creating standards in a wide variety of fields including data communications. (p. 10)

American Standard Code for Information Interchange (ASCII)   A 7-bit code set commonly used for data representation in computers and on communications lines. (p. 10/Fig. 2-2)

Amplifier   An electronic device that increases the strength of an analog signal. (p. 24)

Amplitude   The relative strength or power of a signal; the stronger the signal, the greater the amplitude. (p. 21/Fig. 4-3)

Amplitude modulation (AM)   A modem modulation technique in which the amplitude of the carrier signal is altered in a systematic way to represent data from the DTE. Typically, one amplitude is used to represent binary zeros and a second amplitude is used to represent binary ones. (p. 128/Fig. 11-3)

Analog signal   An electrical signal in which the amplitude varies continuously. An analog signal is usually drawn as a sine wave. (p. 23/Fig. 3-2)

ANSI   See **American National Standards Institute.**

Application layer   Layer 7 of the OSI Reference Model; provides application users with access to all OSI services. (p. 43/Fig. 5-3)

ARPANET   A network developed under contract to the U.S. Department of Defense in the 1960s to interconnect computers and communications equipment from a multitude of vendors. ARPANET was one of the first networks to use packet-switching techniques. (p. 103)

ASCII   See **American Standard Code for Information Interchange.**

Async   Short for **Asynchronous.**

Async protocol   A class of simple data link layer protocols that employs asynchronous transmission and has only a few, very basic rules for communicating data. Also called TTY protocol. (p. 61/Fig. 6-4)

Asynchronous transmission   A transmission mode in which there is no time relationship between transmitted characters. Each character is packaged separately between a start bit and one or more stop bits. Contrast with **Synchronous transmission**. (p. 29/Fig. 4-10)

Attenuation   The weakening of electrical signals as they travel through a transmission medium. (p. 22/Fig. 4-4)

Autodial   Feature of either a DTE or a DCE that allows it to dial a switched line connection. (p. 136)

Automatic calling unit (ACU)   A device that dials a telephone connection when instructed to do so by a DTE; usually refers to older-style hardware that used the RS-366 interface between DTE and ACU. (p. 137)

B channel   Bearer channel; one of the 64 Kbps user channels on an ISDN interface. See also **ISDN** and **D channel**. (p. 211)

Balanced electrical interface   An electrical interface on which each circuit consists of a separate pair of wires. A balanced electrical interface generally allows data to be transmitted over longer distances than an **unbalanced electrical interface**. (p. 122)

Bandsplitting   A technique for dividing the bandwidth of a circuit into multiple, independent channels for use in one or both transmission directions. (p. 135)

Bandwidth   The carrying capacity, or size, of a communication channel; usually expressed in hertz for analog circuits and bits per second for digital circuits. (p. 19)

Baseband   A transmission technique in which digital signals are placed directly onto the medium without first modulating a carrier signal. Baseband transmission allows only one signal to be present at any given moment. Contrast with **Broadband**. (p. 215/Fig. 17-1)

Basic rate interface   An ISDN interface with two B channels (64 Kbps each) and one D channel (16 Kbps). See **ISDN, B channel, D channel**. (p. 211)

Baud rate   The rate of signaling speed of a transmission medium; that is, the number of times that some characteristic of the electrical signal can be changed each second and still have those changes be distinguishable by the receiver on the circuit. Each baud can carry one or more bits of data depending on the modulation technique used. (p. 16)

Bearer channel   See **B channel**.

Bell operating companies (BOC)   The local telephone companies that were part of the Bell Telephone System prior to the divestiture of AT&T and are now owned by the **Regional Bell operating companies**. (p. 202)

BERT See **Bit error rate tester.**

Binary A counting system in which all numbers are expressed as combinations of two digits, zero and one. (p. 9)

Bisync (BSC) A family of IBM data link layer protocols. (p. 68/Fig. 7-1)

Bit A *binary* dig*it*; the smallest unit of data in the binary counting system. A bit either has a value of zero or one. (p. 9)

Bit error rate tester (BERT) A device that generates and transmits a known bit pattern and can compare a received version of the same signal with the original; used in conjunction with loopback testing to validate the various components on a circuit. (p. 242)

Bit-oriented protocol A class of data link layer protocols that employs a standard frame format (see **Frame**) regardless of whether the frame carries user data, control information, or a combination of the two. Bits within the address and control fields are used instead of separate control characters, and data transparency is achieved by bit stuffing. (p. 63/Fig. 6-6)

Bit stuffing A technique used with bit-oriented protocols to achieve data transparency. Bit stuffing is accomplished by having the transmitter insert extra zero bits according to a strict set of rules; the receiver deletes the extra bits by applying the same rules in reverse. (p. 64/Fig. 6-7)

Bits per second (bps) A measure of the actual data transmission rate; The bps rate may be equal to or greater than the baud rate depending on the modulation technique used to encode bits into each baud interval. Often expressed as Kbps (thousands) or Mbps (millions). (p. 17)

Block A collection of characters that makes up one transmission unit in a character-oriented protocol. (p. 61/Fig. 6-5)

Blocked async protocol A class of data link layer protocols that improves on the efficiency of simple async protocols by using the more sophisticated error-detection techniques of character- or bit-oriented protocols on an asynchronous circuit. Also called Protected async protocol. (p. 66)

Block mode transmission Another name for **Synchronous transmission.** (p. 31)

BOC See **Bell operating company.**

bps See **Bits per second.**

Branching tree topology A local area network topology that joins each cable segment to the previous one in the same manner that branches are joined to a tree. All transmissions from any device travel to the headend (that is, the base of the tree) and are then retransmitted out all branches of the tree. (p. 218/Fig. 17-3)

Breakout box A device used to examine and possibly modify the state of the control signals on a DTE to DCE interface. (p. 235/Fig. 19-2)

BRI See **Basic rate interface.**

Bridge Generally refers to a device that connects two local area networks of the same type at the data link layer, for example, two Ethernet networks, by retransmitting frames from one network to the other. (p. 223)

Broadband A transmission technique in which digital signals are first converted to analog form and are then modulated onto one of the many carrier signals. Broadband transmission allows multiple, simultaneous signals to be carried over a single transmission medium. Contrast with **Baseband.** (p. 215/Fig. 17-2)

BSC See **Bisync.**

Bus topology A local area network topology consisting of a single segment of cable to which all computer devices are directly connected. (p. 218/Fig. 17-3)

Bypass Any of a variety of techniques to provide telephone or data communications service without using the facilities of the local telephone company. (p. 203/Fig. 16-1)

Byte count protocol A class of data link protocols in which each frame has a header that contains a count of the total number of data characters in the body of the frame. (p. 66)

Byte-oriented protocol See **Character-oriented protocol.**

C band A range of radio frequencies used for satellite transmission. The uplink frequency is at 6 GHz and the downlink is at 4 GHz. Contrast with **Ku band.** (p. 207)

Carrier A constant-frequency sine wave that is modulated, using one or a combination of techniques, in order to carry data signals generated by a computer. (p. 16/Fig. 3-2)

Carrier detect (CD) An RS-232 signal used by the DCE to inform the DTE of the presence of an incoming carrier signal on the telephone line. Also known as Data carrier detect (DCD). (p. 114/Fig. 10-4)

Carrier sense multiple access with collision detection (CSMA/CD) The method used by IEEE 802.3 local area networks, among others, to control access to the transmission medium. (p. 220/Fig. 17-4)

CCITT   See **Consultative Committee on International Telephony and Telegraphy.**

CD   See **Carrier detect.**

Cellular telephone   A type of radio-telephone service in which the calling area is divided into many small cells, each of which contains a low-powered transmitter/receiver. Cellular telephone service permits many more simultaneous calls within a given geographic area as compared to older techniques that used one high-powered transmitter/receiver for the entire calling area. (p. 208/Fig. 16-2)

Central office (CO)   The location of telephone company switching equipment. (p. 125/Fig. 16-1)

Centrex   A service from the local telephone company that provides PBX-like functions directly from the central office switch. (p. 236)

Channel   A path for communications. Same as circuit or link. (p. 19)

Character-oriented protocol   A class of protocols in which selected characters are given special meaning in order to control the flow of information on a line. (p. 61/Fig. 6-5)

Check digit   An extra digit that is added to a message to allow the integrity of the message to be validated by the receiver; more than one check digit may be added to a message. (p. 60)

Circuit   A path for communications. Same as Channel or Link. (p. 19)

Circuit switching   A type of switching in which a physical connection is established between the calling and called parties on demand. Contrast with **Store and forward switching.** (p. 156/Fig. 13-5)

Clear to send (CTS)   An RS-232 signal used by the DCE to give the DTE permission to transmit. (p. 114/Fig. 10-4)

Clear to send delay   For RS-232, the interval between the time the DTE requests permission to transmit, using Request to Send, and the time that the DCE grants permission, using Clear to Send. Also called RTS-CTS delay. (p. 118/Fig. 10-7)

CO   See **Central office.**

Coax   See **Coaxial cable.**

Coaxial cable   A type of cable in which the center conductor (also called the core) is co-axial with, that is, shares the same axis as, the outer conductor (also called the shield). Also known as Coax. (p. 150/Fig. 13-1)

Codec Stands for coder-decoder; a device that converts analog signals into digital signals. (p. 228)

Color multiplexing Frequency-division multiplexing of light waves on fiber-optic cable to improve transmission efficiency. (p. 170)

Combined station In HDLC protocol, a computer that can send both commands and responses. Contrast with **Primary station** and **Secondary station**. (p. 74)

Conditioned lines Leased telephone lines on which additional electronic equipment has been installed to improve their resistance to specific types of transmission impairments. (p. 134)

Configuration management A set of facilities to create, maintain, and change information about the topology of a network and the entities in the network. One of the Specific Management Functional Areas highlighted in the OSI Management Framework. (p. 232)

Conformance testing The process of testing a vendor's implementation of an international standard to determine whether it matches the specifications. Contrast with **Interoperability testing**. (p. 46)

Connectionless operation A mode of operation for a communications protocol in which a logical connection is not established between communicating devices; instead, each protocol data unit is sent independently through the network. (p. 44)

Connection-oriented operation A mode of operation for a communications protocol in which a logical connection is established between communicating devices. Connection-oriented service is also referred to as virtual-circuit service. (p. 44)

Connectorized cable Usually refers to fiber-optic cable that is purchased with connectors already attached. Connectorized cable is used to circumvent the technical problems associated with splicing and joining fiber-optic cables during installation. (p. 151)

Constellation For some modem modulation techniques, the pattern that results from plotting the combinations of phase angle and amplitude on X-Y axes. (p. 130/Figs. 11-6, 11-7)

Consultative Committee on International Telephony and Telegraphy (CCITT) One of the primary international standards organizations. CCITT is actively involved in all aspects of voice and data communications standardization. (p. 38)

Contention   A technique for controlling access to a transmission medium on which there is no master device; instead, each device begins to transmit whenever it is ready and the channel is available. There must also be a means to resolve conflicts and collisions if more than one device begins to transmit at once. Contrast with **Polling**. (p. 56)

Control character   A character used to regulate the flow of data on a circuit, for example, ACK, ETX. See also **Character-oriented protocol**. (p. 61/ Fig. 2-3)

Control packet   An X.25 packet that is used to regulate the flow of data between two devices and does not contain any user data. For example, RR packets are used to acknowledge receipt of previously transmitted packets. (p. 92)

Corporation for Open Systems (COS)   An independent corporation formed in 1986 to promote and accelerate the development of international standards for communications and to develop and market conformance testing facilities and products. Similar to **Standards Promotion and Acceleration Group**. (p. 46)

COS   See **Corporation for Open Systems**.

CRC   See **Cyclic redundancy check**.

Crossover cables   RS-232 cables that have been wired to provide the functions of a **Null modem**. (p. 140)

CSMA/CD   See **Carrier sense multiple access with collision detection**.

CTS   See **Clear to Send**.

Cyclic redundancy check (CRC)   A technique for ensuring the integrity of trans-mitted data. The transmitter generates one or two characters of data, using a previously defined mathematical formula, and appends these characters to the data message. The receiver performs the same calculation as the data ar-rive, and compares the CRC in the message with the calculated result. (p. 59)

D channel   The channel on an ISDN interface used to carry signaling informa-tion, for example, the phone number to be dialed or the status of the accom-panying B channels. The D channel consists of 16 Kbps for the **Basic rate interface** or 64 Kbps for the **Primary rate interface**. See also **ISDN** and **B channel**. (p. 211)

Data carrier detect (DCD)   See **Carrier detect**.

Data circuit-terminating equipment (DCE)   The signal-conversion device that translates the digital signal from the DTE into a form acceptable to the par-ticular communications medium. (p. 110/Fig. 10-1)

Data communications   The movement of data between computers. (p. 6)

Data compression   A technique for reducing the amount of data to be transmitted or stored by replacing frequently occurring data patterns with shorter patterns. (p. 172/Figs. 14-4, 14-5, 14-6)

Data link escape (DLE)   A control character used in bisync protocol. (p. 69)

Data link layer   Layer 2 of the OSI Reference Model; transforms the physical medium into a reliable channel. (p. 42/Fig. 5-3)

Data over voice (DOV)   A technique that allows data to be multiplexed with voice signals on the same twisted pair wire to and from a PBX. (p. 227/Fig. 18-2)

Data packet   An X.25 packet that contains user data. (p. 92)

Data set   In data communications, another name for a **Modem**. (p. 114)

Data set ready (DSR)   An RS-232 signal used by the DCE to inform the DTE that the DCE is powered on and functional. (p. 113/Fig. 10-4)

Data switch   A PBX-like device designed for switching data circuits in a local area. (p. 228)

Data terminal equipment (DTE)   The computer equipment on an RS-232 interface. (p. 110/Fig. 10-1)

Data terminal ready (DTR)   An RS-232 signal used by the DTE to inform the DCE that the DTE is powered on and functional. (p. 113/Fig. 10-4)

Dataphone Digital Service (DDS)   The name of a family of AT&T digital communications services. (p. 159)

Datascope   See **Line monitor**.

DB25 connector   The 25-pin connector used for the RS-232 and RS-366 interface standards. (p. 111/Fig. 10-2)

DCD   Data carrier detect. See **Carrier detect**.

DCE   See **Data circuit-terminating equipment**.

DDS   See **Dataphone Digital Service**.

De facto standards   Standards that have come into general acceptance even though they have not been approved by a standards organization. De facto standards often result from product introductions by the dominant vendor in a particular marketplace, for example, IBM's SDLC data link protocol. (p. 37)

Decimal   A counting system in which all numbers are represented by combinations of ten digits, zero through nine. (p. 9)

Dedicated line   A telephone circuit that is allocated solely for the use of a single customer. Also called a Leased line. (p. 158)

Demultiplexer   See **Multiplexer.**

Dialup line   A temporary circuit that is available on demand; it is established either by manually dialing a telephone or by having a computer or a modem perform the dialing. (p. 156)

Dibit   The result of a modem modulation technique that places 2 bits of data into each baud interval. (p. 130/Fig. 11-3)

Digital service unit (DSU)   A conversion device used for connecting a DTE to a digital communications line, for example, AT&T's Dataphone Digital Service. (p. 145)

Digital signal   An electrical signal in which the amplitude has one of two discrete values at any point in time, typically described as zero and one or on and off. A digital signal is usually drawn as a square wave. (p. 9/Fig. 4-6)

Divestiture   The U.S. government-mandated separation of the former Bell Telephone System into several parts. Divestiture resulted in the formation of the seven Regional Bell operating companies. (p. 202)

DLE   See **Data link escape.**

DOD protocol architecture   A name sometimes used to describe the collection of protocols created for use within the U.S. Department of Defense community. See **TCP/IP, TELNET, SMTP.** (p. 103)

DOV   See **Data over voice.**

Downlink   The downward path from a satellite to an earth station and the opposite of **Uplink.** (p. 153)

DS-1, DS-1C, DS-2, DS-3, DS-4   The levels of the AT&T digital service hierarchy corresponding to 1.544, 3.152, 6.312, 44.736, and 274.176 Mbps. DS-1 is also referred to as **T-1.** (p. 161/Fig. 13-7)

DSR   See **Data set ready.**

DSU   See **Digital service unit.**

DTE   See **Data terminal equipment.**

DTR   See **Data terminal ready.**

Dual-cable network   A form of branching tree topology local area network in which each branch of the network consists of two separate coax cables. One cable carries signals toward the headend and the other carries signals in the opposite direction. Contrast with **Single-cable network**. (p. 218)

Dumb terminal   An inexpensive terminal with only basic communications capabilities. (p. 8/Fig. 2-1)

Duplex   See **Full duplex**.

EBCDIC   See **Extended Binary Coded Decimal Interchange Code**.

Echo canceling   An electronic technique used to suppress the echoes that occur on telephone lines. Also refers to the technique used in some newer modems to provide full-duplex communications over a two-wire circuit. (p. 136)

EIA   See **Electronic Industries Association**.

Electronic Industries Association (EIA)   An organization that sets standards for many aspects of electronic equipment. EIA created the RS-232 and RS-449 interface standards among others. (p. 110)

Encapsulation   The process in which each layer in a network architecture takes information from the next higher layer, adds its own header (and possibly a trailer), and passes the result to the next lower layer. (p. 41/Fig. 5-3)

End of text (ETX)   A bisync control character marking the end of a message block.

End of transmission (EOT)   A bisync control character used to terminate all preceding activity and reset all communications functions. (p. 69)

Enveloping   See **Encapsulation**.

EOT   See **End of transmission**.

Equalizer   Electronic equipment designed to improve data transmission quality by compensating for certain transmission impairments. (p. 134)

ETC   See **External transmit clock**.

ETX   See **End of text**.

Even parity   See **Parity**.

Extended Binary Coded Decimal Interchange Code (EBCDIC)   IBM's 8-bit code set commonly used for data representation in computers and on communications lines. (p. 10/Fig. 2-5)

External transmit clock (ETC)   An RS-232 lead used when synchronous clock signals are provided by the DTE instead of the DCE. (p. 114/Fig. 10-4)

Fault management   The aspect of network management related to the detection, isolation, and repair of failures. One of the Specific Management Functional Areas highlighted in the OSI Management Framework. (p. 232)

FCC   See **Federal Communications Commission.**

FCS   See **Frame check sequence.**

FDM   See **Frequency-division multiplexing.**

FDX   See **Full duplex.**

FEC   See **Forward error correction.**

Federal Communications Commission (FCC)   The U.S. government commission responsible for regulating interstate electronic communications and foreign communications that originate or terminate in the United States. (p. 205)

FEP   See **Front-end processor.**

Fiber-optic cable   A cable composed of glass or plastic fibers that carries data by superimposing the data onto pulses of light. (p. 150)

Fiber-optic modem   A conversion device used for connecting a DTE to a fiber-optic cable. (p. 144)

File Transfer, Access, and Management (FTAM)   International Organization for Standardization recommendation for file movement and access in a network of open systems. (p. 98)

Flag   The bit pattern (0111 1110) used to indicate the beginning and end of a link layer frame in bit-oriented protocols such as HDLC and SDLC. (p. 63/ Fig. 6-6)

Flow control   The process of regulating the movement of data on a communications channel.

FM   See **Frequency modulation.**

FM subcarrier transmission   A simplex communication circuit created by multiplexing data onto a portion of a standard FM radio signal. (p. 210)

Footprint   In satellite communications, the portion of the earth's surface than can broadcast to or receive from a given satellite. (p. 153/Fig. 13-3)

Forward error correction (FEC)   A technique that transmits sufficient redundant information with the outgoing data to allow the receiver not only to detect errors but to automatically correct them without requiring retransmission. (p. 60)

Four-wire circuit A telephone circuit that consists of four wires, thereby providing the full 4-KHz bandwidth in each direction.

Frame The basic data link layer transmission unit for bit-oriented protocols; consists of an opening flag, an address field, a control field, an information field, a frame check sequence, and a closing flag. (p. 63/Fig. 6-6)

Frame check sequence (FCS) The cyclic redundancy check field in bit-oriented protocols. (p. 78/Fig. 6-6)

Frequency The number of oscillations, or cycles, per second of an electronic waveform; measured in hertz (Hz), where 1 Hz equals 1 cycle per second.

Frequency-division multiplexing (FDM) A multiplexing technique that divides the total bandwidth of the circuit into several smaller bandwidth channels by allocating specific frequency ranges to each. Contrast with **Time-division multiplexing**. (p. 168/Fig. 14-2)

Frequency modulation (FM) A modem modulation technique in which the frequency of the carrier signal is altered in a systematic way to represent the data from the DTE. Typically, one frequency is used to represent a binary zero and a second frequency is used to represent a binary one. (p. 129/ Fig. 11-3)

Frequency shift keying (FSK) A type of **Frequency modulation.**

Front-end processor (FEP) A special-purpose computer used to offload data communications-related processing from the main processor. (p. 7)

FSK See **Frequency shift keying.**

FTAM See **File Transfer, Access, and Management.**

Full duplex (FDX) A transmission mode in which data can move in both directions simultaneously. FDX is sometimes called two-way simultaneous transmission. (p. 21/Fig. 4-2)

Full-duplex protocol A protocol, such as HDLC, that does not force the transmitter to stop and wait for an acknowledgment for each unit of transmitted data, thereby allowing data to move in both directions at once. (p. 57/ Fig. 7-9)

Gateway A device that connects two networks by performing appropriate protocol and format conversions at all or most of the layers of the network architecture. (p. 224)

Geosynchronous orbit A satellite orbit (approximately 22,300 miles above the earth) in which the satellite circles the earth at the same rate that the earth is rotating so that the satellite appears to remain stationary above a fixed location. (p. 152/Fig. 13-3)

Guard band   A narrow frequency band used to separate the information-carrying channels on a frequency-division multiplexed circuit. (p. 127/Fig. 11-2)

Half duplex (HDX)   A transmission mode in which data can move in both directions, but only one at a time. HDX is sometimes called two-way alternate transmission. (p. 21/Fig. 4-2)

Half-duplex protocol   A protocol, such as bisync, that forces the transmitter to stop and wait for an acknowledgment for each unit of transmitted data, thereby allowing data to move in only one direction at a time. Do not confuse with half- and full-duplex transmission; a half-duplex protocol may operate over either a half- or full-duplex circuit. (p. 57/Fig. 7-8)

HDLC   See **High-level Data Link Control.**

HDX   See **Half duplex.**

Headend   The "root of the tree" for a branching tree topology local area network. The headend is the location on the network where all incoming transmissions are looped around and retransmitted in the outbound direction. (p. 218/Fig. 17-2)

Hertz (Hz)   A measure of the frequency of a waveform; 1 Hz equals 1 cycle per second. Often expressed as kilohertz (thousands), megahertz (millions), or gigahertz (billions). (p. 20)

High-level Data Link Control (HDLC)   A bit-oriented data link layer protocol created by ISO as a superset of IBM's SDLC. HDLC is widely implemented throughout the non-SNA world. (p. 63)

Huffman encoding   A data-compression technique in which frequently occurring characters or data patterns are replaced by shorter bit patterns, thereby reducing the overall number of bits to be transmitted. (p. 173/Fig. 14-6)

Hybrid circuit   A telephone circuit that consists of four wires between telephone company central offices, but consists of two wires at the customer premises.

Hz   See **Hertz.**

IEEE   See **Institute of Electrical and Electronic Engineers.**

I-frame   See **Information frame.**

Information field   The portion of an HDLC frame that contains the data from the network layer. (p. 77/Fig. 6-6)

Information frame (I-frame)   The HDLC frame type that carries information from the network layer across the data link. (p. 74/Fig. 7-5)

Institute of Electrical and Electronic Engineers (IEEE)   A professional engineering society, one of whose many functions has been to create local area network standards via the 802 Committee. (p. 100)

Integrated Services Digital Network (ISDN)   A totally digital network providing separate channels for telephone company signaling information and user data or voice traffic through a single interface to the user premises. (p. 211)

Interexchange carrier   A telephone company that is allowed to provide long-distance telephone services between LATAs but not within any one LATA. See **LATA**. (p. 203)

Interface   In a layered network architecture, the boundary between two adjacent layers. In general, the boundary between any two adjacent entities in a network, for example, the RS-232 interface between DTE and DCE. (p. 39)

International Organization for Standardization (ISO)   An international standards organization working in many areas, but very active in data communications. (p. 38)

Internet   A general name for a collection of interconnected local and wide area networks. (p. 104/Fig. 9-3)

Internet Protocol (IP)   A network layer protocol developed for use in the U.S. Department of Defense community to allow simple internetworking for multiple vendors' computers connected over multiple networks. See also **Transmission Control Protocol**. (p. 103/Fig. 9-3)

Interoperability testing   Testing performed by two communications product vendors to ensure that their products will communicate with each other. Contrast with **Conformance testing**. (p. 47)

IP   See **Internet protocol**.

ISDN   See **Integrated Services Digital Network**.

ISO   See **International Organization for Standardization**.

Ku band   A range of radio frequencies used for satellite transmission. The uplink frequency is at 14 GHz and the downlink is at 12 GHz. Contrast with C band. (p. 208)

LAN   See **Local area network**.

Land line   See **Terrestrial link**.

LAP   See **Link Access Procedure**.

LAPB See **Link Access Procedure Balanced.**

Last mile Common expression for the connection between the customer premises and the nearest telephone company central office. The last mile is also called the local loop. (p. 201/Fig. 16-1)

LATA See **Local access transport area.**

Layer protocol The protocol for communication between peer layers of a network architecture running on two different computers, for example, network layer to network layer or application layer to application layer. (p. 40)

LCN See **Logical channel number.**

Lead Common expression for the pins, or wires, of an RS-232 interface. (p. 112)

Leased line A telephone circuit that is allocated solely for the use of a single customer. A leased line is also called a dedicated line. (p. 158)

LED See **Light emitting diode.**

Light emitting diode (LED) A semiconductor light source used for indicator lights on electronic equipment. LEDs are also used as the light source for some types of fiber-optic cables. (p. 150)

Limited-distance modem (LDM) A special-purpose conversion device designed to connect two DTEs over a relatively short distance, typically up to several miles. An LDM is not really a modem since it does not perform a digital-to-analog conversion, but transmits a special type of digital signal to the other LDM on the circuit. Also called a line driver or short-haul modem. (p. 143)

Line A communication path or circuit. (p. 19)

Line driver See **Limited-distance modem.**

Line monitor A device used to observe and sometimes record traffic on a DTE-to-DCE interface. (p. 237/Fig. 19-3)

Link A path for communications. Same as circuit or channel. (p. 19)

Link Access Procedure (LAP) A set of procedures used in early versions of X.25 to establish and terminate logical link connections over a physical link. LAP was superseded by **LAPB.** (p. 74)

Link Access Procedure Balanced (LAPB) A set of procedures used in X.25 to establish and terminate logical link connections over a physical link. (p. 184/Fig. 15-6)

Loading coils Equipment added to a circuit by the telephone company to improve the quality of voice transmissions. (p. 205)

Local access transport area (LATA) The calling area served by one Bell operating company or other local telephone company. LATAs were created as part of the divestiture of AT&T and typically contain one area code, but may contain more than one. (p. 202)

Local area network (LAN) A network used to connect devices within a building or in a small geographic area, usually at relatively high speeds (hundreds of kilobits per second to hundreds of megabits per second). (p. 214)

Local loop Common expression for the connection between the customer premises and the nearest telephone company central office. The local loop is also called the last mile. (p. 201/Fig. 16-1)

Logical channel number (LCN) The unique number assigned to each of the separate, simultaneous conversations that can take place at the X.25 packet layer. (p. 186/Fig. 15-1)

Loopback testing A technique used to isolate problems on a data circuit by transmitting a known signal, intercepting it at one of several places on the circuit, retransmitting it back to the source, and then comparing the results. (p. 240/Fig. 19-5)

Longitudinal parity See **Longitudinal redundancy check.**

Longitudinal redundancy check (LRC) An error-detection scheme in which an extra character is added to each transmitted block of data in order to allow the receiver to verify the integrity of the data. See also **Parity.** (p. 58/Fig. 6-3)

LRC See **Longitudinal redundancy check.**

Manufacturing Automation Protocol (MAP) A protocol standardization effort founded by General Motors to define a complete seven-layer set of protocols for use in the manufacturing environment. (p. 102)

MAP See **Manufacturing Automation Protocol.**

Mark In telegraph communications, refers to the presence of electrical current on a circuit. In data communications, refers to a binary one. The transmission of continuous one bits, called marking the line, is used whenever a synchronous line is idle. Contrast with **Space.** (p. 30)

Matrix switch A computerized means of connecting DTEs and DCEs such that alternate connections can be easily made by entering commands to the computer. Compare with **Patch panel.** (p. 240)

Message switching A type of store and forward switching in which entire messages are stored and forwarded intact. Contrast with **Packet switching.** (p. 178/Fig. 15-1)

MFJ   See **Modified Final Judgment.**

Microwave   A transmission medium that employs radio frequency waves traveling through the air between tower- or building-mounted antennas. (p. 151/Fig. 13-2)

Modem   A signal-conversion device used to convert digital signals from a computer into analog signals that can be transmitted across the telephone network. Modem is a contraction of *mo*dulator-*dem*odulator. (p. 15/Fig. 3-1)

Modem eliminator   A device used to simulate the presence of two modems and the intervening telephone network when two DTE are relatively close to each other. Also called a **Null modem.** (p. 140/Figs. 12-1, 12-2, 12-3)

Modified Final Judgment (MFJ)   The Modified Final Judgment of Judge Harold Greene served as the basis for the divestiture of AT&T. (p. 202)

Modulation   A process in which one or more of the properties of a carrier signal (amplitude, frequency, or phase) is varied in accordance with another signal. In data communications, a signal-conversion device modulates a carrier signal based on the data from the DTE. (p. 17/Fig. 3-2)

Modulo arithmetic   A circular counting scheme in which counting reverts to the lowest number after reaching the highest number. For example, modulo eight counting, as used for numbering HDLC frames, proceeds as follows: 0, 1, 2, 3, 4, 5, 6, 7, 0, 1, 2, 3, ... (p. 79)

Multichannel modulation   A modem modulation technique in which the telephone bandwidth is broken into dozens, or even hundreds, of narrow-bandwidth channels to achieve faster overall transmission speeds. (p. 134)

Multiplex   To combine multiple input signals into one output signal for transmission; used to improve utilization of communications lines. (p. 126/ Fig. 14-2)

Multiplexer (MUX)   A device used to combine multiple data or voice signals onto a single circuit to improve transmission efficiency. A corresponding **Demultiplexer** must be used at the other end of the circuit. Also spelled multiplexor. (p. 167/Fig. 14-1)

MUX   See **Multiplexer.**

NAK   See **Negative acknowledgment.**

National Bureau of Standards (NBS)   Former name of the **National Institute of Standards and Technology.** (p. 46)

National Institute of Standards and Technology (NIST)   The agency within the U.S. Department of Commerce that monitors and evaluates standards for the federal government. NIST was formerly called the National Bureau of Standards. (p. 46)

NBS   See **National Bureau of Standards.**

Negative acknowledgment (NAK)   A message or indication used by a receiving device to notify the sending device that data have been received with errors and must be retransmitted. (p. 56)

Network   A collection of computers and circuits.

Network architecture   An overall framework for data communications that includes protocols for all aspects of communication from the physical wire up to the application that performs the desired function for the user. (p. 37)

Network layer   Layer 3 of the OSI Reference Model. The network layer is concerned with routing data through the network. (p. 42/Fig. 5-3)

NIST   See **National Institute of Standards and Technology.**

Noise   Electrical interference that can cause the corruption of data transmission. (p. 23/Figs. 4-4, 4-7)

Nonwireline carrier   FCC regulations restrict providers of cellular telephone service in any given market to one wireline carrier (the local telephone company) and one nonwireline carrier (any company other than the local telephone company). (p. 209)

N_R or N(R)   See **Receive sequence number.**

N_S or N(S)   See **Send sequence number.**

Null modem   A device used to simulate the presence of two modems and the intervening telephone network when two DTEs are relatively close to each other. Also called a **Modem eliminator.** (p. 140/Figs. 12-1, 12-2, 12-3)

Octet   A group of 8 bits in an HDLC frame. (p. 63)

Odd parity   See **Parity.**

Open system   A computer that communicates using the principles of the OSI Reference Model. (p. 42)

Open System Interconnection (OSI)   The Open System Interconnection Reference Model was created by ISO to serve as a layered network architecture for communication among various vendors' equipment. (p. 38)

OSI/OSI Model/OSI Reference Model/OSI Seven Layer Model   See **Open System Interconnection.**

Packet A unit of data that is handled in one piece in a store and forward network. The packet is the data unit created by the X.25 packet layer. (p. 92)

Packet assembler/disassembler (PAD) A device that allows the connection of start-stop mode terminals to a packet-switching network. (p. 190/Fig. 15-17)

Packet layer The term used by CCITT to describe the network layer in the X.25 recommendation. (p. 92)

Packet switching A type of store and forward switching in which the data to be transmitted are first broken into small packets, typically 64, 128, or 256 octets long, before transmission. Contrast with **Message switching.** (p. 179/Fig. 15-3)

Packet-switching network (PSN) A network that uses packet-switching techniques. (p. 179/Fig. 15-3)

Packet-switching node (PSN) One of the computers inside a packet-switching network that is responsible for the routing and switching of data packets. (Fig. 15-3)

PAD See **Packet assembler/disassembler.**

Parallel transmission Data transmission in which there is a separate wire for each bit of a character. Parallel transmission is generally used only for short distances, for example, within a computer system. Contrast with **Serial transmission.** (p. 19/Fig. 4-1)

Parity An error-detection method in which an additional bit is added to each transmitted character according to a simple bit-counting scheme. The receiver uses the same scheme to count incoming bits and compares the result with the transmitted parity bit for consistency. The parity bit may be set to ensure that each character has an even number of bits (even parity) or an odd number of bits (odd parity). (p. 57/Fig. 6-2)

Parity bit The bit added to each transmitted character for error detection. See **Parity.** (p. 57/Fig. 6-2)

Parity error The error that results when the parity bit setting expected by the receiver of a character does not match the transmitted parity bit. (p. 58/Fig. 6-3)

Patch panel A manual means of connecting DTEs and DCEs such that alternate connections can be easily made using sockets and patch cords. Compare with **Matrix switch.** (p. 239/Fig. 19-4)

PBX See **Private branch exchange.**

PDN See **Public data network.**

PDU   See **Protocol data unit.**

Peer   An equal partner. In data communications, a peer is a communications device that has equal rights with the other devices on the network; that is, there is no master/slave relationship among the devices. (p. 184)

Peer layer   In a layered architecture, the corresponding layer in another open system, for example, the session layer in system A and the session layer in system B are peer layers. (p. 40)

Performance management   The process of collecting data about network operations such that the performance of the network can be analyzed. One of the Specific Management Functional Areas highlighted in the OSI Management Framework. (p. 232)

Permanent virtual circuit (PVC)   A virtual circuit through a packet-switching network that is always in place; that is, it does not require an explicit call request. Contrast with **Switched virtual circuit.** (p. 92)

Phase   The relative position of a waveform within a single cycle, measured in degrees. (p. 129)

Phase modulation (PM)   A modem modulation technique in which the phase of the carrier signal is altered in a systematic way to represent the data from the DTE. (p. 129/Fig. 11-3)

Phase shift keying (PSK)   A type of **Phase modulation.** (p. 130)

Photodiode   A light-sensitive semiconductor device often used as the light receptor on fiber-optic cables. (p. 150)

Physical layer   Layer 1 of the OSI Reference Model. The physical layer moves bits across a transmission medium. (p. 42/Fig. 5-3)

Ping-Pong multiplexing   See **Time-compression multiplexing.**

PM   See **Phase modulation.**

Point of presence (POP)   The access point to a long-distance carrier's facilities within a **Local Access Transport Area.** (p. 203/Fig. 16-1)

Polling   An access control method in which one device, called the master or the primary, issues special messages to the other devices, referred to as slaves or secondaries, inviting them to transmit one at a time. Compare with **Contention;** see also **Selecting.** (p. 54/Fig. 6-1)

Poll/final bit   Bit 5 in the control field of an HDLC frame. (p. 76/Fig. 7-5)

Polling protocol   A data communications protocol that uses polling to control access to a link. See **Polling** and **Selecting.** (p. 54/Fig. 6-1)

POP   See **Point of presence.**

Postal, telephone, and telegraph authority (PTT)   A quasi-governmental organization in many countries outside of North America that controls postal, telephone, and telegraph services. (p. 38)

Presentation layer   Layer 6 of the OSI Reference Model. The presentation layer is concerned with the format of the data being exchanged between application users. (p. 43/Fig. 5-3)

PRI   See **Primary rate interface.**

Primary rate interface   An ISDN interface with 23 B channels (64 Kbps each) and one D channel (64 Kbps) in North America and Japan, and 30 B channels plus one D channel in the most of the rest of the world. See **ISDN, B channel, D channel.** (p. 212)

Primary station   In HDLC, the controlling station on a link that issues commands to a secondary station. Contrast with **Secondary station** and **Combined station.** (p. 74)

Private branch exchange (PBX)   A device for switching telephone calls, usually within a building or a small number of buildings, that is typically owned by the company using it. (p. 226)

Private data network   A network that is owned and used exclusively by one company. (p. 178)

Private line   See **Dedicated line.**

Protected async protocol   See **Blocked async protocol.**

Protocol   A set of rules for communicating data. (p. 7)

Protocol converter   A device used to allow two computers that do not share a common protocol to communicate. See also **Protocol emulator.** (p. 86/Figs. 17-14, 17-15)

Protocol data unit (PDU)   A group of logically related data conforming to the protocol for a given layer of a network architecture. A PDU usually consists of a protocol header, data, and, optionally, a protocol trailer. Examples include an HDLC frame (data link layer), an X.25 packet (network layer), and a session PDU (session layer). (p. 40)

Protocol emulator   Software that runs on one computer to make it look like a second type of computer with which it does not share a common protocol, thereby allowing communications to take place. See also **Protocol converter.** (p. 87/Figs. 17-16, 17-17)

Protocol header   The information added to the beginning of a protocol data unit by one layer in a network architecture in order to communicate with its peer layer in another system. (p. 41)

PSK   See **Phase shift keying.**

PSN   See **Packet-switching network** or **Packet-switching node.**

PTT   See **Postal, telephone, and telegraph authority.**

Public data network (PDN)   A network that is maintained by a company in the business of providing network transmission services to individuals and companies. (p. 178)

PVC   See **Permanent virtual circuit.**

QAM   See **Quadrature amplitude modulation.**

Quabit or **Quadbit**   The result of a modem modulation technique that places 4 bits of data into each baud interval. (p. 130/Fig. 11-5)

Quadrature amplitude modulation (QAM)   A modem modulation technique in which combinations of phase and amplitude changes of the carrier signal are used to represent the data from the DTE. (p. 130/Fig. 11-3)

Radio frequency (RF) modem   A special-purpose modem used to convert computer signals into analog, radio frequency signals for transmission. (p. 144)

RBHC   Regional Bell holding company. See **Regional Bell operating company.**

RBOC   See **Regional Bell operating company.**

RC   See **Receive clock.**

RD   See **Receive data.**

Receive clock (RC)   An RS-232 signal used by the DCE to tell the DTE when to read the next bit from the receive data (RD) lead. RC is used for synchronous transmission only. (p. 114/Fig. 10-4)

Receive data (RD)   An RS-232 signal used by the DCE to send data received from the telephone line to the DTE. (p. 113/Fig. 10-4)

Receive sequence number   The counter in an HDLC control field that is used to keep track of the number of the next frame expected by a receiving station. (p. 78/Fig. 7-5)

Regenerator   See **Repeater.**

Regional Bell operating company (RBOC)   One of the seven holding companies created by divestiture to own the various local Bell telephone companies. The RBOCs are Nynex, Bell Atlantic, BellSouth, Ameritech, US West, Pacific Telesis Group, and Southwestern Bell Corporation. RBOCs are also called Regional Bell holding companies. (p. 202)

REJ frames   HDLC frames used to request retransmission of previously transmitted frames. (p. 82/Fig. 7-12)

Repeater   A device that increases the strength of a digital signal; its input is a noisy, attenuated digital signal, and its output is a clean square wave. A repeater provides a similar function for digital signals that an amplifier provides for analog signals. A repeater is also called a regenerator. (p. 26)

Request to send (RTS)   An RS-232 signal used by the DTE to request permission from the DCE to transmit data. (p. 114/Fig. 10-4)

Residual error   An error in the network that is neither corrected by the network layer nor reported to the transport layer. (p. 95)

Reverse channel   A portion of the telephone line bandwidth that is reserved for communication in the opposite direction, usually at a much lower speed. (p. 135)

RF modem   See **Radio frequency modem.**

Ring topology   A local area network topology in which each device is connected to a central ring of wire or cable. (p. 220/Fig. 17-3)

RNR frame   Receiver not ready frame. This HDLC frame notifies the transmitter that previous frames have been received, but instructs it not to send any additional frames at this time. (p. 81/Fig. 7-11)

Router   A device used to connect two networks by performing required protocol and format conversions at the network layer and below. (p. 224)

RR frame   Receiver ready frame; this HDLC frame notifies the transmitter that previous frames have been received and that it may continue to transmit. (p. 81/Fig. 7-10)

RS-232   Widely used EIA standard for the interface between data terminal equipment (DTE) and data circuit-terminating equipment (DCE). (p. 110/Figs. 10-1 through 10-7)

RS-366   EIA standard used with autocalling units to dial connections over the public switched telephone network. The need for RS-366 has been largely eliminated by smart modems that can dial calls directly. (p. 137)

RS-422   Balanced electrical interface used with RS-449. (p. 122/Fig. 10-10)

RS-423   Unbalanced electrical interface used with RS-449. (p. 122/Fig. 10-10)

RS-449   EIA standard for the interface between data terminal equipment (DTE) and data circuit-terminating equipment (DCE). RS-449 features higher speeds and longer DTE-DCE distances than RS-232. (p. 119/Figs. 10-8, 10-9)

RTS   See **Request to send.**

RTS-CTS delay   See **Clear to send delay.**

Run-length encoding   A data-compression scheme in which repeated occurrences of a character are replaced by one occurrence of the character, plus a counter containing the number of repetitions that were in the original. (p. 173/Fig. 14-5)

S/N ratio   See **Signal-to-noise ratio.**

SABM   See **Set asynchronous balanced mode.**

Satellite   An electronic device orbiting the earth that can be used to relay signals from one point on the earth to another. (p. 152/Fig. 13-3)

SDLC   See **Synchronous Data Link Control.**

SDN   See **Software-defined network.**

Secondary station   In HDLC, a station that operates under the control of a primary station and can only send responses to commands from the primary. Contrast with **Primary station** and **Combined station.** (p. 74)

Security management   The part of network management that relates to controlling access to network resources and to the management system itself. Security management is one of the Specific Management Functional Areas highlighted in the OSI Management Framework. (p. 232)

Selecting   The process by which a master device asks a slave device whether it is able to receive data. See also **Polling.** (p. 54/Fig. 6-1)

Semi-octet   Half of an octet; 4 bits. (p. 63)

Send sequence number   The counter in an HDLC control field that is used to number each frame sent by a transmitting station. (p. 78/Fig. 7-5)

Serial transmission   Data transmission in which there is only one physical path for all bits, so that they follow each other sequentially down the wire. Contrast with **Parallel transmission.** (p. 19/Fig. 4-1)

Session layer   Layer 5 of the OSI Reference Model. The session layer establishes and regulates a logical connection between two application entities. (p. 43/Fig. 5-3)

270

Set asynchronous balanced mode (SABM) An HDLC command used to establish a link between two combined stations. (p. 83/Fig. 7-13)

Seven-layer model See **Open System Interconnection.**

Short-haul modem (SHM) See **Limited-distance modem.**

Signal-to-noise ratio (S/N) A measure of the relative strength of the information-carrying signal to the background noise. (p. 24)

Signaled error A network error that is detected and reported to the transport layer. (p. 95)

Signaling terminal (STE) The switching computer used to route packets from one X.25 network to another using X.75. See **X.75.** (p. 92/Fig. 15-20)

Simple Mail Transfer Protocol (SMTP) A rudimentary electronic mail protocol developed for use in **TCP/IP** networks. (p. 106)

Simple Network Management Protocol (SNMP) A protocol for transfer of network management information. SNMP was created for use in **TCP/IP** networks.

Simplex A transmission mode in which data can only move in one direction. (p. 21/Fig. 4-2)

Single-cable network A form of branching tree topology local area network in which each branch of the network consists of one coax cable. The single cable is split into two frequency bands, one of which carries signals toward the headend and the other carries signals in the opposite direction. Contrast with **Dual-cable network.** (p. 218)

Smart terminal A terminal that has local processing capability in addition to one or more types of communication capability. (p. 8/Fig. 2-1)

SME See **Synchronous modem eliminator.**

SMFA See **Specific Management Functional Area.**

SMTP See **Simple Mail Transfer Protocol**

SNA See **Systems Network Architecture.**

SNMP See **Simple Network Management Protocol.**

Software-defined network (SDN) A network that gives the appearance of a private, leased line network but that is implemented using the public switched telephone network. (p. 165)

SOH See **Start of header.**

Space   In telegraph communications, refers to the absence of electrical current on a circuit. In data communications, refers to a binary zero. Contrast with **Mark**. (p. 30)

SPAG   See **Standards Promotion and Acceleration Group**.

Specific Management Functional Area (SMFA)   One of the five sets of management facilities needed for management of OSI networks as specified in the OSI Management Framework [ISO 7498/4]. The five SMFAs are configuration, fault, accounting, security, and performance management. (p. 232)

SREJ   Selective reject, an HDLC frame used to request retransmission of a specific information frame. (p. 83/Fig. 7-12)

Stack   The collection of protocols that implements a network architecture, for example, the OSI stack or the SNA stack. (p. 38/Fig. 5-1)

Standards Promotion and Application Group (SPAG)   A European consortium established to accelerate the development and use of communications standards. Similar to **Corporation for Open Systems**. (p. 46)

Star topology   A local area network topology in which each device is connected to a central hub. (p. 219/Fig. 17-3)

Start bit   In asynchronous communication, a zero bit added to the beginning of each transmitted character. The start bit alerts the receiver to the arrival of the next incoming character. (p. 30/Fig. 4-10)

Start of header (SOH)   A bisync control character marking the beginning of a message block.

Start of text (STX)   A bisync control character marking the beginning of the text portion of a message block.

Start-stop mode terminal   A terminal that communicates using asynchronous transmission. (p. 195/Fig. 15-18)

Station   General term for a device at the end of a communication line.

Statistical multiplexer   A multiplexer that dynamically assigns bandwidth to input lines as it is needed, rather than on a predetermined, fixed basis. Also called a Statistical time-division multiplexer. (p. 170/Fig. 14-2)

Statistical time-division multiplexer (STDM)   See **Statistical multiplexer**.

Statmux   See **Statistical multiplexer**.

STDM   Statistical time-division multiplexer. See **Statistical multiplexer**.

STE   See **Signaling terminal.**

Store and forward switching   A switching technique in which there is no physical connection between the communicating parties. Instead, units of data are received, stored, and then forwarded when an outgoing path is available. Contrast with **Circuit switching.** See also **Message switching** and **Packet switching.** (p. 177)

Stop bit   In asynchronous communication, a one bit added to the end of each transmitted character. (p. 30/Fig. 4-10)

STX   See **Start of text.**

Superconductor   A device that offers zero resistance to the flow of electrons. (p. 22)

Supervisory frame (S-frame)   The HDLC frame type used to control the flow of information frames on the link. (p. 74)

SVC   See **Switched virtual circuit.**

Switched virtual circuit (SVC)   A temporary virtual circuit through a packet-switching network that is established in response to a call request packet and is terminated in response to a clear request packet. Contrast with **Permanent virtual circuit.** (p. 92)

SYN   See **Sync character.**

Sync character   A control character that is used in synchronous transmission to allow the receiver to synchronize its clock with that of the transmitter. (p. 31/Fig. 7-1)

Synchronous Data Link Control (SDLC)   A bit-oriented data link layer protocol created by IBM as part of their Systems Network Architecture. (p. 63)

Synchronous modem eliminator (SME)   A modem eliminator that provides clock signals to the DTE and, therefore, can be used on a synchronous circuit. See also **Modem eliminator.** (p. 143/Fig. 12-3)

Synchronous transmission   A transmission mode in which there is a fixed time relationship between transmitted characters and characters are always transmitted in blocks. Also called block mode transmission. Contrast with **Asynchronous transmission.** (p. 31)

Systems Network Architecture (SNA)   IBM's network architecture which is the most widely implemented network architecture in the world. (p. 38/ Fig. 5-5)

T-1 circuit   A circuit operating at 1.544 Mbps in North America and Japan and at 2.048 Mbps in most of the rest of the world. (p. 161/Fig. 13-7)

T-carrier   Another name for a **T-1 circuit.**

TC   See **Transmit clock.**

TCM   See **Time-compression multiplexing** or **Trellis-coding modulation.**

TCP   See **Transmission Control Protocol.**

TCP/IP   See **Transmission Control Protocol** and **Internet Protocol.**

TD   See **Transmit data.**

TDM   See **Time-division multiplexing.**

Technical Office Protocol (TOP)   A protocol standardization effort founded by Boeing Computer Services to define a complete seven-layer set of protocols for use in the technical office environment. (p. 103)

Telecommunications   The transmission of information by electronic means. Some people use this term to refer specifically to voice communications as distinct from data communications, but generally it refers to any electronic exchange of information. (p. 6)

Teletype   A terminal, usually consisting of a keyboard and a printer, used for communications. (p. 61)

TELNET   A virtual terminal protocol developed for use in the U.S. Department of Defense community. (p. 104)

Terminal   A device that is capable of communicating with a computer. (p. 8)

Terrestrial link   A communication circuit that does not include a satellite link. Also called a land line. (p. 72)

Time-compression multiplexing (TCM)   A technique for achieving full-duplex transmission by means of extremely fast half-duplex transmission. Data are transmitted more than twice as fast as the expected data rate, first in one direction and then in the other, with virtually no delay in switching from one direction to the other. TCM is used to implement full-duplex, 56 Kbps, switched digital circuits. Also called Ping-Pong multiplexing. (p. 135)

Time-division multiplexing (TDM)   A multiplexing technique in which the total bandwidth of the circuit is divided into several smaller bandwidth channels by allocating specific time slots to each. Contrast with **Frequency-division multiplexing.** (p. 170/Fig. 14-2)

Timeout   The amount of time that hardware or software waits for an expected event before taking corrective action. (p. 53)

Token   A special data pattern used to grant permission to transmit. See also **Token passing**. (p. 222/Fig. 17-5)

Token passing   A technique for controlling access to a transmission medium by passing a data pattern called a token to each device in its turn. A device may transmit only when it owns the token. (p. 222/Fig. 17-5)

Token ring   A ring topology local area network that uses the token-passing access method. (p. 222/Fig. 17-3)

TOP   See **Technical Office Protocol**.

Topology   The physical configuration of a network showing how the network would look if it were laid out flat and viewed from above. (p. 218)

Transmit clock (TC)   An RS-232 signal used by the DCE to inform the DTE when to place the next bit onto the transmit data lead (for synchronous transmission only). (p. 114/Fig. 10-4)

Transmit data (TD)   An RS-232 signal used by the DTE to transmit data to the DCE. (p. 113/Fig. 10-4)

Transparency   A protocol feature that allows any pattern of bits to be transmitted such that ordinary data cannot be mistakenly interpreted as control information by the receiving device. See **Bit stuffing**. (p. 63)

Transponder   A device in a satellite that receives signals from an earth station on one frequency and retransmits them back down on a separate frequency. A satellite typically contains 12 to 24 transponders. (p. 153)

Transmission Control Protocol (TCP)   A transport layer protocol developed in the U.S. Department of Defense community for communication among multiple vendors' computers. See also **Internet Protocol**. (p. 103/Fig. 9-3)

Transport layer   Layer 4 of the OSI Reference Model. The transport layer provides a reliable end-to-end connection independent of the number or quality of the underlying networks. (p. 42/Fig. 5-3)

Trellis-coding modulation (TCM)   A modem modulation technique in which sophisticated mathematics are used to predict the best fit between the incoming signal and a large set of possible combinations of amplitude and phase changes. TCM provides for transmission speeds of 14,400 bps and above. (p. 131)

Tribit   The result of a modem modulation technique that places 3 bits of data into each baud interval. (p. 130/Fig. 11-4)

Trunk circuit   A large bandwidth circuit connecting two locations. Calls are typically multiplexed on a trunk to improve transmission efficiency. (p. 126/Fig. 11-1)

TTY protocol   See **Async protocol.**

Twisted pair   Transmission medium in which two insulated wires are wrapped around each other. (p. 149)

Two-wire circuit   A telephone circuit consisting of two wires.

Unbalanced electrical interface   An electrical interface on which every circuit shares a common ground wire. Transmission distances are usually shorter over an unbalanced electrical interface than over a balanced electrical interface. (p. 112)

Unnumbered frame (U-frame)   The HDLC frame type used to initiate and terminate a logical link connection across a physical link. (p.74)

Uplink   The upward path between an earth station and a satellite and the opposite of **Downlink.** (p. 153)

V.24   CCITT recommendation for the DTE-to-DCE interface; equivalent to RS-232. (p. 110)

V.35   CCITT recommendation for a higher-speed DTE-to-DCE interface than V.24.

Value-added network (VAN)   A network that provides additional services beyond raw bandwidth, for example, error correction, speed conversion, and protocol conversion. (p. 178)

VC   See **Virtual circuit.**

Very small aperture terminal (VSAT)   A relatively small diameter satellite antenna, typically 1.5 to 3.0 meters in diameter. (p. 208)

Virtual circuit (VC)   A logical connection through a packet-switching network; may be a **Switched virtual circuit** or a **Permanent virtual circuit.** (p. 186/Fig. 15-10)

Virtual terminal (VT)   A universal terminal. The ISO VT protocol is designed to describe the operation of a so-called universal terminal in order to allow any terminal to talk with any host computer. (p. 98)

Voice communications   The movement of voice conversations over transmission media. (p. 6)

Voice-grade lines   A telephone line of the quality usually provided for voice conversations. (p. 126)

VSAT   See **Very small aperture terminal.**

VT   See **Virtual terminal.**

WAN   See **Wide area network.**

Wide area network (WAN)   A network that connects devices spread over a large geographic area, typically at low to medium speeds (several kilobits per second to 1 or 2 megabits per second).

Window size   In packet switching, the number of frames or packets that may be sent before the transmitter must stop and wait for an acknowledgment from the receiver. (p. 79)

Wireline carrier   FCC regulations restrict providers of cellular telephone service in any given market to one wireline carrier (the local telephone company) and one **nonwireline carrier** (any company other than the local telephone company). (p. 209)

X.21   CCITT recommendation for the DTE-to-DCE interface for synchronous operation over public data networks. (p. 122)

X.21 bis   An interim CCITT recommendation that may used in lieu of X.21; allows use of **RS-232, V.24, RS-449,** or **V.35.** (p. 183)

X.25   CCITT recommendation for the DTE-to-DCE interface for connection of packet mode devices to a public data network. (p. 92/Fig. 15-5)

X.28   CCITT recommendation for communication between a start/stop mode terminal and a PAD. (p. 196/Fig. 15-18)

X.29   CCITT recommendation for communication between a packet mode DTE and a PAD or between two PADs. (p. 196/Fig. 15-18)

X.3   CCITT recommendation for operation of a PAD. (p. 195/Fig. 15-18)

X.75 CCITT recommendation for interconnection of two packet-switching networks. (p. 92/Fig. 15-20)

X.200   CCITT recommendation for open system interconnection; equivalent to the OSI reference model. (p. 38)

X.400   CCITT recommendation for message-handling systems, for example, electronic mail. (p. 98)

BIBLIOGRAPHY

NOTE: Most of the ISO and CCITT standards documents listed here are subject to periodic revision. Before relying on the publication dates listed here, check for more recent versions.

ANSI	*American National Standard Code for Information Interchange*. New York: American National Standards Institute, Inc., 1977.
Black	Black, Uyless D., *Data Communications and Distributed Networks* (2nd ed.). Englewood Cliffs, N.J.: Prentice-Hall, Inc., A Reston Book, 1987. Technical but readable introductory text; good focus in latter portions on distributed applications and databases.
Brodd	Brodd, Wayne D., "HDLC, ADCCP, and SDLC: What's the Difference?", *Data Communications*, August 1983, p. 115.
CCITT X.25	"Interface between Data Terminal Equipment (DTE) and Data Circuit-terminating Equipment (DCE) for Terminals Operating in the Packet Mode and Connected to Public Data Networks," *CCITT Red Book*, Fascicle VIII.3, p. 108. Geneva: Consultative Committee on International Telegraphy and Telephony, 1984.
CCITT X.28	"DTE/DCE Interface for a Start-stop Mode Data Terminal Equipment Accessing the Packet Assembly/Disassembly Facility (PAD) in a Public Data Network Situated in the Same Country," *CCITT Red Book*, Fascicle VIII.3, p. 243. Geneva: Consultative Committee on International Telegraphy and Telephony, 1984.
CCITT X.29	"Procedures for the Exchange of Control Information and User Data between a Packet Assembly/Disassembly (PAD) Facility and a Packet Mode

DTE or Another PAD," *CCITT Red Book*, Fascicle VIII.3, p. 280. Geneva: Consultative Committee on International Telegraphy and Telephony, 1984.

CCITT X.3   "Packet Assembly/Disassembly Facility (PAD) in a Public Data Network," *CCITT Red Book*, Fascicle VIII.2, p. 17. Geneva: Consultative Committee on International Telegraphy and Telephony, 1984.

CCITT X.75   "Terminal and Transit Call Control Procedures and Data Transfer System on International Circuits between Packet-switched Data Networks," *CCITT Red Book*, Fascicle VIII.4, p. 152. Geneva: Consultative Committee on International Telegraphy and Telephony, 1984.

CCITT X.200   "Reference Model of Open Systems Interconnection for CCITT Applications," *CCITT Red Book*, Fascicle VIII.5, p. 1. Geneva: Consultative Committee on International Telegraphy and Telephony, 1984.

CCITT X.213   "Network Service Definition for Open Systems Interconnection (OSI) for CCITT Applications," *CCITT Red Book*, Fascicle VIII.5, p. 60. Geneva: Consultative Committee on International Telegraphy and Telephony, 1984.

CCITT X.214   "Transport Service Definition for Open Systems Interconnection (OSI) for CCITT Applications," *CCITT Red Book*, Fascicle VIII.5, p. 97. Geneva: Consultative Committee on International Telegraphy and Telephony, 1984.

CCITT X.215   "Session Service Definition for Open Systems Interconnection for CCITT Applications," *CCITT Red Book*, Fascicle VIII.5, p. 122. Geneva: Consultative Committee on International Telegraphy and Telephony, 1984.

CCITT X.224   "Transport Protocol Specification for Open Systems Interconnection for CCITT Applications," *CCITT Red Book*, Fascicle VIII.5, p. 202. Geneva: Consultative Committee on International Telegraphy and Telephony, 1984.

CCITT X.225   "Session Protocol Specification for Open Systems Interconnection for CCITT Applications," *CCITT Red Book*, Fascicle VIII.5, p. 292. Geneva: Consultative Committee on International Telegraphy and Telephony, 1984.

CCITT X.400   "Message Handling Systems: System Model-Service Elements," *CCITT Red Book*, Fascicle VIII.7, p. 3. Geneva: Consultative Committee on International Telegraphy and Telephony, 1984.

CCITT X.409   "Message Handling Systems: Presentation Transfer Syntax and Notation," *CCITT Red Book*, Fascicle VIII.7, p. 62. Geneva: Consultative Committee on International Telegraphy and Telephony, 1984.

CommWeek   "VSATs: Coping with the Special Challenges," a Closeup Supplement to *CommunicationsWeek*, January 18, 1988.

Cypser   Cypser, R. J., *Communications Architecture for Distributed Systems*. The Systems Programming Series. Reading, Mass: Addison-Wesley Publishing Company, 1978. Has never been updated, but remains a basic reference on SNA.

daCruz   da Cruz, Frank, and Christine Gianone, "Shopping for Software That Lets PCs Chat with Mainframes," *Data Communications,* December 1987, p. 155.

DDN   Feinler, Elizabeth, and others, eds., *DDN Protocol Handbook.* Menlo Park, Calif.: DDN Network Information Center, SRI International, 1985. Contains copies of standards specified for use in the Defense Data Network.

EIA 232D   *EIA Standard RS-232-D: Interface between Data Terminal Equipment and Data Circuit-Terminating Equipment Employing Serial Binary Data Interchange.* Washington, D.C.: Electronic Industries Association, 1987.

EIA 449   *EIA Standard RS-449: General Purpose 37-Position and 9-Position Interface for Data Terminal Equipment and Data Circuit-Terminating Equipment Employing Serial Binary Data Interchange.* Washington, D.C.: Electronic Industries Association, 1977.

FitzGerald   FitzGerald, Jerry, *Business Data Communications: Basic Concepts, Security, and Design* (2nd ed.). New York: John Wiley & Sons, Inc., 1988.

Folts   Folts, Harold C., ed., *McGraw-Hill's Compilation of Data Communications Standards* (3rd ed.), Data Communications Book Series. New York: McGraw-Hill Information Systems Company, 1986. A three volume set containing copies of dozens of standards from CCITT, ISO, ANSI, and others.

Freeman   Freeman, Roger L., *Telecommunication System Engineering, Analog and Digital Network Design.* New York: John Wiley & Sons, Inc., 1980. Fundamental reference for telephone networks and general telephony.

Gartner   "SNA/DECnet Hybridization: Where Are the Boundaries?", Local Area Network Communications Key Issues K-246-367.1, Gartner Group, Inc., July 31, 1987.

Glasgal   Glasgal, Ralph, *Techniques in Data Communications.* Norwood, Mass.: Artech House, Inc., 1983. Full of engineering details about data communications hardware, e.g., modems, muxes, test equipment; not easy reading.

Gurugé   Gurugé, Anura, *SNA: Theory and Practice.* Maidenhead, Berkshire, England: Pergamon Infotech Ltd., 1984.

Held1   Held, Gilbert, and Ray Sarch, *Data Communications: A Comprehensive Approach,* Data Communications Series. New York: McGraw-Hill Publications Company, 1983.

Held2   Held, Gilbert, "Making the Most of the Versatile Breakout Box," *Data Communications,* March 1988, p. 167.

ISO 3309   *Information Processing Systems-Data Communication-High-level Data Link Control Procedures-Frame Structure* (3rd ed.). Geneva: International Organization for Standardization, 1984.

ISO 4335   *Information Processing Systems-Data Communication-High-level Data Link Control Elements of Procedures* (3rd ed.). Geneva: International Organization for Standardization, 1987.

ISO 7498   *Information Processing Systems-Open Systems Interconnection-Basic Reference Model.* Geneva: International Organization for Standardization, 1984.

ISO 7498/4   *Information Processing Systems-Open Systems Interconnection-Basic Reference Model Part 4-OSI Management Framework.* Geneva: International Organization for Standardization, 1987.

ISO 8072   *Information Processing Systems-Open Systems Interconnection-Transport Service Definition.* Geneva: International Organization for Standardization, 1986.

ISO 8073   *Information Processing Systems-Open Systems Interconnection-Connection Oriented Protocol Specification.* Geneva: International Organization for Standardization, 1986.

ISO 8326   *Information Processing Systems-Open Systems Interconnection-Basic Connection Oriented Session Service Definition.* Geneva: International Organization for Standardization, 1987.

ISO 8327   *Information Processing Systems-Open Systems Interconnection-Basic Connection Oriented Session Protocol Specification.* Geneva: International Organization for Standardization, 1987.

ISO 8571   *Information Processing Systems-Open Systems Interconnection-File Transfer, Access and Management.* Geneva: International Organization for Standardization, 1986.

ISO 8648   *Information Processing Systems-Open Systems Interconnection-Internal Organization of the Network Layer.* Geneva: International Organization for Standardization, 1988.

ISO 8822   *Information Processing Systems-Open Systems Interconnection-Basic Connection Oriented Presentation Service Definition.* Geneva: International Organization for Standardization, 1986.

ISO 8823   *Information Processing Systems-Open Systems Interconnection-Basic Connection Oriented Presentation Protocol Specification.* Geneva: International Organization for Standardization, 1986.

ISO 8824   *Information Processing Systems-Open Systems Interconnection-Specification of Abstract Syntax Notation One (ASN.1).* Geneva: International Organization for Standardization, 1987.

ISO 8825   *Information Processing Systems-Open Systems Interconnection-Specification of Basic Encoding Rules for Abstract Syntax Notation One (ASN.1).* Geneva: International Organization for Standardization, 1987.

ISO 8878   *Information Processing Systems-Data Communications-Use of X.25 to Provide the OSI Connection-mode Network Service.* Geneva: International Organization for Standardization, 1987.

Korzeniowski   Korzeniowski, Paul, "A New Net Goes Down Under," *Network World,* September 15, 1986, p. 39.

Kreager	Kreager, Paul S., *Practical Aspects of Data Communications*. New York: McGraw-Hill Book Company, 1983. Very practical; covers facility design, running cables, necessary documentation to run a network, etc.; no coverage of the usual introductory topics.
LiCalzi	LiCalzi, Pamela, "Information Providers Tune Up, Send More Data over FM Nets," *CommunicationsWeek,* January 4, 1988, p. 35.
Marney-Petix	Marney-Petix, Victoria C., *Networking and Data Communications*. Englewood Cliffs, N.J.: Prentice-Hall, Inc., 1986.
Martin	Martin, James, with Joe Leben, *Data Communication Technology*. Englewood Cliffs, N.J.: Prentice-Hall, Inc., 1988.
McNamara	McNamara, John E., *Technical Aspects of Data Communication* (2nd ed.). Bedford, Mass.: Digital Press, 1982. Strong hardware orientation, but an excellent book to have on your shelf for reference.
Meijer	Meijer, Anton, and Paul Peeters, *Computer Network Architectures*. Electrical Engineering Communications and Signal Processing Series. Rockville, Md.: Computer Science Press, 1982. Solid treatment of OSI model and related standards but somewhat dated; good collection of vendor network architecture information.
Omnicom	*The Omnicom Index of Standards for Distributed Information and Telecommunication Systems*. Vienna, Va.: Omnicom, Inc., 1986. Extensive index to standards documents.
Payton	Payton, John, and Shahid Qureshi, "Trellis Encoding: What It Is and How It Affects Data Transmission," *Data Communications*, May 1985, p. 143.
Rey	Rey, R. F., technical ed., *Engineering and Operations in the Bell System* (2nd ed.). Murray Hill, N.J.: Bell Telephone Laboratories, Inc., 1983. Contains every nitty-gritty detail about the internal aspects of the Bell system network; full of valuable charts and pictures; divestiture has not changed the value of the technical information, although information on organizational structure of AT&T is now out of date.
Rosner	Rosner, Roy D., *Packet Switching: Tomorrow's Communications Today*. Belmont, Calif.: Lifetime Learning Publications, 1982.
Schwartz	Schwartz, Mischa, *Telecommunication Networks: Protocols, Modeling and Analysis*, Addison-Wesley Series in Electrical and Computer Engineering. Reading, Mass.: Addison-Wesley Publishing Company, 1987. Very comprehensive book but requires significant mathematical background to read; in the author's words, "the stress throughout ... is on the quantitative performance evaluation of telecommunication networks and systems."
Seyer	Seyer, Martin D., *RS-232 Made Easy: Connecting Computers, Printers, Terminals and Modems*. Englewood Cliffs, N.J.: Prentice-Hall, Inc., 1984.
Sherman	Sherman, Kenneth, *Data Communications: A User's Guide* (2nd ed.). Englewood Cliffs, N.J.: Prentice-Hall, Inc., 1985. This edition is reasonably good and is readable; don't bother with the first edition.

Spotlight1   "Spotlight on Modems," *Computerworld*, March 30, 1987. Collection of articles on modem technology, customer application profiles, product comparisons; six pages of comparison charts of digital service units and fiber-optic modems.

Spotlight2   "Spotlight on T1 Technology," *Computerworld*, April 27, 1987. Collection of articles on T-1 technology, including good description of AT&T digital hierarchy; three pages of comparison charts of T-1 multiplexers.

Stallings1   Stallings, William, *Data and Computer Communications* (2nd ed.). New York: Macmillan Publishing Company, 1988. Very comprehensive, but extremely technical; not easy reading.

Stallings2   Stallings, William, *Local Networks: An Introduction*. New York: Macmillan Publishing Company, 1984.

Tanenbaum   Tanenbaum, Andrew, *Computer Networks* (2nd ed.). Englewood Cliffs, N.J.: Prentice-Hall, Inc., 1988. A classic in the field; one of the earliest books to be organized around the OSI model; very technical, yet quite readable. More than half of the second edition is completely new; the remainder has been heavily updated; provides significant new coverage of the OSI upper layers, MAP, LANs, ISDN, and other topics.

Terplan   Terplan, Kornel, *Communication Networks Management*. Prentice-Hall Computer Communication Series. Englewood Cliffs, N.J.: Prentice-Hall, Inc., 1987.

von Taube   von Taube, Eugene, and Karl W. Seitz, "Modem Design Boosts Data Processing Throughput," *Computer Design*, April 15, 1986, p. 71.

INDEX

Page numbers in italics indicate the location of the definition or the primary discussion of the indexed item. Italics are not used when there is only one reference listed for an index entry.

Synonyms, abbreviations, or acronyms for an index entry are listed in parentheses following the entry. Most acronyms are indexed under their fully spelled out form. The exceptions are those acronyms that are commonly used only in their short form, for example, HDLC and CCITT.